MW00849443

Dr. Schmidt is a master teacher. I was mesmerized by his wonderful apology for Christianity and its matchless positive contributions to society and the world in How Christianity Changed the World.

Now the good doctor has produced another classic. This book treats the distinctives of genuine Lutheranism in a palatable yet sufficiently thorough manner to provide information for the neophyte, while providing deep, yet clear, understanding for the person wanting to stretch his or her maturing knowledge of the faith. You'll love this book. Read it and give it to a friend.

—Pastor Matthew C. Harrison
President, The Lutheran Church—Missouri Synod

This is a remarkable compilation of Lutheran wisdom by Professor Schmidt. It is both comprehensive and deep, offering the reader a complete account of Lutheran beliefs and practices.

—Robert Benne
Jordan Trexler Professor Emeritus of Religion
and Research Associate, Roanoke College, Salem, VA
Professor of Christian Ethics, Institute of Lutheran Theology, Brookings, SD

How many Lutherans understand the nature of their church and its theology? Sociologists tell us that among Lutherans, as among people of other denominations, the church is often viewed chiefly as a social phenomenon—a place to belong among folks of similar background and tastes. This may be inevitable in church bodies that have lost touch with their theological roots and the need to connect with the teachings of Holy Scripture and Gospel proclamation. Lutherans, however, should have no excuse for substituting sociology for theology. Dr. Schmidt's book offers a clear and comprehensive corrective to this endemic danger.

—John Warwick Montgomery, PhD, DThéol, LLD
Director, International Academy of Apologetics, Evangelism and Human Rights,
Strasbourg, France

I don't think many confessional Lutherans know how much the rest of the Church needs them. Therefore, it is all the more urgent that Lutherans themselves know what they believe and why they believe it. I'm glad to learn from this book and highly recommend it to insiders and outsiders alike.

—Michael Horton
J. Gresham Machen Professor of Theology, Westminster Seminary California

How many erudite scholars do you know who are so brilliant that they are able to write simple English sentences to express their thoughts? That list is a very short one (including, for example, C. S. Lewis). But Dr. Schmidt avoids linguistic obscurantism like the plague! Few have the breadth of education to tackle what is such a "well-trodden path," communicate to us lowly ones fact after fact, and weave it into a book that is consummately readable. But that is exactly what Dr. Schmidt has done.

—Rod Rosenbladt
Professor of Theology and Christian Apologetics (retired), Concordia University Irvine

Noting that many within the Lutheran community lack a broader familiarity with the theological tradition of which they are a part, Dr. Alvin Schmidt focuses on the hallmarks of Lutheran theology as faithfully confessed since the sixteenth century. Aimed specifically at a lay audience, the targeted and concise topics that make up this volume cover the Lutheran waterfront—from understanding the Scriptures and Confessions, to the history of the Church, to matters of practice. In the end, appropriately, all find their focus in Christ. Dr. Schmidt's volume of vignettes on key Lutheran themes will prove invaluable for Lutheran pastors, teachers, and lay leaders as they guide people into an understanding of their rich story.

—Rev. Dr. Lawrence R. Rast Jr.
President, Concordia Theological Seminary, Fort Wayne, IN

Alvin Schmidt's careful account of "Lutheran identity" offers readers a welcome explanation of the enduring contributions from Martin Luther's legacy. The book is an attractive introduction to the main principles of Lutheranism for those with little earlier acquaintance but also a helpfully comprehensive refresher for Lutherans and others who may have already studied Luther's catechisms or have some knowledge of Lutheran traditions after Luther.

—Mark Noll
Emeritus Professor of History, University of Notre Dame
Author of Protestantism: A Very Short Introduction

Dr. Schmidt, with his extensive academic and parish experience, writes at a level that can be understood by the layman while challenging those with a theological degree on issues that present themselves to the present-day Church. I especially liked the chapters on the biblical canon, worship, and the two kingdoms. With the provided questions at the end of each chapter, I can see this book used as a supplement in adult catechism training as well as for Bible classes. This work seems to fit well with other books produced by Concordia Publishing House, such as The Lutheran Difference, Lutheranism 101, and Being Lutheran, which along with Dr. Schmidt's most recent tome, would all be useful for any Lutheran to have on his shelf. One might ask if the unique differences of Lutheran doctrine and practice—the hallmarks of Lutheran identity—are worth maintaining, and Dr. Schmidt shows from the Scriptures and the Confessions that this is most certainly true!

—Rev. Mark A. Miller
President of the Central Illinois District of the Lutheran Church—Missouri Synod

Author Alvin Schmidt does not shy away from the important yet challenging topics Christians face today. From Islam and Mormonism to cremation and the positive influence of Christianity on Western civilization, he has brought his experience, insight, and the truth of the Bible and the Book of Concord to challenge, inform, comfort, and delight his readers.

After reading Lutheranism 101, The Spirituality of the Cross, Has American Christianity Failed?, or Being Lutheran, read Concordia's Hallmarks of Lutheran Identity on your way to a more comprehensive reading of the Lutheran Confessions and your faithful reception of the Lord's gifts of Word and Sacrament in the Divine Service.

Schmidt's personal knowledge, extensive research, passion for the subject, and winsomeness help the reader better understand the solas of the Reformation, Lutheran theological emphases, faithful Lutheran practices, and Lutheran confessional documents, all truly "hallmarks of Lutheran identity."

—Rev. Paul J Cain
Pastor, Immanuel Lutheran Church, Sheridan, WY
Headmaster, Martin Luther Grammar School and Immanuel Academy, Sheridan, WY
Wyoming District Education Executive
Editor, Lutheran Book Review

In a day of generic and watered-down Christianity, Alvin Schmidt shows the beauty and treasure of the great Lutheran hallmarks. Christ is at the center, and everything flows from Him. For some, this material may be basic, but for most readers, the rich and dynamic quotes from Luther, the Church Fathers, and more recent theologians will resource and engage. This book is not superficial, but it also does not get the reader stuck in irrelevant detail. The author writes with conviction and passion.

Hallmarks of Lutheran Identity covers the great Lutheran themes and offers insight and thoughtful application for the local congregation and an individual's devotional life. This work will fill in the gaps for many Lutheran teachings and practices that might be assumed or too readily dismissed. I read this book with interest and along the way, my curiosity grew. Lutheran theology at its best will lead to a faithful and passionate mission for the sake of those disconnected from the Church and the spiritually lost.

I am grateful for the confession of this book. While I did not come to all the conclusions and applications Schmidt does, that's okay. It is a worthwhile read!

—Rev. Allan Buss
Senior Pastor, Immanuel Lutheran Church, Belvidere, IL

With the heart of a pastor and the mind of a scholar, Alvin J. Schmidt provides a welcome resource for Lutherans living in a diverse culture. Do you want a clear and thorough understanding of Lutheran "hallmarks" such as the distinction of Law and Gospel, the blessing of the Sacraments, and life as sinner and saint? Schmidt has done a remarkable job of covering the ground. That he is able to bring this knowledge forward in such a full and accessible way is a true benefit to Lutheran laity and families.

—Rev. Warren Graff, STM
Pastor, Grace Lutheran Church, Albuquerque, NM

Dr. Schmidt addresses what has become an all-too-common problem in the Lutheran Church, especially in America, with many Lutherans "not knowing or not being conscious that they possess a theological heritage that is significantly different from other Christian denominations" (p. 11). This deficiency in Lutheran identity among Lutherans often results in their sacrificing that heritage—but they do so without realizing that they are losing a valuable and truly biblical and evangelical heritage. Schmidt sets out to halt and reverse this drift away from a genuine Lutheran piety and ethos, wishing to see instead the emergence of "an observable Lutheran mystique" among an informed Lutheran laity. Anyone who shares these concerns, as well as these hopes for a renewal of Lutheran consciousness and commitment, will find this book to be an extremely helpful resource and tool.

—David Jay Webber, STM
Pastor, Redeemer Lutheran Church, Scottsdale, AZ

This book addresses a serious predicament even within committed Lutheran churches, and that is the biblical and confessional ignorance so widespread in our time. With clear words, Alvin Schmidt opens the door for Lutheran Christians to reclaim their spiritual heritage. Careful reflection on the topics he presents will contribute to a growth in the maturity of Christ's people, making their confession more honest because they've gained a clearer understanding of what it means. Parish pastors will find plenty of useful material here for Bible class and other adult discussion groups.

—Rev. Dr. Robert Bugbee
President, Lutheran Church—Canada

CONCORDIA PUBLISHING HOUSE • SAINT LOUIS

HALLMARKS
of LUTHERAN
IDENTITY

Alvin J. Schmidt

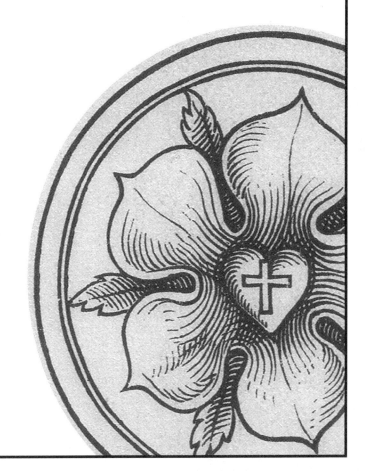

Published by Concordia Publishing House
3558 S. Jefferson Ave., St. Louis, MO 63118-3968
1-800-325-3040 · www.cph.org

Cover art: iStockphoto.com

Manufactured in the United States of America

Library of Congress Cataloging-in-Publication Data
Names: Schmidt, Alvin J., author.
Title: Hallmarks of Lutheran Identity / Alvin J. Schmidt.
Description: St. Louis : Concordia Publishing House, 2017.
Identifiers: LCCN 2016041655 (print) | LCCN 2016046422 (ebook) | ISBN 9780758655578 | ISBN 9780758655585
Subjects: LCSH: Lutheran Church--Doctrines.
Classification: LCC BX8065.3 .S36 2017 (print) | LCC BX8065.3 (ebook) | DDC 230/.41--dc23
LC record available at https://lccn.loc.gov/2016041655

2 3 4 5 6 7 8 9 10 11   28 27 26 25 24 23 22 21 20 19

CONTENTS

ABBREVIATIONS

AE	Luther's Works: American Edition
KJV	King James Version of the Bible
LSB	*Lutheran Service Book*
NIV	New International Version of the Bible
NKJV	New King James Version of the Bible
RSV	Revised Standard Version of the Bible
TLH	*The Lutheran Hymnal*

ABBREVIATIONS FOR DOCUMENTS IN THE BOOK OF CONCORD

AC Augsburg Confession

Ap Apology of the Augsburg Confession

Ep Epitome of the Formula of Concord

FC Formula of Concord

LC Large Catechism of Martin Luther

SA Smalcald Articles

SC Small Catechism of Martin Luther

SD Solid Declaration of the Formula of Concord

Tr Treatise on the Power and Primacy of the Pope

Dedication

To my grandsons, J. P. Schmidt and Will Schmidt

Acknowledgments

In my previously published books, I expressed gratitude and appreciation to my wife, Carol, for her patience in tolerating my social isolation while writing those books. She extended her patience again as I wrote the present book, and she also proofread the manuscript before it went to the publisher. I would be remiss if I did not thank her again. So, many kind thanks, Carol.

Considerable gratitude is also due to Beth Hoeltke, Public Service Administrator at the library at Concordia Seminary, St. Louis. She helped me obtain some special interlibrary materials. I also appreciate the assistance Lyle Buettner, Special Collections Librarian at Concordia Seminary, provided me with German and Latin books authored by some sixteenth- and seventeenth-century Lutheran theologians. My research also benefited from the helpfulness I received from Daniel Harmelink, Laura Marrs, and Todd Zittlow at Concordia Historical Institute, St. Louis. I also thank the personnel at St. Louis University's rare book collection for making available a thirteenth-century papal document. And not to be overlooked is my appreciation for the help received from several librarians at Washington University, St. Louis. And finally, I was impressed with the professional editing done by Laura Lane, Scot Kinnaman, and Barbara Shippy, along with designer Vicky Schaeffer. They were superb.

FOREWORD

Five hundred years on, does the Lutheran Reformation matter to most Americans? The sociological evidence is rather sobering. According to a recent study of American religiosity, there has been a sharp increase in the "nones," those who identify with no particular religious affiliation.[1] This includes a minority of confessed atheists and agnostics, but most of the nones simply reject the idea that it really matters which religious tradition one follows, either because they think religion in general is unimportant or because they see no value in any specific set of religious teachings. And the problem does not end there. A decade ago, Christian Smith and Melinda Denton showed that many American youth who do claim a religious affiliation are either ignorant of, or indifferent toward, the central doctrines that define their tradition. Instead, their main guiding belief is *moralistic therapeutic deism*. This eclectic set of convictions directly conflicts with the most basic Christian teachings. It "is not a religion of repentance from sin . . . of building character through suffering . . . of basking in God's love and grace. . . . It is about attaining subjective well-being . . . and getting along amiably with other people."[2] On this view, people are basically good (not infected with original sin), God is not involved in most of our lives (deism), and when He is, it is only as life-coach and therapist, not as our only hope of salvation.

It is difficult to imagine attitudes further removed from the clear, biblical confessions of the Lutheran Reformation. Evidently, many people do not understand the incredible achievement of the Lutheran reformers in recovering and articulating God's truth about our

---

1   Pew Research Center, May 12, 2015, "America's Changing Religious Landscape." Accessed 12/29/2016. http://assets.pewresearch.org/wp-content/uploads/sites/11/2015/05/RLS-08 -26-full-report.pdf.

2   Christian Smith and Melinda Denton, *Soul Searching: The Religious and Spiritual Lives of American Teenagers* (New York: Oxford University Press, 2005), 163–64.

sinful condition and Christ as our only Savior. Nothing, therefore, is more desperately needed than a book like this one: a fresh, accessible account of the great teachings of the Lutheran Reformation that explains why they are not outdated cultural relics but rather faithful expositions of the Word of God with eternal value, a gift to Lutherans and non-Lutherans alike.

Alvin Schmidt is known to many for his combination of a highly accessible style with meticulous historical research, as evidenced by such splendid works as *How Christianity Changed the World*, *The Great Divide*, and *The American Muhammad*. In the present volume, Dr. Schmidt uses the same approach, giving a clear and concise presentation of distinctive Lutheran contributions to the Christian faith, and also noting many misconceptions that persist even among contemporary confessional Lutherans. Dr. Schmidt makes it very clear where he stands on disputed matters, and even if some readers disagree, they will learn why the issue is important.

As one might expect, Dr. Schmidt begins with an exposition of the three great *solas*—we are saved *sola gratia* (by grace alone), *sola fide* (by faith alone), and *sola Scriptura* (by Scripture alone). But he points out that these three affirmations are actually subordinate to a fourth, *solus Christus* (Christ alone), which emphasizes that for Lutherans, *all* theology is rooted in Christ. It is in Christ alone that the true God is revealed to us, and it is by attending to Christ and His actions that we come to know God, not by speculations about the "God of the philosophers." And it is the centrality of Christ that accounts for what is distinctive in Lutheran theology. We see this in Luther's central "breakthrough": our works make no contribution to our salvation, but we are saved purely by Christ's works and the loving, gracious gift of His righteousness. And we see it in Luther's understanding of the contents of the New Testament canon, which depended not only on a text's apostolicity but also on whether it preaches Christ. It is also vital in understanding the proper distinction between Law and Gospel, Word and Sacraments as Means of Grace, and the real presence of Christ in, with, and under the elements of Holy Communion.

Along the way, Dr. Schmidt points out where Lutherans disagree with the teachings of the Roman Catholic Church and other Protestant denominations. Commendably, he seeks to show that these differences emerged because Lutherans insist we should take Christ at His Word, neither altering nor adding to His teaching. This explains why Lutherans accept Christ's real (supernatural) presence in Communion without adopting a man-made theory of *how* He becomes present, and why Lutherans follow Scripture in affirming single (not double) predestination.

The Lutheran reformers believed there could be no reformation of the church without a reformation of education, and they not only promoted universal education but also created pedagogical materials of tremendous enduring value. Schmidt provides expositions of the purpose and contents of Dr. Luther's Small Catechism and Large Catechism, as well as Luther's contributions to music and liturgy and the main concepts of Reformation theology. The last includes the ideas that Christians are simultaneously sinners, condemned by the Law, and saints, saved by grace; that God governs His people in two ways: by coercion and Law in the secular sphere, but by the free gift of grace in the spiritual sphere; that all Christians are priests; and that all our stations and occupations in life are sacred and God-pleasing vocations, through which we love our neighbor as God provides for His people. Dr. Schmidt also provides helpful introductions to important doctrinal statements, including the Augsburg Confession, which gave birth to the Lutheran Church, and the Book of Concord, a handbook including all of the Lutheran confessions.

Alvin Schmidt's timely book will admonish and inspire, correct and encourage faithful Lutherans. And it will provide an accessible introduction to Lutheranism for non-Lutherans who know it is only *God's* opinion about the human condition and how we are saved that matters, and who may realize that making that opinion crystal clear was the whole point of the Lutheran Reformation.

Dr. Angus Menuge, Professor and Chair of Philosophy,
Concordia University Wisconsin

INTRODUCTION

Throughout my career, at various speaking engagements over the past four to five decades, I have interacted with numerous Lutherans in different parts of the country. In these contexts, I have often observed that many Lutheran laypeople do not know (or even believe) that their personal theological beliefs are at odds with the biblical teachings Lutheran theology has historically confessed and taught. My observations, of course, are not unique. In 1970, a nationwide representative survey asked Lutherans what they believed as members of the American Lutheran Church (ALC), the Lutheran Church in America (LCA), and The Lutheran Church—Missouri Synod (LCMS), all three bodies representing about nine million Lutherans. Two years later, the survey's findings appeared in *A Study of Generations.* The study reported that many Lutherans held a number of beliefs incompatible with basic Lutheran theology. For example, it stated, "The humanity of Jesus is a hollow, empty humanity for most Lutherans."[1]

Most surprisingly, the study revealed that four in ten Lutherans believed they were saved and justified by works, rather than by faith alone in Jesus Christ.[2] The magnitude of this finding shocked many Lutheran pastors, given that ever since the Reformation in the 1500s, faithful Lutheran pastors had taught and preached the words of St. Paul: "For by grace you have been saved through faith. And this is not your own doing; it is the gift of God, not a result of works, so that no one may boast" (Ephesians 2:8–9).

Then, in 1997, Lutheran Brotherhood published a study that surveyed 2,247 American Lutherans from the The Lutheran Church—Missouri Synod (LCMS), the Evangelical Lutheran Church in America (ELCA), the Wisconsin Evangelical Synod (WELS), and other Lutherans. One of the questions asked, though not exactly the same as the one asked in 1970, was quite similar. The results revealed that 56.2 percent of the Lutherans surveyed believed that "God is satisfied if a person lives the best life one can."[3] Among Lutherans under the age of 35, the figure was even higher: 67.4 percent felt that way. Clearly, these respondents believed they were saved by their works.

Thus, there appears to be a need for Lutheran laypeople to have access to a book in nontechnical language that states and explains what confessional Lutheran theology has taught and practiced since the time of the Reformation in the sixteenth century. This book focuses on the hallmarks of Lutheran theology that in most instances are also hallmarks of Lutheran identity. Most of the hallmarks are the Lutheran Church's major theological teachings. They distinguish Lutherans from Christians of other denominations. And when Lutherans recognize and know these hallmarks, they have the answer to the question "What do we Lutherans believe?"

Many laypeople who ask what Lutherans believe have been members of a Lutheran Church since infancy. In confirmation classes, students (usually in seventh or eighth grade) receive doctrinal instruction that commonly includes memorizing and explaining much of Luther's Small Catechism.

Having served for nearly four decades as a college and seminary professor, I, as a Lutheran pastor, was privileged to preach in numerous congregations in six American states and also in Canada, usually filling in for pastors on vacation. When asked to teach the adult Bible class, I discovered that sometimes half of those in attendance had never even seen Luther's Small Catechism. This seemed to indicate that many of these individuals likely became members of the church as adults who had received minimal or abbreviated instruction, frequently without Luther's Small Catechism—traditionally thought of as the basic text for instruction in the faith.

But even Lutherans who received good instruction as junior catechumens were really too young at

This book focuses on the hallmarks of Lutheran theology that in most instances are also hallmarks of Lutheran identity.

HALLMARKS OF LUTHERAN IDENTITY

the time to understand fully what they learned. Then, soon after the Rite of Confirmation, many Lutherans fail to keep their knowledge from going dormant by not attending Bible classes, taught Sundays in most Lutheran parishes. Most confirmed members also fail to use Luther's Small Catechism as a prayer book, even when they take time for home devotions. Thus, in time, much of what Lutherans once learned is soon forgotten, and so it is not surprising that many Lutherans sometimes ask, "What do we Lutherans believe?"

In 1992, Mark A. Noll published an article titled "The Lutheran Difference."[4] The article noted Lutherans in America have made little or no difference in American culture, in spite of Lutheran theology being notably different than the culture in which it finds itself. Noll does not say, but one wonders whether the reason Lutherans have not made any real difference in American culture is perhaps the result of their not knowing or not being conscious that they possess a theological heritage that is significantly different from other Christian denominations.

Not long after Noll's essay appeared, Lutheran author Robert Benne, in his book *The Paradoxical Vision* (Fortress, 1995), wondered whether the Lutheran difference (he could have said "Lutheran hallmarks") would survive among Lutherans, particularly in regard to the relevancy of Lutheran theology concerning America's social and political issues. Benne's question implies that American Lutherans either do not know what the Lutheran difference (to use Noll's term) is or, if they do, they are not very interested in maintaining and defending it.

Apparently, Lutherans living in the presence of America's large numbers of non-Lutheran Protestants, whose beliefs and values differ notably from Lutheran theology, have been affected by them, even though these non-Lutheran bodies have very different views regarding some basic Christian doctrines. For example, they usually put more emphasis on sanctification (being or becoming holy) than on justification (being declared righteous before God because of a Christian's faith in Jesus Christ). They see less value in the symbolism of the cross in church services or in church art and architecture. Many tend to confuse the two spheres of government (sacred and secular) in regard to social and political issues. They also lack the Lutheran understanding of work and vocation that contends God sees all work having equal value, for He does not assign social status to different kinds of work, as most societies do. Nor do they see God hidden in people's work (Luther referred to this as "His mask") by which He keeps His created world functioning. These non-Lutheran Protestant beliefs and values, which in many ways are a part of American culture, have deterred numerous Lutherans from being conscious of their church's distinctively different teachings, the hallmarks of their theology and identity.

Historically, Lutherans have been blessed with doctrines and practices drawn from the Holy Scriptures and reinforced by the Lutheran Confessions in the Book of Concord. These Lutheran doctrines and practices are often seen by many non-Lutherans as the hallmarks of Lutheran theology. Since these hallmarks are recognized by many non-Lutherans, it seems fitting to cite and explain them to Lutheran laypeople, many of whom do not seem to be conscious of them. Lutheran pastors may also appreciate the discussion in this book, which they can share with their parishioners. These hallmarks, if more consciously recognized, stand to benefit Lutherans in today's American culture with its diverse, often conflicting, religious beliefs and practices, many of which run counter to the historic hallmarks of Lutheran theology.

It is said that Roman Catholics have a mystique; namely, a complex of quasi-mystical beliefs and practices. This mystique is evident as Catholics revere the pope, adore and pray to Mary, pray the rosary, celebrate the Mass (the Roman Church's term for celebrating the Lord's Supper), bless themselves with the sign of the cross, do not allow their priests to marry, value the work of nuns, believe in purgatory, have cardinals who elect the pope, and do not want to be like Protestants. This mystique is recognized by both Catholics and non-Catholics.

Lutherans, however, do not seem to have a mystique, though they certainly have the ingredients for one; namely, *solus Christus* (Christ alone), *sola*

> Lutherans have been blessed with doctrines and practices drawn from the Holy Scriptures and reinforced by the Lutheran Confessions in the Book of Concord.

HALLMARKS OF LUTHERAN IDENTITY

gratia (by grace alone), *sola fide* (by faith alone), *sola Scriptura* (by Scripture alone), the sacramental presence of Christ's body and blood in the Lord's Supper, Law and Gospel, Luther's Small Catechism, the doctrine of two spheres of government, the theology of the cross, an outstanding musical heritage that includes Luther's well-known hymn "A Mighty Fortress Is Our God," an annual celebration of Reformation Day, and so on. These are all distinctive Lutheran hallmarks that merit being seen and recognized as the Lutheran mystique. But thus far these hallmarks have not resulted in an observable Lutheran mystique in the minds of Lutherans or in the perceptions of non-Lutherans. Sometimes it appears many Lutherans do not mind being identified with Protestants in general. Apparently, many Lutherans do not know or believe they have a theological heritage that differs from non-Lutheran Protestants.

This book seeks to help Lutheran laity come to know, understand, and appreciate their church's treasured teachings and help them not to be tempted to think it makes little or no difference whether they or their children remain Lutheran in our diverse culture. To help today's Lutherans overcome the latter temptation, the book seeks to inform and encourage them to understand, to believe, and to hold fast to the historic Lutheran teachings.

The title of each chapter bears the name of an important Lutheran doctrine; namely, one of its hallmarks. Some chapters also have hallmarks within the more prominent hallmark named in the chapter's title. For instance, Luther's contention that apart from Jesus Christ the Bible would be largely a meaningless book is a hallmark within the hallmark of *solus Christus* in chapter 1. And the frequent Lutheran assertion in the Formula of Concord, "We believe, teach, and confess" is a hallmark within the hallmark of the Book of Concord (see chapter 19).

Regarding this book's use of the term *hallmark*, readers will notice that often it refers to both Lutheran theology and its adherents' identity. Occasionally, in some contexts, the term refers only to one or the other. This book also discusses some key biblical concepts that today are in need of clarification. One example is the current use of the word *faith* in our culture. Chapter 3 documents that the word *pistis* (Greek for "faith") is a Christian innovation because *pistis* had no religious meaning in the ancient Greek culture. The chapter further shows how our English-speaking culture has given the word *faith* meanings that are biblically foreign and thus widely misused when, for instance, non-Christian religions today are referred to as "people of faith," referring to people who are affiliated with any kind of religious group. This practice contradicts Ephesians 4:5, where Paul told the Ephesian Christians there was only "one faith"—Christianity.

This book also notes that, over time, some Lutheran hallmarks have become less prominent and have essentially disappeared from Lutheran theology. Chapters 5 and 6, for example, discuss this phenomenon in connection with the longstanding concern Lutheran theologians had regarding the canonicity of some books in the New Testament. These chapters are intended to help today's Lutherans gain a better understanding of the important historical, theological background of the New Testament's canonicity, and also help them answer the question "What do we Lutherans believe?"

Also noted is that numerous hallmarks are often not known even to lifelong Lutherans, one example being these words spoken in the historic Lutheran liturgy: "I, a poor, miserable sinner, confess unto You all my sins and iniquities." These words are not heard in other denominations; they are uniquely Lutheran. Additionally, most Lutherans are not aware that when Luther and his new bride, Katharina, received the former Augustinian Black Cloister building as a gift, it became the first family parsonage in Christendom, the likes of which soon became an admiral institution in most Protestant denominations. This book also notes why the Lutheran Church became known as "the singing church," initially not a compliment.

If members of the Lutheran Church take the hallmarks of Lutheran identity to heart and internalize their abiding Christian value, they will not just be Lutherans out of mere social conformity but out of a God-pleasing conviction. This is the prayerful objective of the present book.

To further help Lutherans know and better understand the various hallmarks of their Lutheran theology and identity, this book offers questions at the end of each chapter for group discussion. They are questions suitable for Bible classes and other educational contexts.

Soli Deo Gloria

CHAPTER 1

SOLUS CHRISTUS (CHRIST ALONE)

"I am the way, and the truth, and the life. No one comes to the Father except through Me." —Jesus Christ; John 14:6

Solus Christus (Christ alone), along with *sola gratia* (by grace alone), *sola fide* (by faith alone), and *sola Scriptura* (by Scripture alone), became one of the four slogans of the Reformation. To Luther and his followers, *solus Christus* was the first and most important Christian truth. It can thus be rightly called the number one hallmark of Lutheran theology. Yet, many Lutherans, similar to other Protestants, have often only seen (or heard of) *sola gratia, sola fide*, and *sola Scriptura* on posters, banners, and printed signs. The slogan *solus Christus* is almost always overlooked when these three are shown. This omission is not only common but also seems largely unrecognized. It is an unfortunate omission, for *solus Christus* should not only be cited with the other three slogans but also listed first, for without *solus Christus* the other three really have no theological value.

Sometimes people ask why *solus Christus* is not written as *sola Christus*, given the other three have the word *sola* preceding them. The reason for this difference lies in the Latin rule that requires an adjective to agree with the noun it describes. The Latin words *gratia, fide*, and *Scriptura* are feminine nouns, and thus each takes the feminine adjective, *sola*. On the other hand, *Christus* is a masculine noun, and so the adjective also has to be masculine—namely, *solus*.

Given that the next three chapters focus on *sola gratia, sola fide*, and *sola Scriptura*, respectively, some readers may wonder why this book does not have a chapter on *Soli Deo Gloria* ("To God Alone the

Glory"), given that this slogan was sometimes used during and after the Reformation years. In fact, Johann Sebastian Bach would write "S. D. G." (*Soli Deo Gloria*) on his musical compositions to thank and honor God. He also penned additional abbreviations on his manuscripts; namely, "J. J." (*Jesu Juva*, meaning "Help Me, Jesus") or "I.N.J." (*In Nomine Jesu*, meaning "In the Name of Jesus"). *Soli Deo Gloria* is a Christian expression of gratitude to God rather than a biblical doctrine. Thus, this book does not include *Soli Deo Gloria* as a Lutheran hallmark.

SOLUS CHRISTUS AND THE BIBLE

The doctrine of *solus Christus* has several facets. First, Lutheran theology, reflecting Luther's description of the Bible, sees the Bible as the cradle of Christ.

Although non-Lutheran Protestants do not deny this understanding of the Bible, it is not a commonly found emphasis in their theological literature, especially when compared to Lutheran theology. Luther contended that the Bible was revealed by God in order to make Jesus Christ known and that without Christ the Bible would largely be an unclear book. Here is how Luther put it: "To him who has the Son Scripture is an open book; and the stronger his faith in Christ becomes, the more brightly will the light of Scripture shine for him."[1] Commenting on Romans 10:4, which states, "Christ is the end of the law so that there may be righteousness for everyone who believes," Luther said that in this passage St. Paul indicates "that all Scripture finds its meaning in Christ."[2]

Arguing that the Bible is the cradle of Christ was not a new teaching introduced by Luther. Christ Himself taught this doctrine. Walking with two men on the road to Emmaus the day He arose from the dead, Christ said, "Everything written about Me in the Law of Moses and the Prophets and the Psalms must be fulfilled" (Luke 24:44). Similarly, the apostle John quotes Christ saying the Scriptures "bear witness about Me" (John 5:39). And Luke, in his Gospel, referring to the risen Christ's conversation with the men on the way to Emmaus, says, "beginning with Moses and all the Prophets, He [Christ] interpreted to them in all the Scriptures the things concerning Himself" (24:27).

So strong was Luther's conviction concerning the Bible being the cradle of Christ, he once said, "Whoever does not have or want to have this Man properly and truly who is called Jesus Christ, God's Son, whom we Christians proclaim, must keep his hands off the Bible."[3] Another time, in responding to Erasmus, the man with whom Luther disagreed much, he stated: "Take Christ out of the Scriptures, and what will you find left in them?"[4] To Luther, the Bible was only valuable because it proclaimed Jesus Christ and His redemptive work. And thus since Luther's time, *solus Christus* has been a distinctive Lutheran hallmark.

Solus Christus and Knowing God

The second aspect of *solus Christus* states that God can only be known through His Son, Jesus Christ. Luther maintained that "he who does not find or receive God in Christ will never find Him. He will not find God outside of Christ, even should he mount up above the heavens or descend below hell itself, or go beyond the limits of the world."[5] At the Marburg Colloquy in 1529, Luther said, "I do not know of any God except who was made flesh, nor do I want to have another."[6]

Although Luther can rightly be credited with accenting the concept of *solus Christus*, he was not entirely alone in holding this position. Erasmus said something similar to Luther when he once stated, "Nothing is to be sought in Scripture but Christ."[7] But it was Luther's strong emphasis on *solus Christus* that received the most attention during the Reformation and later as well. A hundred years after Luther, Blaise Pascal echoed him, saying, "We know God only through Jesus Christ."[8] And more recently, Wolfhart Pannenberg stated, "As Christians we know God only as he has been revealed in and through Jesus."[9]

As with the teaching that Jesus Christ is the focus of the Bible, the teaching that God can only be known or found in His Son comes from Christ Himself. When His disciple Philip asked to be shown the Father, Jesus replied, "Have I been with you so long, and you still do not know Me, Philip?" Then He declared, "Whoever has seen Me has seen the Father. How can you say, 'Show us the Father?'" (John 14:9). To make sure Philip would not miss the point, Jesus further stated, "Believe Me that I am in the Father and the Father is in Me, or else believe on account of the works themselves" (14:11).

For centuries, countless people have searched for God but have not found or come to know Him. The ancient Greeks and Romans thought they knew God to be present in humanly crafted idols; others thought they found Him by worshiping the sun or the moon. Today, many think they have found God in the teachings of Buddha or in the Hindu deities of Brahma, Shiva, and Vishnu; others think they have found Him in the teachings of Islam's Qur'an. But Jesus says God can only be known by people believing in the Son of God. "If you had known Me, you would have known My Father also. From now on you do know Him and have seen Him" (John 14:7).

To Luther, as Hermann Sasse has noted, "God who is hidden (*Deus absconditus*) outside of Christ [is] revealed (*Deus revelatus*) in Christ only."[10] In short, God can only be known through *solus Christus*. Thus, the Islamic concept of god as Allah, the three gods of Hinduism (Brahma, Shiva, and Vishnu), or "The True Name" in the religion of Sikhism are false. For Christ stated, "Whoever has seen Me has seen the Father" (John 14:9), or in the words of St. Paul, "For in Him [Christ] the whole fullness of deity dwells bodily" (Colossians 2:9).

Today's multiculturalists or religious pluralists do not want to hear that God cannot be found apart from Jesus Christ. They think it is bigoted to teach and believe such a doctrine. But that is precisely what Christ taught and preached, and that was also what the early Christians firmly believed and proclaimed. It was this message that not only made them highly unpopular but also often resulted in their being tortured, imprisoned, and sometimes even executed for refusing to participate in Rome's religiously syncretistic, polytheistic activities. Had the early Christians agreed to participate in pagan Rome's inclusive religious practices, Christianity would surely have disappeared in a relatively short period of time. This conclusion Lutherans need to ponder when asked to participate in today's many religiously syncretistic activities that often take place on civic holidays or other events that publicly ignore *solus Christus*.

SOLUS CHRISTUS: THE ONLY WAY TO ETERNAL LIFE

The third component of *solus Christus* in Lutheran theology maintains that no one can obtain eternal life without faith in Jesus Christ's work of salvation. This doctrine stems from what Jesus Himself taught: "I am the way, and the truth, and the life. No one comes to the Father except through Me" (John 14:6). Christ not only said that He was the only way to eternal life but He also taught that "Whoever believes in Him [Christ] is not condemned, but whoever does not believe is condemned already, because he has not believed in the name of the only Son of God" (3:18). Similarly, Christ Himself underscored *solus Christus* when He told the Pharisees, "Unless you believe that I am He you will die in your sins" (8:24).

The teaching of *solus Christus* was boldly proclaimed by the apostle Peter to the temple's council in Jerusalem when he declared salvation could only be obtained in Jesus Christ. "And there is salvation in no one else, for there is no other name under heaven given among men by which we must be saved" (Acts 4:12). In regard to this biblical reference, Luther said, "it is impossible that there should be more saviors, ways, or means to be saved than through the one righteousness which our Savior Jesus Christ is and has bestowed upon us, and has offered to God for us as our one mercy seat."[11]

Despite Jesus having clearly taught there is no salvation outside of faith in Him, many Christians, including some modern Lutherans, do not accept this biblical teaching. In 1972, a nationwide study of Lutherans in the United States (noted earlier in the Introduction) revealed that 72 percent of Lutherans in America believed that "although there are many religions in the world, most of them lead to the same God."[12] And when in 1997 a similar question was asked once again, 67 percent of Lutherans in America said most religious beliefs led to the same God.[13] This means approximately seven out of ten American Lutherans presently do not appear to believe in *solus Christus* when it comes to human beings obtaining eternal life. Clearly, the ideology of multiculturalism and related forces are having powerfully negative effects on large numbers of today's American Lutherans.

Solus Christus and Christian Prayers

The fourth component of *solus Christus* means that Christians are to pray in Christ's name. Jesus said, "Whatever you ask in My name, this I will do" (John 14:13). Countless Christians have heeded these words from the Church's earliest days by beginning or ending their prayers in the name of Jesus Christ.

Today, however, it is not uncommon to hear some Christians pray Christless prayers by omitting the name of Jesus Christ, often when they pray in a civic setting, where apparently they do not want to give offense to those who are not Christians. These prayers usually begin with the words "Dear God." Then, after the petitions and thanks have been expressed, the person praying concludes by saying, "We pray these things in Your name."

There is an unrecognized oddity about this kind of prayer, for God's name was not mentioned. The word *God* is merely used as a generic term for a divine being. Thus, Christians want to name Jesus Christ in their prayers. But some may ask, "What about the Lord's Prayer, which does not include Jesus' name?" True, but it is His prayer, and so when Christians pray that prayer, they are honoring Him, even though Christ's name is not specifically mentioned.

Using the name Jesus Christ in our prayers is important for at least three reasons. First, such prayers follow Christ's command (John 14:13). Second, praying in the name of Christ gives a Christian witness and confession to all present. Third, it tells those hearing the prayer(s), contrary to what is believed by many in today's pervasive climate of multiculturalism and political correctness, Christians do not pray as non-Christians pray. Christians pray in the name of Jesus Christ; that is, *solus Christus*.

Christians pray in the name of Jesus Christ; that is, *solus Christus*.

Given the biblical and Lutheran accent on praying in the name of Jesus Christ, it behooves Lutheran parents to teach their children to pray in His name. Similarly, Lutheran Sunday Schools, parochial schools, and sermons need to teach this important way to pray. If Lutherans are not specifically taught to pray in the name of Jesus Christ, given today's pervasive accent on political correctness, they may unwittingly pray Christless prayers, such as is often heard on radio and television and on civic holidays, such as Memorial Day, Fourth of July, Veterans' Day, and Thanksgiving Day.

Often Christians end their prayers with the words "We ask this in Jesus' name." This is fine, but it is even better also to include the name of "Christ." To say "Christ" along with the name "Jesus" accents His messianic role. When praying in the latter way, we Lutherans are following the example of St. Paul, who most frequently used the name Jesus Christ or Christ Jesus in his epistles. Similarly, Luther commonly used both names when he prayed. When he used only one name, he usually used the name Christ. Although Paul and Luther are noble examples to imitate, a Lutheran should never feel guilty if he or she prays only in the name of Jesus.

The manner in which the Church, for centuries, prayed its collects in its historic liturgy are also great examples to follow. These brief prayers have typically concluded their petitions to God with the words "through Jesus Christ, Your Son, our Lord." These final words in most collects underscore the deity of Christ in opposition to the Arian heresy[14] of the fourth century that did not consider Jesus as God, but rather as a special being created by God.

We also find Martin Luther consistently praying in the name of Jesus Christ. He rarely separated the name Christ from the name Jesus in his prayers. For instance, his well-known Morning and Evening Prayers in his Small Catechism begin: "I thank You, my heavenly Father, through Jesus Christ, Your dear Son . . ." Praying in this manner is additional evidence of Luther's strong belief in *solus Christus*. It is a noble example for Lutherans to imitate. And it is also important to note that the first thesis of Luther's Ninety-Five Theses (1517), which sparked the Reformation, begins, "Our Lord and Master Jesus Christ . . ."

Solus Christus in Christian prayers further means Christians are not to pray to departed saints, a practice common in the Roman Catholic Church and also in the Eastern Orthodox churches. The Augsburg Confession (1530) of Lutheran theology states, "But the Scriptures do not teach that we are to call on the saints or to ask the saints for help. Scripture sets before us the one Christ as the Mediator, Atoning Sacrifice, High Priest, and Intercessor. He is to be prayed to" (AC XXI 2–3). In not praying to saints, Lutheran theology cites St. Paul, who told Timothy, "For there is one God, and there is one mediator between God and men, the man Christ Jesus" (1 Timothy 2:5).

SOLUS CHRISTUS AS HUMAN AND DIVINE

According to *A Study of Generations*, Lutheran laypeople strongly emphasized Jesus' divinity but underemphasized His human nature. The study correctly pointed out that believing in the divinity of Christ does not indicate what a person believes about the humanity of Jesus. Given that the majority of Lutherans underemphasize Jesus' human nature, the study also stated that "Lutherans as a group are Nestorians; that is, they reflect the ancient heresy of separating the two natures of Christ."[15] Thus, they either do not know, remember, or believe what the Council of Chalcedon in AD 451 declared: "We confess one and the same Jesus Christ, the Son and Lord only begotten, in two natures without mixture, without change, without division, without separation."

Solus Christus and the Roman Catholic Church

While most Protestant denominations do not deny or reject *solus Christus* as a basic Christian doctrine, they do not all explicitly teach that it is necessary to believe in Jesus Christ in order to obtain eternal salvation. Whether someone can obtain eternal life without faith in Christ is a question often left unanswered. Outside the Protestant realm, however, the Roman Catholic Church has specifically asked whether there is salvation outside of Jesus Christ and has answered in the affirmative.

The official Roman Catholic statement on this matter is found in the papal declaration of *Lumen Gentium* (1964), cited in the *Catechism of the Catholic Church* (1994). It states, "Those who, through no fault of their own, do not know the Gospel of Christ or His Church, but who nevertheless seek God with a sincere heart, and, moved by grace, try in their actions to do His will as they know it through the dictates of their conscience—those too may achieve eternal salvation."[16] This Roman Catholic teaching was already strongly underscored by Pope Pius IX, who held the papal office from 1846 to 1878. He decreed,

> It is known to Us [sic] and to you that those who labor in invincible ignorance concerning our most holy religion and who, assiduously observing the natural law and its precepts which has inscribed in the hearts of all, and being ready to obey God, live an honest and upright life can, through the working of divine light and grace, attain eternal Life.[17]

This statement contradicts the words of Jesus in John 14:6, which clearly state, "I am the way, and the truth, and the life. No one comes to the Father except through Me." It also contradicts another statement of His, "Whoever believes in the Son has eternal life; whoever does not obey the Son shall not see life, but the wrath of God remains on him" (3:36). As noted above, the doctrine of *solus Christus* in regard to salvation is also stated unequivocally by St. Peter in Acts 4:12: "And there is salvation in no one else, for there is no other name under heaven given among men by which we must be saved." These passages unmistakably declare eternal life can only be obtained through faith in Jesus Christ.

Despite these clear biblical references, the Roman Catholic Church, in effect, denies *solus Christus* in regard to people obtaining eternal life. Thus, according to Rome's *Lumen Gentium* and its catechism of 1994, it really makes no difference whether individuals are Muslims, Hindus,

Sikhs, Buddhists, or astral worshipers; they all will obtain eternal life even though they do not have faith in Jesus Christ. Thus, the Lutheran hallmark of *solus Christus* is not accepted in Roman Catholic theology.

❧❧

CONCLUSION

Luther, in his strong accent on solus Christus, said anything that diminishes Christ is heresy. Unfortunately, there are a number of ways Christ is often diminished. He is diminished when people think they can obtain eternal life without Him; when people think all religions honor and pray to the same God; when individuals believe they are saved by good works, or by good works combined with faith in Christ; when they intentionally pray Christless or deistic prayers; or when they see Christ primarily as a great teacher but not as God.

As Lutherans, we hold to the hallmark of *solus Christus* because the Holy Spirit has convinced us that there is no salvation outside of Him, just as the Holy Spirit convinced Peter to say, "Lord, to whom shall we go? You have the words of eternal life" (John 6:68). By believing in *solus Christus*, we also take seriously Jesus' words, "Whoever believes in Him [Jesus] is not condemned, but whoever does not believe is condemned already, because he has not believed in the name of the only Son of God" (3:18).

Finally, as faithful followers of Christ, we Lutherans want to (1) remember that Christ is the light in which the Bible must be read and understood; (2) make a consistent, conscious effort always to pray in the name of Jesus Christ; (3) remember there is no salvation outside of Jesus Christ; and (4) recall Luther's words from his hymn "A Mighty Fortress Is Our God," where he says, "Ask ye, Who is this? Jesus Christ it is, Of Sabaoth Lord, And there's none other God" (*LSB* 656:2). *Solus Christus* is indeed a hallmark of Lutheran theology and identity.

> Luther, in his strong accent on *solus Christus*, said anything that diminishes Christ is heresy.

1. Why do *sola gratia, sola fide,* and *sola Scriptura* have no real spiritual or theological value without *solus Christus*?

2. How did Luther view the Bible in relation to Jesus Christ?

3. Research shows many Christians do not believe that Jesus Christ is the only way human beings can obtain eternal life. Why do you think this erroneous belief is so common among many people today, including some Lutherans?

4. What biblical passages can you cite to show that there is no salvation outside of Jesus Christ?

5. Why is it so easy in our Western culture today to say prayers that fail to mention the name of Jesus Christ?

6. Why should Christians always pray and make their petitions known to God by specifically praying in the name of Jesus Christ?

7. Cite some biblical passages that teach Christians to pray in the name of Jesus Christ.

8. Does God receive prayers that deliberately are not spoken in the name of Jesus Christ? Why or why not?

9. Why do you think, even in Lutheran contexts, we often hear or see *sola gratia, sola fide,* and *sola Scriptura,* but not *solus Christus*?

10. When did the Roman Catholic Church officially state that non-Christians could obtain eternal life without faith in Jesus Christ?

11. How can parents teach their children—or how can Christians teach the next generations—to be more conscious of the biblical fact that there is no salvation outside of Jesus Christ?

12. Why does the Bible theologically have no value apart from *solus Christus*?

CHAPTER 2

SOLA GRATIA (BY GRACE ALONE)

"But if it is by grace, it is no longer on the basis of works."
—St. Paul; Romans 11:6

GRACE: GOD'S MERCIFUL DISPOSITION

The concept of *sola gratia*, a prominent biblical concept, is underscored in several biblical passages, most specifically in Ephesians 2:8, which states, "For by *grace* you have been saved through faith" (emphasis added). *Grace* means "undeserved mercy, prompted by God's love shown by Jesus Christ." In order to gain a better understanding of God's love underlying His mercy, as shown in the New Testament, it is helpful to note the Greek language has three words for *love*. (1) *Eros* refers to erotic love. (2) *Philos* is love between friends. (3) *Agape* is the highest and most exalted form of love, a love that in reality only God is capable of exercising. Yet, there are numerous times that God in His Word wants Christians to exercise this exalted form of love; for example, "You shall love [*agape*] your neighbor as yourself" (Matthew 19:19b). "Love [*agape*] your enemies, do good to those who hate you" (Luke 6:27b). "Husbands, love [*agape*] your wives, as Christ loved [*agape*] the church and gave Himself up for her" (Ephesians 5:25). John 3:16 asserts, "For God so *loved* the world, that He gave His only Son, that whoever believes in Him should not perish but have eternal life" (emphasis added). The word *loved* in this verse is the past tense of *agape*.

In conformity with John 3:16, the apostle Paul told the Christians in Ephesus they were not saved by any of their good works but through their faith in Jesus Christ, whom God through grace sacrificed for their sins. Hence, *sola gratia* is solely and completely an act of God's merciful disposition, prompted by His love (*agape*).

God's grace is completely divorced from anything that any human being, even the most noble, is capable of meriting. For the apostle Paul says grace is "the gift of God, not a result of works, so that no one may boast" (Ephesians 2:8–9).

The grace of God is always active and present. It is not an idle emotion or compassion on God's part, but a disposition that prompts Him to save all those who repent and believe in His Son, Jesus Christ. Moreover, there is nothing in the universe or in mankind, except His love, that moves God to be gracious to those who believe in the merits of His Son's death and resurrection.

The grace of God is always active and present.

SOLA GRATIA AND GRATIA INFUSA

God's grace is not infused in Christians, as is officially taught in Roman Catholic theology by its concept of *gratia infusa*. The *Catechism of the Catholic Church* teaches, "The grace of Christ is the gratuitous gift that God makes to us of his own life, infused by the Holy Spirit into our soul to heal it of sin and sanctify it. It is the *sanctifying* or *deifying* [sic] *grace* received in Baptism."[1]

Lutheran theology teaches that if grace were infused in persons, they would then be capable of doing something for their salvation because at least some of the grace would come from the infused grace within them, and thus grace alone (*sola gratia*) would be diminished or nullified, in that the human being is contributing something to his or her salvation, hence, a human work (contribution) that is accepted as works-righteousness by God. As Edward Koehler has aptly stated, "The slightest injection of man's merit and worthiness utterly destroys the concept of grace."[2] Here it is also well to remember the words of St. Paul: "But if it is by grace, it is no longer on the basis of works; otherwise grace would no longer be grace" (Romans 11:6).

It needs to be underscored that while any and all "merits of man are indeed excluded from the concept of grace, the merits of Christ must necessarily be included."[3] This is consistent with the words spoken by Paul in Romans 3:22–24: "For there is no distinction: for all have sinned and fall short of the glory of God, and are justified by His grace as a gift, through the redemption that is in Christ Jesus."

When grace is understood and accepted as being an exclusive quality of God's gracious disposition, the Christian can be absolutely certain of its validity. On the other hand, if some part of it were to come from within the person, or what he or she has to do to merit grace, then there could never be total certainty, for the person would not know for sure whether he or she has done enough good works to obtain eternal salvation.

The Lutheran doctrine of *sola gratia* (by grace alone) gives all glory and honor to God. If human beings, even in the smallest way, could contribute to God's grace by any human efforts, it would not only deprive God of His glory and honor but also destroy the comforting doctrine of *sola gratia*. Hence, Lutheran theology, since the time of Martin Luther, has always accented and underscored *sola gratia* as a vitally important hallmark of Lutheran theology.

The Lutheran doctrine of *sola gratia* (by grace alone) gives all glory and honor to God.

Attributes of Saving Grace

God's saving grace has a number of attributes. To note and briefly discuss them provides us Christians an enriched and better understanding of the Gospel of Jesus Christ.

God's Grace Extends Back to Eternity[4]

God's grace is not a recent or ephemeral phenomenon. The apostle Paul underscored this important point when he told his co-worker Timothy that God "has saved us and called us with a holy calling, not according to our works, but according to His own purpose and grace which was given to us in Christ Jesus *before time began*" (2 Timothy 1:9 NKJV, emphasis added).

GOD'S GRACE IS UNIVERSAL

Despite mankind's sinful condition, God offers His saving grace to all people so that they would have available to them eternal life and salvation. As St. Paul assured Titus, "the grace of God has appeared, bringing salvation for all people" (Titus 2:11). Similarly, the apostle John wrote, "God so loved the world, that He gave His only Son, that whoever believes in Him should not perish but have eternal life" (John 3:16). And in the Old Testament, the prophet Ezekiel wrote, "As I live, declares the Lord GOD, I have no pleasure in the death of the wicked" (33:11).

God's grace for eternal salvation is available for all mankind, including for those who reject and spurn it by their unbelief. As Stephen, the first Christian martyr, said to his executioners as they stoned him, "You stiff-necked people, uncircumcised in heart and ears, you always resist the Holy Spirit. As your fathers did, so do you" (Acts 7:51). Similarly, Jesus lamented, "O Jerusalem, Jerusalem, the city that kills the prophets and stones those who are sent to it! How often would I have gathered your children together as a hen gathers her brood under her wings, and you were not willing!" (Luke 13:34).

GOD'S GRACE IS SERIOUS AND EFFICACIOUS

Along with Christians being saved by grace alone, Lutheran theology, in conformity with Scripture, also teaches God's universal grace is genuinely serious and efficacious, even though we know from Jesus' own words the way to eternal life is through a narrow gate, "and the way is easy that leads to destruction, and those who enter by it are many" (Matthew 7:13). This biblical fact sometimes prompts some to ask, "Why, then, are some converted while others are not, even though all people are by nature equally sinful and corrupt?"

In the Protestant world consisting of Lutherans and the Reformed (Calvinists and many Evangelicals), there are two very different answers to this question. The Calvinists[5] answer this question by citing Calvin, who taught that "God has always been at liberty to bestow His grace on whom He would."[6] Calvin further taught "that God, in His eternal counsel, chose those whom He pleased unto life eternal, and left those whom He pleased to eternal destruction."[7] Theologically, Calvin's teaching that denies God's universal, saving grace is known as double predestination, meaning God predestines (elects) some to salvation and some to damnation. The latter, according to Calvin, never had God's universal, saving grace extended to them. Thus, he denied that God's grace is serious and efficacious.

Devout adherents of Calvin's double predestination doctrine are sometimes referred to by the acronym of TULIP; namely, all people are born *totally* depraved but some are *unconditionally* elected; these are recipients of *limited* atonement, accept God's *irresistible* grace, and *persevere* as God's saints.

In contradistinction to Calvinism, it is important to note that Lutheran theology teaches single predestination, as taught in Scripture. This means all who die believing in Christ were predestined (elected) by God in His grace and mercy, as the apostle Paul told the Ephesian Christians that God "chose us in Him [Christ] before the foundation of the world, that we should be holy and blameless before Him" (Ephesians 1:4). Our Lutheran Confessions underscore these words spoken by Paul, for they say, "Predestination, or God's eternal election, covers only the godly, beloved children of God. It is a cause of their salvation, which He also provides" (FC Ep XI 5).

Single predestination asserts that God wants all people to be saved, and thus He does not elect or predestine anyone to damnation. As Francis Pieper has said, "Christians owe their whole Christian state in time, specifically also their faith, to their eternal election; but with the same clarity and emphasis Scripture also excludes the thought that the unbelief of the lost can be traced to a predestination to damnation."[8] To underscore this biblical teaching, some Lutherans have used the word *fault* to accent single predestination, indicating when people are eternally

Single predestination asserts that God wants all people to be saved, and thus He does not elect or predestine anyone to damnation.

lost, it is entirely their fault, and with regard to those who attain eternal life, it is entirely God's "fault."

While Calvinism, with its doctrine of double predestination, denies God's universal grace, many Evangelicals (often known as Arminians[9]), deny *sola gratia* by teaching that individuals in their conversion cooperate with God. This teaching is known as synergism, from the Greek *syn-ergo*, meaning "work with"; that is, working with God in their conversion. Hence, those who are predestined worked with God to become converted, while many did not. In this context, it is interesting to note that Roger E. Olson, a defender of synergism, states that most Protestant churches (Lutherans exempted) today are synergistic.[10]

Synergism teaches that before conversion "a person is not absolutely dead to good in spiritual things, but is badly wounded and half dead. . . . The will can do something toward salvation; it can help and cooperate in it and can qualify itself for it. The will can apply itself to grace, can grasp and accept it, and can believe the Gospel" (FC SD II 77). Hence, the Book of Concord rightly maintains that synergism denies *sola gratia* (by grace alone).

The Lutheran rejection of synergism in the Book of Concord was largely a response to Philip Melanchthon[11] and several other Lutherans who espoused this erroneous doctrine after Luther's death in 1546. Contrary to these Lutheran synergists, Luther was a monergist, one who contends God alone directs events in His world, including the act of converting a person to faith in Jesus Christ. The synergism of Melanchthon and his associates, however, was not a new phenomenon in the history of the Christian Church, for some Church Fathers in the Early Church and also later had espoused synergistic beliefs. Thus, the Lutheran opposition to synergism is a hallmark of Lutheran theology.

Synergists, on the other hand, answer that there is a difference in people because some unbelievers before conversion cooperate or offer less resistance in coming to faith in Jesus Christ, and for this reason, God in His foreknowledge predestined them to eternal life. This answer also denies *sola gratia* (by grace alone). Both groups use human reason, rather than Scripture, to resolve a divine mystery why God does not predestine or elect all people. Our Lutheran Confessions reject both Calvinism and synergism as contrabiblical, for "He [God] has revealed nothing to us about it in His Word, much less commanded us to investigate it with our thoughts. Instead, He has seriously discouraged us from that (Romans 11:33–35). Therefore, we should not reason in our thoughts, draw conclusions, or inquire curiously into these matters, but we should cling to His revealed Word, to which He points us" (FC SD XI 55).

Sola Gratia and the Means of Grace

There are a number of teachings that notably distinguish Lutheran theology from that of other Protestant denominations. One of them is what Lutherans call the "Means of Grace." From the time of Luther to the present day, Lutheran theology has always taught that God works through means in converting and also keeping Christians in His kingdom of grace, whereas some non-Lutheran Protestants teach that God converts people directly, apart from any means. In fact, since the Reformation, Lutheran theology has called this teaching "Enthusiasm" ("*Schwärmerei*" in German). Luther condemned Enthusiasm in his treatise "Against the Heavenly Prophets" (1525) and in the Smalcald Articles (1537), in which he stated, "God does not want to deal with us in any other way than through the spoken Word and the Sacraments. Whatever is praised as from the Spirit—without the Word and Sacraments—is the devil himself" (SA III VIII 10). These latter words by Luther are especially important for us to remember when we sometimes hear well-meaning Christians say that God spoke to them and gave them specific information relative to a particular concern of theirs, whether physical or spiritual. In short, God does not speak to us outside of His divinely inspired Word.

In order for Christians to benefit from His grace, God made it available through given means. One of the means is the Word of God. As St. Paul declared, "So faith comes from hearing, and hearing through the word of Christ" (Romans 10:17). In short, God's grace is revealed and made known to us by reading or hearing His divinely inspired Word.

Another means of God's grace available to us is the sacrament of Baptism, in which God's Word, connected with water, brings the baptized individual into the kingdom of grace and forgiveness. In Baptism, the individual—by daily repentance and faith in the promises of Baptism—receives the grace of God's forgiveness, as St. Peter proclaimed it on the Day of Pentecost: "Repent and be baptized every one of you in the name of Jesus Christ for the forgiveness of your sins, and you will receive the gift of the Holy Spirit" (Acts 2:38).

A third Means of Grace is the sacrament of the Lord's Supper. By its use, repentant Christians through faith in Christ obtain God's grace as they receive Christ's body and blood in this sacrament. His Word assures repentant recipients that their sins are forgiven when in faith they believe Christ's words, "Take, eat; this is My body," followed by the words "Drink of it, all of you, for this is My blood of the covenant, which is poured out for many for the forgiveness of sins" (Matthew 26:26–28).[12]

CONCLUSION

As noted earlier, according to Ephesians 2:8–9, all those who die and receive eternal life receive it only as a result of God's saving grace through faith that accepts and relies solely on the merits of God's only-begotten Son, Jesus Christ, who was crucified and raised from the dead for our justification (Romans 4:25). This doctrine is the core of the Christian theology around which the Lutheran Reformation revolved. It distinguishes the Christian religion from all others, even though there are really only two: the *Done Religion* (Christianity) and the *Do Religion* (all non-Christian religions). In Christianity, God in Jesus Christ has *done* everything necessary for man's eternal salvation, whereas in the *Do Religions*, every person is told to *do* something in order to obtain salvation.

CHAPTER 2 DISCUSSION QUESTIONS

1. What is meant by the concept of grace?

2. How does Lutheran theology differ from Roman Catholic theology in regard to the concept of grace?

3. What is infused grace (*gratia infusa*)? How does it conflict with Romans 11:6?

4. How is the Roman Catholic concept of infused grace related to works-righteousness?

5. Why does Lutheran theology teach that the Word of God, Baptism, and the Lord's Supper are the three Means of Grace?

6. How does God convey His saving grace to Christians?

7. Some individuals during the Reformation believed and taught that God bestowed His saving grace upon people apart from the Word of God, Baptism, and the Lord's Supper. By what name do the Lutheran Confessions call these individuals?

8. What dangerous implication is there in believing that God's saving grace is or can be received apart from the Word of God, Baptism, and the Lord's Supper?

9. What was one of the core doctrines of the Lutheran Reformation?

10. Why do so many people, including some erring Lutherans, believe they have to do good works in order obtain eternal life?

CHAPTER 3

SOLA FIDE (BY FAITH ALONE)

"For by grace you have been saved through faith. And this
is not your own doing; it is the gift of God, not a result
of works, so that no one may boast."
—St. Paul; Ephesians 2:8–9

In the above biblical passage, the apostle Paul told the Christians in Ephesus[1] that they as Christians were saved through faith in Jesus Christ, not by any human efforts or their good works. Similarly, he told Christians in Rome, "For we hold that one is justified by faith apart from works of the law" (Romans 3:28). To the Christians in Galatia, he declared, "We know that a person is not justified by works of the law but through faith in Jesus Christ, so we also have believed in Christ Jesus, in order to be justified by faith in Christ and not by works of the law, because by works of the law no one will be justified" (Galatians 2:16). These were the three cardinal passages in the Bible upon which Luther during the Reformation based his teaching of *sola fide* (by faith alone), meaning that man is justified before God through faith alone in Jesus Christ. This biblical doctrine is a major Lutheran hallmark.

EXAMPLES OF FAITH FALSELY DEFINED OR UNDERSTOOD

The word *faith* in today's English-speaking world is used frequently in the context of religion, but it is never defined. As J. Gresham Machen, a conservative Presbyterian theologian, once said, "These preachers speak about faith, but they do not tell what faith is."[2] Thus, faith is largely understood as a subjective experience; namely, believing something that is independent of any supporting historical facts or evidence. Our secular culture has underscored this erroneous concept of faith, and Westerners (including many Christians) have generally and unwittingly accepted this faulty understanding that largely stems from liberal theology.

Paul Tillich taught this erroneous view of faith. According to him, "The truth of faith cannot be made dependent on the historical truth of the stories and legends in which faith has expressed itself. It is a disastrous distortion of the meaning of faith to identify it with the belief in the historical validity of the Biblical stories." Tillich further argued that "faith cannot be shaken by historical research even if its results are critical of the traditions in which the event is reported."[3]

Rudolf Bultmann argued much the same way. "Let it be most emphatically stated that it is of absolutely no importance for the Christian faith to prove the possibility or historicity of the miracles of Jesus as events of the past, but on the contrary, this would only be a confusion of the issue."[4]

Interestingly, Dietrich Bonhoeffer held a similar erroneous view of faith. He argued that history does not provide any absolute grounds for faith, saying, "The historical approach to finding Jesus in history cannot be linked to faith."[5] He further said, *"Vita Jesu scribi non potest"* (the life of Jesus cannot be written).[6] Simply stated, to Bonhoeffer, Jesus existed only in the eyes of His disciples' "faith."

Briefly summarized, Tillich, Bultmann, and Bonhoeffer promulgated radical theology, yet still called themselves Lutheran, even though they did not see the miracles Jesus performed or His bodily resurrection as historical events. They saw Christ's resurrection as a theological myth that conveyed some truth or value, but believed there is no historical evidence to corroborate it. These three theologians reflected the influence of the Enlightenment's philosophy that appeared in the eighteenth century when many philosophers and theologians rejected the reality of miracles cited in the New Testament, including the greatest miracle of all, the bodily resurrection of Christ. Thus it was that Tillich, Bultmann, and Bonhoeffer saw faith as unrelated to any miracles recorded in the Bible. Hence, Bonhoeffer argued, "The resurrection [of Christ] occurred in the sphere of faith [*in der Sphäre des Glaubens*]."[7] To see Christ's resurrection as a historical phenomenon, he argued, was "senseless and crude" [*sinnlos und grob*].[8] Bultmann's,

Tillich's, and Bonhoeffer's concept of faith comes remarkably close to Mark Twain's reputed definition: "faith is believing what one knows is not true."

Biblically speaking, this is a heretical understanding of faith. It ignores and denies the experience of Christ's apostles, whose faith was anchored in their having seen Him a number of times after His bodily resurrection. Here it is helpful to note that before the eleven apostles chose a replacement for Judas, they stipulated that the candidate had to be someone who had actually seen the risen Christ (Acts 1:21–23). This requirement shows how important the empirical, bodily resurrection of Jesus Christ was to the disciples.

The contrabiblical, subjective definition of faith by Tillich, Bultmann, and Bonhoeffer, however, is not just confined to liberal theologians. On occasion, one even finds some Lutherans today defining faith in a similar manner. For instance, I have personally heard some conservative Lutheran pastors say that faith is believing without the benefit of a person's five senses (seeing, touching, tasting, smelling, or hearing). For if any of these are involved, one's belief is no longer faith. This definition of faith is similar to the definition of the three German theologians just mentioned. For if faith is unrelated to any human senses, then doubting Thomas, who upon seeing and touching the wounds of the resurrected Christ, did not have faith when he said, "My Lord and my God," because Jesus had asked him to use two of his five senses (sight and touch), prompting him to make the greatest confession of faith recorded in the entire Bible. Liberal theologians clearly contradict the biblical evidence just cited above. Their concept of faith that denies Christ's miracles and His resurrection is fideistic— meaning, it is faith in faith without any factual, historical evidence.

Faith: An Exclusive Christian Concept

When the apostle Paul told the Ephesians, "For by grace you have been saved through faith" (2:8), he used the Greek word *pistis*, translated as *faith* in English. By doing so, he and the other New Testament writers gave the word *pistis* a new meaning, a theological meaning not known to the Greeks or Romans. For as ancient history scholar Dieter Lührmann shows, "'Faith,' as a central category of Greek religious language did not exist."[9] He also notes, "Faith is a peculiarly Christian concept. While other religious traditions have aspects of what the churches have come to name 'faith,' none has the specific quality of intellectual assent that distinguishes faith from fidelity."[10] Lührmann further states that early Christianity, in contrast to other religions, used faith (*pistis*) to "define itself."[11]

There is another point worth noting with regard to the concept of *pistis* (faith), in light of the ancient Greeks' conception of it. They had a negative view of *pistis*; they saw it as "the lowest grade of cognition; it was the state of mind of the uneducated, who believe[d] things on hearsay without being able to give reasons for their belief."[12] This, of course, is notably different from the New Testament's portrayal of faith the early Christians manifested. For the New Testament's writers gave reasons and pointed to factual, empirical evidence for their faith, as St. Paul did in 1 Corinthians 15, regarding Christ's bodily resurrection.

Similarly, the apostle Peter argued the faith of Christians was not without factual, corroborating evidence when he urged the first-century recipients of his epistle to always be "prepared to make a defense [*apologia*] to anyone who asks you for a reason for the hope that is in you" (1 Peter 3:15). In short, the faith of the first Christians was not the lowest grade of cognition based on hearsay, but a phenomenon that was defended by Paul and Peter because it was based on factual, historically reliable evidence. (For a further discussion of the word *pistis*, see pp. 46–48.)

The validity of the faith of Christians, as portrayed in the New Testament, rests upon the historical fact of Christ's bodily resurrection. Hence, it is totally different from all non-Christian religions that use the term *faith* without any such evidence. When Muhammad, for instance, said the angel Gabriel spoke to him, neither he nor his followers could point to any witnesses who had heard Gabriel speak to him. Whereas the New Testament's apostles—for example, John and Peter—declared, "We cannot but speak of what we have seen and heard" (Acts 4:20). Similarly, on the Day of Pentecost, Peter preached, "This Jesus God raised up, and of that we all are witnesses" (2:32). And Paul, standing before King Agrippa, told him, "This thing [Christ's resurrection] was not done in a corner" (26:26 NKJV). These and other similar citations from the apostles clearly indicate that not one of them ever argued for the veracity of Christ's bodily resurrection on the basis of their faith. To them, it was not their faith that made Christ's resurrection true. Rather, it was the empirical fact of their having seen and witnessed with their own eyes His live and resurrected body, which they had seen on a number of occasions, that made their faith true and valid. This important point, unfortunately, is often overlooked by many Christians in light of today's erroneous understanding of faith; namely, that faith is unrelated to the empirical, historical fact of Christ's bodily resurrection.

The stalwart, eye-witnessing posture of the apostles, who put their lives on the line for what they had seen and heard, prompted Blaise Pascal to say he would rather believe Christianity than some other religion that has no such record and can make no such claim. In today's world of multiculturalism that considers all religions equally valuable or true, we Lutherans need to remember Pascal's confession and also make it our confession. To do so is to uphold an important Lutheran hallmark and identity.

Lutheran Definition of Faith

The Lutheran reformers in the sixteenth century put forth a notably different definition of faith than the one of today's widespread, erroneous understanding of faith as a subjective phenomenon, divorced from any historical evidence. They said faith consists of historical knowledge (*notitia* in Latin) and a person's assent (*assensus*), along with trust (*fiducia*) regarding God's redemptive acts in Jesus Christ. Thus, the Augsburg Confession states that a Christian's faith consists of believing "the history, but also the effect of the history. In other words, it believes this article: the forgiveness of sins. We have grace, righteousness, and forgiveness of sins through Christ" (XX 23). A Christian's faith is not merely a subjective experience independent of factual, historical evidence.

But some may ask, "What about Hebrews 11:1-2?" This reference says, "Now faith is the assurance of things hoped for, the conviction of things not seen." Sometimes this passage is cited to argue that the faith of Christians is unrelated to any historical facts. But that is not what this passage says. The early Christians knew for a *fact* that Christ had risen from the dead. Thus, these words in this epistle speak only about the effects or benefits of Christ's redemptive work—namely, the forgiveness of sins and eternal life—that which the early Christians hoped for, but could not visually see.

If faith were unrelated to or independent of Christ's many miracles, and especially His bodily resurrection, why did He reveal Himself physically to His disciples? Why did He after His resurrection on one occasion eat fish in their presence? (Luke 24:43). Why did Paul in

1 Corinthians 15:6 note that some five hundred people, most of them still alive, had seen the risen Christ, if He had not in fact risen from the dead?

Moreover, whether it is true that Christ rose from the dead is not a matter of faith but a fact in history, similar to other facts or events that have occurred in history. In the biblical context, faith is accepting the *effects* or *benefits* of Christ's bodily resurrection, not whether He rose from the dead on Easter Sunday. It was not the faith of the apostles that established the veracity of Christ's resurrection. Rather, Christ's bodily resurrection established and undergirded their faith, as it did in the case of doubting Thomas. (More details about Thomas's experience in the next section.)

Merely knowing and accepting the historical fact of Christ's suffering, death, and resurrection, however, is not enough for saving faith. Wolfhart Pannenberg correctly said, "Mere knowledge of God's revelation does not yet make one a participant in the salvation included therein. Only when a man relies upon this in that he trustingly takes this event as the ground on which he stands does he receive a share in that. Salvation is only received in the act of trust."[13] Pannenberg's words echo the Lutheran concept of trust (*fiducia*) as part of a Christian's faith, along with historical knowledge (*notitia*).

Faith Founded on Factual Evidence: The Doubting Thomas Incident

Many well-meaning Christians sometimes cite the last words Jesus spoke to Thomas, "Blessed are those who have not seen and yet have believed" (John 20:29), in a manner as though Thomas was a "bad boy" for wanting to see empirical evidence that Christ had indeed risen from the dead. He should have simply believed his fellow apostles. This kind of thinking, however, implies that Christ's bodily resurrection is merely a matter of faith without any factual evidence undergirding it. This is a misreading of the text, for Jesus did not say or imply that the veracity of His resurrection was a matter of faith. If that had been what He meant, He would not have asked Thomas to see and touch His crucified wounds.

In connection with the Thomas account, Christians sometimes ask what Jesus meant by saying, "Blessed are those who have not seen and yet have believed." Some think these words imply that faith needs no evidence. Biblically speaking, that is a false conclusion. Rather, Jesus' words refer to all individuals (including us today) who, unlike Thomas, have not seen Him, the risen Lord, but who do accept and believe the empirical reports of the disciples who *in fact did see Him* after He rose from the grave and saw Him a number of times before He ascended to heaven.

In short, Christ's words to Thomas regarding those who are blessed, but have not seen and still believe, do not mean the benefits of Christ's resurrection are valid apart from it having factually occurred in history. Expressed another way, a Christian's faith does not establish the benefits or veracity of Christ's resurrection any more than faith establishes the veracity of any other event that occurred in history—for instance, the existence of Christopher Columbus. Whether Christ's bodily resurrection happened, similar to the past existence of Columbus, is a fact of history, not a matter of faith. Only the *benefits* or the *effects* of Christ's resurrection are received through faith. Faith does not make Christ's bodily resurrection historically true.

Given Thomas's experience and his confession, Christians can be confident that Christ did in fact rise from the dead. Thomas's exclamation of "my Lord and my God," is an excellent example that shows, as John Calvin said, "Faith rests upon knowledge, not upon pious ignorance."[14] Similarly, John Warwick Montgomery states, "The Christian faith is not blind faith or credulity; it is grounded in fact."[15]

Christ's giving Thomas the empirical evidence for His bodily resurrection supports the Lutheran position that faith includes biblically based historical knowledge (*notitia*). It is important for Lutherans to remember this fact in today's culture that increasingly defines faith as a subjective phenomenon independent of any facts in history. Hence, it is unfortunate when some well-meaning Christians say they know Christ rose from the dead because He lives in their hearts.

Here we are also reminded of a popular Gospel song titled "He Lives" by Alfred H. Ackley. Two of its sentences say, "You ask me how I know He lives? He lives within my heart." These words have no biblical basis. They are completely subjective, an example of fideism; namely, faith in faith without factual evidence. As J. Gresham Machen once wrote, "Christian experience is rightly used when it confirms the documentary evidence. But it can never possibly provide a substitute for the documentary evidence."[16]

The Importance of Faith
Founded on Fact

Regarding the modern conception of divorcing faith from factual evidence, it is helpful to cite Wolfhart Pannenberg again. "If . . . historical study declares itself unable to establish what 'really' happened on Easter, then all the more, faith is not able to do so; for faith cannot ascertain anything about events of the past that would perhaps be inaccessible to the historian."[17] In short, Pannenberg says the Bible is not just a book of faith. It is also a book of historical facts. But this view of the Bible is no longer accepted in today's secular culture, as is evident from a recent article in *The Economist* magazine, which stated, "Arguably, even talking about the 'facts' of the Bible is a statement of faith."[18]

If the veracity of Christianity were linked only to its moral or ethical teachings, as is true of all non-Christian religions, it would make little or no difference whether the faith of Christians is dependent on the historical fact of Jesus' bodily resurrection. For instance, it is not important whether the founder of Hinduism, Sikhism, or Islam rose from the dead or whether these religious founders performed any miracles because these religions rest their teachings entirely on ethical or moral precepts. But Christianity stands or falls with the historical veracity of Christ's physical resurrection. Without His empirical resurrection, the entire Christian religion, including the faith of all Christians, collapses like the proverbial house of cards. Thus, the apostle Paul told the Christians in Corinth, "If Christ has not been raised, your faith is futile and you are still in your sins" (1 Corinthians 15:17).

Christianity stands or falls with the historical veracity of Christ's physical resurrection.

In support of Paul's words, Luke proclaimed that the resurrected Christ "presented Himself alive after His suffering by many *infallible proofs*, being seen by them [the apostles] during forty days and speaking of the things pertaining to the kingdom of God" (Acts 1:3 NKJV, emphasis added). The Greek word in this text translated as "infallible proofs" is *tekmeriois*. This is the same word the Greek philosopher Aristotle used for demonstrable evidence that could not factually be denied in his classic work *The Art of Rhetoric*.[19] If non-Christian religions had such evidence, then—and only then—could their followers be seen as having faith similar to that of the Christians. If this were true, then the word *faith* could rightly be appended as a suffix to the name of non-Christian religious groups, discussed below in the section titled "Faith Misused" (see p. 46).

FAITH AND THE ROLE OF THE HOLY SPIRIT

Christian apologetics, defending the veracity of the biblical evidence, is sometimes criticized by those who say it ignores the role of the Holy Spirit in its attempts to persuade unbelievers on the basis of evidence to become Christians. This criticism reveals a wrong understanding of Christian apologetics, for when apologists (defenders) point non-Christians to the biblical facts that happened in history—for example, the doubting Thomas incident—the Holy Spirit is invariably operative. Also, when the biblical facts of Christ's life, death, and resurrection are defended, God's Word comes into play. And when God's Word is operative, the Holy Spirit is present, seeking to create faith in the hearers by moving them to believe and accept the benefits of Christ's death and resurrection.

In today's world of multiculturalism, with its concomitants of cultural and moral relativism, Lutherans need to be more active in Christian apologetics, for they have sometimes been criticized for being strong in polemics (finding fault with given positions) but weak in apologetics (defending the validity of given positions). Here it is important to remember it is often through the method of Christian apologetics that faith is ignited in the hearts of unbelievers. And it is equally important to remember that when we defend the foundations of the Gospel, we are imitating the apostle Paul, who told the Christians in Philippi that he was engaged in the "defense [*apologia*] and confirmation of the gospel" (Philippians 1:7). Similarly, St. Peter told the early Christians to always be "prepared to make a defense [*apologia*] to anyone who asks you for a reason for the hope that is in you" (1 Peter 3:15).

When Christians believe in the merits and benefits of Christ's death and bodily resurrection, it is the result of the Holy Spirit having worked faith in them through the Word of God, preached or read.

The Holy Spirit was also active when Thomas confessed, "My Lord and my God!" (John 20:28). For as St. Paul said, "No one can say 'Jesus is Lord' except in the Holy Spirit" (1 Corinthians 12:3). Thus, when Christ showed Thomas the empirical evidence that he demanded, the Holy Spirit was also at work, prompting him to believe when Jesus said, "Do not disbelieve, but believe" (John 20:27). The New Testament also presents other examples of how the Holy Spirit moved individuals to believe in Christ; for example, upon their seeing miracles performed. Thus, when the apostle Peter in Joppa raised Tabitha from her death, "many believed in the Lord" (Acts 9:42).

SOLA FIDE (BY FAITH ALONE) AND ROMAN CATHOLICISM

Although the Roman Catholic Church teaches that Christians are saved by faith, it does *not* teach they are saved through faith *alone*. This is an important point to remember because sometimes we hear Catholics also believe they are saved by faith alone. Although some individual Catholics may indeed believe they are saved by faith alone, that is not what the Catholic Church officially teaches. At the Council of Trent (1545–63), the Roman Church officially rejected and condemned the teaching of *sola fide* (by faith alone). It strongly reprimanded Lutherans:

> If anyone shall say that by *faith alone* the sinner is justi-
> fied, so as to understand that nothing else is required to
> cooperate in the attainment of the grace of justification,
> and that it is in no way necessary that he be prepared and
> disposed by the action of his own will: let him be *anathema*
> [damned]. (Canon 9, emphases added)[20]

In making this declaration against the doctrine of *sola fide*, a doctrine clearly taught in Scripture (see Romans 3:28), the Council of Trent firmly spurned Article VI of the Augsburg Confession, even though this article cited St. Ambrose[21] to show that *sola fide* was not a Lutheran innovation. Ambrose, similar to Luther, also taught *sola fide gratis* (faith alone by grace.) Nevertheless, the Council of Trent "leveled its heaviest artillery against the Lutheran doctrine of justification by faith alone."[22]

A key Scripture passage Rome uses to reject the biblical, Lutheran doctrine of *sola fide* is from James 2:24: "You see that a person is justified by works and not by faith alone." But to use this passage from James's epistle to counter and reject *sola fide* at the time of Luther presented a major problem to Rome, for the Book of James did not have canonical status. Thus, when Rome convened the Council of Trent in December 1545, it soon decreed on April 8, 1546, the Book of James as canonical, along with six other antilegomena books. (*Antilegomena* [Greek "spoken against"] refers to certain books of the New Testament that were disputed canonically.) This decree ignored the historical reality that the Early Church, and the Church for centuries after, declined to recognize James as a canonical writing of the New Testament. (Chapter 5 provides more information regarding Trent's arbitrary decree.)

FAITH AND GOOD WORKS

Given the Lutheran emphasis on the doctrine of *sola fide*, some Lutherans are occasionally confused when asked, "Are good works necessary in the life of a Christian?" Some say no. This answer, of course, is wrong. For while no one is saved by faith *and* good works, good works are indeed necessary in every Christian's life. St. Paul, right after Ephesians 2:8–9, reminds Christians, "For we are His workmanship, created in Christ Jesus for good works, which God prepared beforehand, that we should walk in them" (v. 10). Consistent with these words, Christ said, "If you love Me, you will keep My commandments" (John 14:15), and He further expounded, "Whoever abides in Me and I in him, he it is that bears much fruit" (15:5).

Thus, we Lutherans need to remember it is through our good works that the world can see us as Christians. Jesus said, "Let your light shine before others, so that they may see your good works and give glory to your Father who is in heaven" (Matthew 5:16). In summary, good works are necessary, but not necessary for salvation.

We Lutherans need to remember it is through our good works that the world can see us as Christians.

While good works are not necessary for our salvation, they are, however, necessary because God commands them, for they are the fruits, the evidence of a Christian's faith. Hence, the Augsburg Confession states,

> Our churches teach that this faith is bound to bring forth good fruit [Galatians 5:22–23]. It is necessary to do good works commanded by God [Ephesians 2:10], because of God's will. We should not rely on those works to merit justification before God. The forgiveness of sins and justification is received through faith. (VI 1–2)

Lutherans are sometimes perceived and criticized for emphasizing creeds at the expense of deeds. This assessment, however, does not agree with what Lutheran theology teaches—nor is it what informed, faithful Lutherans believe, as Article VI of the Augsburg Confession shows. One Lutheran pastor rightly said the following: "We are not only saved *from* something, but also *for* something."[23] This means we Lutherans need to encourage one another to do good works each and every day out of gratitude for Christ's redemptive love for us, always remembering that Christians doing good works is a powerful way of showing love for our neighbor. Gustaf Wingren, in explaining Luther's doctrine of vocation, said, "God does not need our good works, but our neighbor does."[24]

Faith Misused

One common misuse of the word *faith* in today's English-speaking culture is using it as a synonym for religion. Thus, people and the media talk about "the Islamic faith" or "the Mormon faith" rather than "the Islamic religion" or "the Mormon religion," and so on. The English word *faith* has even morphed into the expression of "people of faith," which refers to individuals who belong to any religion, Christian or non-Christian.[25]

Using the word *faith* as a synonym for *religion* has been purloined from the New Testament, where it is only a synonym for Christianity or its teachings. The usage of the word *pistis* (faith) as a synonym for any religion was unknown to the ancient Greeks, and the Romans also did not use *fide* (faith) in that manner. Rather, it was the apostle Paul, who, for instance, in Galatians 1:23, wrote about preaching "the faith" (*ten pistis*), referring to Christianity's teachings. Similarly, Luke in Acts 6:7

wrote that "many . . . became obedient to the faith [*ten pistis*]." Hence, Paul, Luke, and other New Testament writers gave "faith" (*pistis*) a meaning it did not previously have. It is also important to note the definite article "the" (*ten*) in these and other references depict only Christianity as *the faith* (*ten pistis*). The New Testament never uses *pistis* in regard to any non-Christian religion. Biblically speaking, the word *faith* (*pistis*) or the phrase "the faith" (*ten pistis*) applies only to Christianity.

We Christians want to remember that St. Paul tells us there is only "one Lord, *one faith*, one baptism" (Ephesians 4:5, emphasis added). And it is also important to know the early Christians referred to the Nicene Creed as "symbol of *the faith*" (*symbolon tns pistews*).

To encourage Lutherans and other Christians to stop using the word *faith* appended to non-Christian religions or groups, to be sure, is easier said than accomplished. For we live in the iron cage of culture from which it is difficult to break out. But it can be done if we consciously discipline ourselves not to imitate the language of our culture that appends the word *faith* to all religious groups. If we want to uphold the biblical meaning of the word *faith* and its Christian uniqueness, we cannot let secular culture have its way.

The misuse of *faith* has also spawned the word *faiths*, pluralizing all religions. This modern neologism finds no support in the Bible. Rather, it contradicts the New Testament's depicting Christianity as *ten pistis* ("the faith").

FAITH AS A SYNONYM FOR RELIGION SLIGHTS CHRISTIANITY

Faith as a synonym for *religion* also implies Christianity is similar to all non-Christian religions—namely, its teachings, like those of non-Christian religions, are also based only on faith for which there is no historical or factual evidence. This is false! The New Testament provides overwhelming evidence that Christianity is the only religion where the faith of its adherents is linked to factual events that happened in history. Biblically speaking, to have faith in presumed spiritual benefits of some teachings for which there is no factual evidence is not faith but the absence of faith as defined and used in the Scriptures. So it is important again to recall the apostle Paul's words that he wrote to the Christians in Corinth, "If Christ has not been raised, your faith is futile" (1 Corinthians 15:17). For without the miraculous, empirical reality of Christ's bodily resurrection, and Christians accepting its spiritual benefits, there is no valid faith.

The faulty
conclusion
that all reli-
gions lead to
eternal life
contradicts
common
sense.

The use of *faith* as a synonym for *religion* also slights Christianity in that it erroneously implies the teachings of non-Christian religions lead to eternal life. This implication, however, is in direct conflict with what Christ taught: "I am the way, and the truth, and the life. No one comes to the Father except through Me" (John 14:6). Additionally, the faulty conclusion that all religions lead to eternal life contradicts common sense. For when we need to drive to a specific location, not every road will take us there. Common sense tells us we need to take the correct road. But when it comes to varying religious beliefs, common sense is often absent, for many want to believe that every religion's teachings, no matter how different, all lead to eternal life.

Faith as Content and Faith as Conviction

When speaking of faith as content (its teachings), Lutheran theologians call it, in Latin, *fides quae creditur*—that is, "the faith" (*ten pistis*); namely, Christianity or its teachings, as St. Paul stated, "the word of faith that we proclaim" (Romans 10:8). Another example is Paul's telling Timothy that "some will depart from the faith" (1 Timothy 4:1). It is the faith that is believed, sometimes also known as objective faith.

Theologians also speak of *fides qua creditur*, the act of believing in Christ and His teachings for life and salvation, as St. Paul taught: "If you confess with your mouth that Jesus is Lord and believe in your heart that God raised Him from the dead, you will be saved" (Romans 10:9). A second example is Jesus saying, "Daughter, your faith has made you well" (Mark 5:34). *Fides qua creditur* in today's language is often known as personal faith. In Luther's words, that "faith is a living, daring confidence in God's grace, so sure and certain that the believer would stake his life on it a thousand times."[26]

CONCLUSION

It is important for us Lutherans to remember that we are saved by grace through faith alone (*sola fide*), as St. Paul so confidently reminded the Christians in his day. This means our good works do not help us acquire salvation; they are the fruits of our faith. And as already noted, Lutherans need to be careful not to accept today's widely held notion that faith is equivalent to believing in something for which there is no historical evidence. Such understanding of faith is not found in the New Testament, and, therefore, it is not found in the Lutheran Book of Concord either.

It is important to remember that *faith* (*pistis*), first used in that manner in the New Testament, was a Christian innovation that made faith an exclusively Christian concept. The New Testament also never uses "the faith" (*ten pistis*) in regard to non-Christian religious content or teachings. Thus, we Lutherans, knowing there is only one faith (Ephesians 4:5), will consciously try to cease and desist using the word *faith* when referring to any non-Christian religion or to its teachings.

Finally, we want to adhere to the biblical doctrine that teaches individuals are saved only through faith in Jesus Christ, a faith founded on the historical fact of Christ's bodily resurrection. As we cling to this faith by God's grace, we want to remember it is a unique Christian doctrine and another noteworthy hallmark of Lutheran theology and identity.

1. What biblical passages teach us that we are saved by faith alone?

2. Why is it wrong to say that we are saved by faith *and* works?

3. Are good works of Christians necessary in the life of Christians? Why or why not?

4. What well-known Roman Catholic council first condemned the biblical teaching that Christians are saved by faith alone?

5. Why is it biblically wrong to say the faith of Christians is independent of historical facts— for example, the resurrection of Jesus Christ?

6. Why is historical knowledge (*notitia*) not enough for a correct understanding of faith?

7. What role does assent (*assensus*) play in the concept of faith?

8. How can the veracity of Christianity's concept of faith be defended on the basis of sound reason and historical evidence?

9. Why is it wrong to say, "The resurrection of Christ is true because of my faith"?

10. Why should Christians not use the term *faith* when referring to non-Christian religions?

11. Why do you think Christians often call non-Christian religions "faith groups"?

12. How is the role of Christian apologetics complementary to the role of the Holy Spirit?

13. Why is the so-called "faith" of all non-Christians based only on hearsay?

14. Why was the faith of the early Christians not the lowest form of cognition?

CHAPTER 4

SOLA SCRIPTURA (BY SCRIPTURE ALONE)

"All of Scripture . . . is pure Christ."[1]

"The Bible is the cradle wherein Christ is laid."[2]

"Unless I am convinced by the testimony of the Scriptures
or by clear reason (for I do not trust either in the pope or
in councils alone, since it is well known that they have
often erred and contradicted themselves), I am bound by
the Scriptures I have quoted and my conscience is captive
to the Word of God. I cannot and I will not retract anything
. . . here I stand, may God help me, Amen."[3]
—Martin Luther (1483–1546)

"You search the Scriptures because you think that in them
you have eternal life; and it is they that bear witness
about Me."—Jesus; John 5:39

Since the Reformation in the sixteenth century, the doctrine of *sola Scriptura* (by Scripture alone) has been widely accepted by most Protestant churches, even though the term itself might not always be commonly uttered by them. The doctrine of *sola Scriptura* is evident when, in theological matters, Christians cite a biblical passage to underscore or support a given theological point or argument. Quite frequently, the citation of a biblical reference is accepted as the authoritative way to support a particular position. In effect, the participants have opted for *sola Scriptura* as their final and only source of authority.

THE ORIGIN OF *SOLA SCRIPTURA*

Although *sola Scriptura* is often called the "Protestant principle," it is Luther who first enunciated this term. German Luther scholar Bernhard Lohse says that although the Early and Medieval Church took for granted the authority of Scripture, the "principle of 'Scripture alone' was never advocated before Luther."[4] Lohse also notes that before Luther invoked the concept of *sola Scriptura*, the church had not addressed "the relationship between Scripture and tradition," nor had it considered how the authority of Scripture was related to the office of the pope.[5]

Lutherans seem to accent or display the slogan *sola Scriptura* most prominently on banners and in church publications. Lutheran pastors are especially accustomed to citing a Scripture reference when they contend for a given theological teaching. And Luther's doctrine of *sola Scriptura* has consistently been portrayed by Luther's many sculptors who have molded statues of him clutching the Bible close to his heart. These examples clearly indicate the concept of *sola Scriptura* is a noteworthy hallmark of Lutheran theology.

In 1229, five hundred years before Luther heralded the concept of *sola Scriptura,* the Synod of Toulouse (France) outlawed Bible reading for lay Christians. This Synod also outlawed Bible translations in vernacular tongues. Laypeople were only permitted to possess the Psalms and a few prayer verses. This drastic action was largely in response to the Waldensians, followers of Peter Waldo (d. ca. 1217). Waldo, independently wealthy, had the Bible translated into the vernacular. The Waldensians had become quite conversant with the Bible, especially with the New Testament. The Synod of Toulouse, under the persuasion of the pope, concluded that had the Waldensian lay Christians not been able to read the translated Bible, they would not have rejected a number of Rome's doctrines, such as purgatory, masses for the dead, indulgences, praying to saints, venerating relics of saints, and the authority of the pope.[6]

In 1233, four years after the Synod of Toulouse (in Gaul, now France), the Synod of Tarragona (in Spain) ruled that no layperson could possess any books of the Old or New Testament. Then some seventy years after Toulouse, Pope Boniface VIII (1294–1301) decreed there was no need for Christians to read the Holy Bible because the pope had all the biblical laws in "the chamber of his heart" ("*Scrinio pectoris*").[7] The Sacred Scriptures were to be "interpreted only by Masters and Doctors of

HALLMARKS OF LUTHERAN IDENTITY

Divinity, and only then in the light of the Fathers and the Scholastics, in which the University of Paris and the Pope claimed to have a monopoly."[8] In 1407, the archbishop of London outlawed the production of Bible translations in English and "condemned to death anyone caught reading a Wycliffe Bible."[9] It is important to remember the man who translated this Bible, John Wycliffe, was condemned twenty-five years earlier (1385), in part for translating Scripture into English.[10]

The decisions of the Synods of Toulouse and Tarragona, Pope Boniface, and the London archbishop meant that for centuries most Christian laypeople never saw a Bible, much less had the freedom to read it. Some historians, for instance, say that Luther, even though he was raised in a pious Christian home, apparently had not seen God's sacred book until he was about fourteen years old, and then only when he attended the cathedral school in Magdeburg. Other historians say he did not see a Holy Bible until he was a university student at the University of Erfurt. The latter argument, however, is found only in Luther's Table Talks, a source not considered scholarly reliable.[11]

Whether Luther first saw a Bible at Magdeburg or at Erfurt is not known for certain. We do know, however, there is no evidence that he used the principle of *sola Scriptura* before he taught at the University of Wittenberg, where he first began teaching on a part-time basis in 1508. Thus, Ernest G. Schwiebert, an American Luther scholar, believes it was at this time (between 1508 and 1509) that *sola Scriptura* became part of Luther's theology.[12] And Schwiebert indicates Luther focused on the *sola Scriptura* principle because "so many pagan streams had emptied their sullied waters into the river of medieval theology, no traditional interpretation of the Schoolmen or even of the western Fathers was reliable."[13] Thus, Luther declared, "For we cannot trust or build on the lives and works of the fathers, but on God's word alone."[14]

In 1512, Luther earned the doctor of theology degree and began giving lectures based on the Bible (*lectura in Biblia*) at the University of Wittenberg.[15] But whether he at this time formally taught the concept of *sola Scriptura* is not definitely known. It is known, however, that in October 1518, when Cardinal Cajetan tried to get Luther to recant in a private meeting in Augsburg, he told the cardinal, "I teach nothing save what is in Scripture."[16] It is also known that he declared his belief in *sola Scriptura* to the entire world in 1521 when he professed before Emperor Charles V and the electors at the Diet of Worms, "Unless I am convicted by Scripture and plain reason—I do not accept the authority of popes and councils, for they have contradicted each other—my conscience is captive to the Word of God. . . . God help me. Amen."[17]

Sola Scriptura and Lutheran Theology

The significance of *sola Scriptura* in Lutheran theology is evident when one reads the Lutheran Confessions. (For details on the Lutheran Confessions as contained in the Book of Concord, see chapter 19.) The writings that make up the Confessions include the Augsburg Confession, the Apology of the Augsburg Confession, the Smalcald Articles, the Treatise on the Power and Primacy of the Pope, the Small Catechism, the Large Catechism, and the Formula of Concord. These documents are replete with biblical documentation. For instance, the Smalcald Articles, written by Luther in 1537, specifically accent *sola Scriptura* by asserting, "God's Word shall establish articles of faith, and no one else, not even an angel can do so" (SA II II 15). Fifty years later (1580), Lutheran theologians, in the preface to the Formula of Concord, similarly declared,

> We believe, teach, and confess that the only rule and norm according to which all teachings, together with ‹all› teachers, should be evaluated and judged [2 Timothy 3:15–17] are the prophetic and apostolic Scriptures of the Old and New Testament alone. . . . However, other writings by ancient or modern teachers—no matter whose name they bear—must not be regarded as equal to the Holy Scriptures. All of them are subject to the Scriptures [1 Corinthians 14:32]. Other writings should not be received in any other way or as anything more than witnesses that show how this ‹pure› doctrine of the prophets and apostles was preserved after the time of the apostles, and at what places. (FC Ep Summary 1–2)

This statement from the Formula of Concord indicates that, for Lutherans, the Holy Scriptures are the only (*sola*) source and authority of Christian theology. It is a major Lutheran hallmark.

Sola Scriptura and the Church Fathers

Although Luther is credited with being the first to enunciate formally the concept of *sola Scriptura*, a number of Church Fathers from the second century into the early Middle Ages also saw Holy Scripture in a similar light, though they did not use the term *sola Scriptura*. So we

HALLMARKS OF LUTHERAN IDENTITY

find Clement of Alexandria (d. ca. 216) saying, "But those who are ready to toil in the most excellent pursuits, will not desist from the search after truth, till they get the information from the Scriptures themselves" (*Stromata* 7:16). Hippolytus of Rome (d. 235) affirmed his belief in the Scriptures, saying, "There is, brethren, one God, the knowledge of whom we gain from the Holy Scriptures and no other source" (*Against the Heresy of One Noetus* 9). In AD 370, Bishop Basil of Caesarea wrote, "Therefore let God-inspired Scripture decide between us; and on which side be found doctrines in harmony with the word of God, in favour of that side will be cast the vote of truth" (*Letter* 189:3). Athanasius (d. 373), the ardent defender of Christ's deity at the Council of Nicaea, said, "The holy Scripture is of all things most sufficient for us" (*To the Bishops of Egypt* 1:4). Bishop Gregory of Nyssa (d. 394) in the Eastern Church declared, "Let the inspired Scripture, then, be our umpire, and the vote of truth will surely be given to those whose dogmas are found to agree with the Divine words" (*On the Holy Spirit: Against the Followers of Macedonius*). And St. Ambrose (d. 397), Bishop of Milan, confidently proclaimed, "For how can we adopt those things which we do not find in the Holy Scriptures?" (*Duties of the Clergy* 1:23).

> . . .they firmly held to the principle that God's inspired Holy Scriptures were the final authority for Christian theology.

Although these Church Fathers did not literally use the term *sola Scriptura*, they firmly held to the principle that God's inspired Holy Scriptures were the final authority for Christian theology.

SOLA SCRIPTURA AND CHRISTIAN TRADITION

Roman Catholic critics of Lutheran theology commonly argue against *sola Scriptura* by saying it ignores or repudiates the value of the traditions of the church. This argument is made rather forcefully by Robert A. Sungenis, a Roman Catholic lay theologian. His book has the imprimatur of the Vicar General of the Archdiocese of Baltimore and is titled *Not by Scripture Alone: A Catholic Critique of the Protestant Doctrine of Sola Scriptura* (1997).[18] Although the

Roman Catholic criticism that *sola Scriptura* ignores the church's tradition is basically true in regard to many Protestant churches, it needs to be qualified in regard to the Lutheran Church. Lutheran theology has always honored many traditions of the historic church, especially if they did not contradict the teachings of Scripture.

One example of the Lutheran respect for tradition is the Lutheran Church's relatively wide use of the historic Christian liturgy in Divine Services. The traditional liturgy incorporates many elements that reach back to the Early Church. The Kyrie, for instance, has its roots in the latter part of the first century; the Gloria in Excelsis goes back to the Eastern Church's life in the second century; and the Gloria Patri comes from the fourth century, both in the Western and Eastern Churches. These and other components of the traditional liturgy have been (and still are) used in numerous Lutheran churches in many countries. It illustrates that tradition of the historic church has an honorable place in Lutheran theology.

Another example of the respect Lutheran theology has for tradition is evident by the continued honor it gives to departed saints, even though Lutherans do not pray to them. Thus, the Lutheran liturgical calendar notes the days of certain saints, and many Lutheran churches honor these saints on appointed Sundays as well. The following are a few examples: St. Timothy (January 24); St. Matthias (February 24); St. Peter and St. Paul (June 29); St. Mary, Mother of our Lord (August 15), and St. Luke (October 18).[19] In addition, Lutherans often name their churches in honor of saints: St. Paul Lutheran Church, St. Timothy Lutheran Church, St. John Lutheran Church, and so on.

Lutheran theology also respects and honors Christian tradition by upholding and regularly confessing the Church's three Ecumenical Creeds: the Apostles' Creed, the Nicene Creed, and the Athanasian Creed.[20] In most publications of the Book of Concord, these three creeds are commonly found preceding the Lutheran Confessions, and unlike some Evangelical churches, who publicly state that they do not have creeds, the Lutheran Church firmly adheres to these historic creeds. These creeds do not conflict with *sola Scriptura* but are complementary to it. Thus the Apostles' Creed or the Nicene Creed is corporately and orally confessed as part of the Divine Service in most Lutheran churches.[21] And in many Lutheran churches, the Athanasian Creed is recited on Trinity Sunday, the Sunday after the Day of Pentecost is observed.

HALLMARKS OF LUTHERAN IDENTITY

Another example of how Lutheran theology honors and upholds Christian tradition is found in its subscribing to the doctrines enunciated by the first four ecumenical councils of the Church: the Council of Nicaea (AD 325), the Council of Constantinople I (AD 381), the Council of Ephesus (AD 431), and the Council of Chalcedon (AD 451).

The Council of Nicaea underscored the doctrine of the Trinity by condemning the teachings of Arius, who denied the deity of Jesus Christ. Arius saw Jesus as the Son of God but not as God. He said there was a time when Jesus, as God's Son, did not exist. The Council of Constantinople I confirmed the decisions made earlier in Nicaea and completed the present wording of the Nicene Creed as it is currently used and confessed in the Divine Service.

The Council of Ephesus condemned the false teaching of Nestorius, Patriarch of Constantinople, for teaching and preaching that Christ was two separate persons, one human and one divine, and that there was no communication between the two. He therefore denied the biblical position that said Christ was a single person with both a human and a divine nature. He also objected to the Virgin Mary being called *theotokos* (bearer of God incarnate); namely, that she gave birth to God in human flesh. Instead, Nestorius argued that Mary was only *Christotokos* (bearer of Christ as only human).

Nestorius's teaching led to the conclusion that in Christ's crucifixion only His human nature died—not also His divine nature. This Nestorian position is contradicted by Acts 20:28, where it states God purchased the Church with His own blood. Nestorius's teaching also contradicted St. Paul, who told the Corinthian Christians that those who had crucified Christ "crucified the Lord of glory" (1 Corinthians 2:8).

Here it seems appropriate to remind Lutherans that they, residing in a predominantly generic Protestant environment, especially in the English-speaking world, probably are not used to hearing that the Virgin Mary gave birth *to God* in human flesh. Thus, some Lutherans are surprised to hear that orthodox, biblical Christianity teaches Mary was the mother of God. Martin Chemnitz offered some helpful comments for Lutherans to remember when he said, "It is neither false nor vain to call Mary the mother of the Lord, for men contended with great seriousness against Nestorius, that we must call Mary the God-bearer (*theotokos* in Greek), and all antiquity concurred."[22]

The Council of Chalcedon, an ecumenical council, reaffirmed the decisions of the Council of Ephesus when it upheld the doctrine of *theotokos* in condemning Nestorius's false teachings. In addition, Chalcedon condemned Eutyches, another false teacher who taught that the human nature of Christ was coalesced (integrated) into his divine nature, and thus Christ had only one nature, the divine nature. His followers were called Monophysites, individuals who taught Christ had only one nature, contrary to the orthodox doctrine that Christ had both a human and a divine nature.

As already noted, Lutheran theology confesses the three Ecumenical Creeds, accepts the first four ecumenical church councils, retains the historic liturgy, and honors the biblical saints. Thus, Lutheran theology honors and respects ancient Christian doctrine and tradition.

Lutheran theology honors and respects ancient Christian doctrine and tradition.

WHY *SOLA SCRIPTURA*?

There were some compelling reasons why Luther tenaciously held to the concept of *sola Scriptura*. He had learned and discovered that while some church councils—for example, the first four ecumenical councils—defended necessary fundamental Christian teachings that preserved the Gospel of Jesus Christ, some later councils often erred and even contradicted themselves. Decisions by the popes often were no better, for many papal proclamations and actions were riddled with errors.

Luther knew and believed that the Holy Scriptures were the inspired words of God because they were written by the apostles or by someone supervised by an apostle. Mark and Luke are of the latter. Luther took Christ at His word when, in His High Priestly Prayer, He said to His Father: "For I have given them the words that You gave me, and they have received them and have come to know in truth that I came from You" (John 17:8). Hence, Scripture alone was the authority in matters of faith and life. In his famous 1519 debate with John Eck[23] in Leipzig, Luther said the church councils had sometimes erred and contradicted themselves.

> I assert that a council has sometimes erred and may sometimes err. Nor has a council authority to establish new articles of faith. A council cannot make divine right out of that which by nature is not divine right. Councils have contradicted each other, for the recent Lateran Council has reversed the claim of the councils of Constance and Basel that a council is above a pope.[24]

He also declared: "As for the pope's decretal on indulgences I say that neither the Church nor pope can establish articles of faith. These must come from Scripture. For the sake of Scripture, we should reject pope and councils."[25]

THE INFLUENCE OF *SOLA SCRIPTURA*

Luther's insistence on *sola Scriptura* has had a broad impact, even on the Roman Catholic Church, which, as shown above, does not look favorably upon this Lutheran concept. Nevertheless, it is now not uncommon for some Catholics, at least in the United States and Canada, to have Bibles (usually Catholic-approved translations) in their homes. Many Catholics who own and read Bibles have to some degree unknowingly been influenced by Luther's concept of *sola Scriptura*. As a result of the Lutheran Reformation, *sola Scriptura* in time overshadowed the stringent prohibitions of owning or reading the Bible, as once decreed by the Synod of Toulouse and the Synod of Tarragona, cited above.

SCRIPTURE INTERPRETS SCRIPTURE

In addition to Lutheran theology saying the Bible is the only source of Christian doctrine, *sola Scriptura* to Lutherans also means the Bible interprets itself. It is a principle that essentially comes from Martin Luther, though Athanasius (d. 373) said something similar: "The sacred and inspired Scriptures are sufficient to declare the truth."[26]

While historical and geographic knowledge can and often should be used to shed additional light on the meaning of given biblical passages, it does not mean that the Bible does not interpret itself. This is especially true in regard to passages in Scripture that are more difficult to understand. Thus, when the latter is true, Lutheran theologians, using the principle that the Bible interprets itself, have always taught that difficult or less-clear biblical passages must be interpreted in light of the Bible's clear passages.

To say Scripture interprets itself also means the Old Testament is interpreted in light of the New Testament. The writers of the New Testament used this principle when they interpreted numerous Old Testament passages as having been fulfilled in the life and deeds of Jesus Christ. An ancient saying (attributed to St. Augustine) states, "The New is in the Old concealed, and the Old is in the New revealed." For instance, when Isaiah prophesied, "The virgin shall conceive and bear a son, and shall call His name Immanuel" (7:14), this prophecy was concealed to many who heard it in Isaiah's time. To whatever degree it once was concealed in the Old Testament, it is now revealed in the New Testament. For Matthew 1:23 quotes Isaiah's prediction showing that the birth of Jesus Christ by the Virgin Mary fulfilled Isaiah's prophecy made some seven hundred years previously. In Mark's Gospel, we find Christ on the cross sorrowfully asking, "My God, My God, why have You forsaken Me?" (Mark 15:34). Here Jesus quotes the very words of Psalm 22:1 that Mark says were fulfilled by Jesus uttering them in His agony on the cross. In Isaiah 53, several predictive verses, made some eight centuries before Christ's birth, are interpreted by the New Testament as fulfilled in Christ's crucifixion; for example, as found in Matthew 8:17; Romans 4:25; and 1 Peter 2:24–25. And in Luke 4:17–21, Jesus says the words of Isaiah 49:8–9 and 61:1–2 are fulfilled in Him. These are examples of Scripture interpreting Scripture. In short, the principle of Scripture interpreting Scripture rests on the doctrine that the Bible is self-authenticating and does not contradict itself.

The Bible is self-authenticating and does not contradict itself.

The Bible as a Book of History and Faith

Since World War I, when men such as Paul Tillich, Rudolf Bultmann, Karl Barth, Dietrich Bonhoeffer, and their followers came on the theological scene, the Bible has increasingly been seen by many merely as a "book of faith." This means its historical accounts and information are minimized or dismissed in regard to providing factual, historical information. So the Bible is primarily a "book of faith."

This liberal view of Holy Scripture is at variance with the doctrine of *sola Scriptura* held by Luther and the Lutheran formulators of the Formula of Concord, who definitely saw the historical accounts cited in the Bible as factual history and not just a book containing statements of faith voiced by the biblical writers. So firm was their conviction that everything in the Bible, written by prophets and apostles, was historically true and correct that they pronounced it as the highest authority of human knowledge and faith, as indicated in the preface to the Formula of Concord, cited earlier.

Conclusion

Although the words *sola Scriptura* come from the lips of Martin Luther, it can be argued they have their origin in the words of Jesus Christ Himself, for it was He who told the Jews (and us too), "Search the scriptures, for in them ye think ye have eternal life; and they are they which testify of Me" (John 5:39 KJV). In short, the Scriptures are the only true source. This KJV translation renders this passage as an imperative statement. In recent years, however, some Bible translations have rendered the word *search* as an indicative verb rather than an imperative, thus making this passage read, "You search the Scriptures because you think that in them you have eternal life."

Here it needs to be noted that in the Greek text of the New Testament the verb *ereunate* (search) can be indicative or imperative. While the context permits both possibilities, the Ancient Church Fathers, however, with apparently only one known exception (Cyril of Alexandria), all saw Christ's use of the word *search* in the imperative sense.[27]

If Christ spoke this passage in the imperative sense, it is another argument in support of *sola Scriptura*. In addition, this passage also accents the importance of *solus Christus*, for Jesus reminded all who heard Him—then and now—that the words of Holy Scripture only make sense if they are viewed through Him because, in the latter part of this verse, Jesus clearly says that "they [the Scriptures] are they which testify of Me" (John 5:39 KJV).

1. Why is it a false argument to say that the doctrine of *sola Scriptura* ignores and nullifies Christian tradition?

2. Why is it incorrect to say Martin Luther was the first one to teach *sola Scriptura*?

3. How has *sola Scriptura* influenced some Roman Catholics, especially in America, even though their church authorities officially reject the doctrine of *sola Scriptura*?

4. How does Lutheran theology that firmly holds to *sola Scriptura* also honor Christian tradition?

5. When *sola Scriptura* is rejected, what other sources of authority are then frequently appealed to?

6. How can the doctrine of *sola Scriptura* be misused?

7. Why does Roman Catholicism not accept *sola Scriptura*?

8. Why do you think the Council of Chalcedon (451) said Mary was the mother of God (*theotokos*)?

9. Why is the term *Christotokos* (Christ-bearer) for Mary inadequate, biblically speaking, as opposed to *theotokos* (God-bearer)?

10. Why do you think some Christians (even some Lutherans) are often not quite sure whether it is correct to say that when the Virgin Mary gave birth to Jesus Christ, she also gave birth to God?

11. Why do you think some recent Bible translations render the word *search* in John 5:39 as a factual statement instead of giving it a sense of an imperative, of something that must be done?

12. How does the Lutheran principle of "Scripture interprets Scripture" often help us understand some difficult biblical passage(s)?

CHAPTER 5

New Testament Canonicity

Early Church, Luther, and the Council of Trent

"But the Helper, the Holy Spirit, whom the Father will send in My name, He will teach you all things and bring to your remembrance all that I have said to you."
—Jesus to His apostles; John 14:26

When I was about twelve years old, I paged through Luther's German Bible that my mother regularly read. I noticed it had a number of books between the Old and New Testament called "Apocrypha." So I asked my mother why her Bible contained these books, because my English Bible did not have them. She shrugged her shoulders and said she really did not know, but added she was once told they were really not a part of the Bible but were okay and good to read. Then some years later, I asked an LCMS pastor about these Apocrypha books. He responded, "They are not inspired." Although I did not know it at the time, I had asked a question about biblical canonicity.

The words *canonicity* and *canonical* are derived from the Greek word *kanon*, meaning "a rule or a guide." The early Christians used the term *kanon* as a rule or guide in regard to which books they accepted as God's revealed, inspired Word. They wanted to know whether every New Testament book in a given canon (or list) was authored by an apostle of Jesus Christ, a matter discussed later on in greater detail.

The present chapter confines itself to discussing only the canonicity of the New Testament. Lutherans and non-Lutheran Protestants have from the days of the Reformation not questioned the authenticity of the Old Testament canon with its thirty-nine books that do not include the Apocrypha. As one renowned biblical scholar has rightly stated, "Almost every book of this literary corpus [the Old Testament] is quoted or alluded to authoritatively by Jesus and the apostles."[1] Similarly, F. F. Bruce, another renowned biblical scholar, has stated that the Old Testament's "canonicity is established for Christians on the testimony of Jesus and his apostles."[2]

THE BIBLE COMPARED TO THE QUR'AN AND THE BOOK OF MORMON

Before the present chapter discusses the various aspects of the New Testament's canonicity, readers will find it helpful to know how the Bible differs from two prominent religious books considered as sacred by their adherents. For brevity's sake, we will only focus on the Qur'an and the Book of Mormon. Regarding the Qur'an, Muslims believe what Muhammad, the founder of Islam, said in the Qur'an; namely, that it is stored on a tablet in heaven. "This is truly a glorious Qur'an written on a preserved Tablet" (Qur'an 85:21–22). One translation of the Qur'an, in a footnote to this reference, says, "God keeps this [tablet] with Him."[3] Similarly, Mormons believe the reputed golden plates that the angel Moroni permitted Joseph Smith to transcribe into the Book of Mormon are back with the angel Moroni in heaven. According to Smith, "I have delivered them [the golden plates] up to him [angel Moroni]; and he has them in his charge until this day."[4]

The beliefs or convictions of Muslims and Mormons are solely derived from hearsay or blind faith without any corroborating empirical evidence.

Here it is important to note the beliefs or convictions of Muslims and Mormons are solely derived from hearsay or blind faith without any corroborating empirical evidence from any reliable eyewitnesses pertaining to the content of these two books. In contrast, informed Christians know the Bible and its teachings did not drop from heaven and are not on a sacred tablet stored in heaven. Rather, it is grounded in factual, historical information recorded by God's chosen prophets in the Old Testament. Many of the prophets published eyewitness reports. And similarly, the New Testament consists of eyewitness accounts written by some of Jesus Christ's apostles, who recorded what they had seen and heard in their empirical interactions with Him, both before and after His bodily resurrection. That is why the apostles Peter and John declared, "For we cannot but speak of what we have seen and heard" (Acts 4:20).

Thus, this and the following chapter provide historically reliable evidence that the Early Church, for its New Testament, only selected writings from the various books in circulation if it was certain the books were penned by Christ's eyewitnesses, His apostles, or by one who was under the supervision of an apostle (Luke and Mark). This selection process reveals the uniqueness of the New Testament's composition and its historical, empirical veracity. Nothing similar characterizes any other book defined as sacred by non-Christian religions.

Various New Testament Canons

The New Testament contains twenty-seven books. Given that its various books did not fall from heaven prompts a rather logical and important question: namely, what criteria did Christians in the Early Church use to determine which books rightfully belonged in the Bible, particularly the books in the New Testament? This question is addressed and discussed in the present chapter and the next, primarily for the spiritual growth and edification of today's Lutherans, and especially for the benefit of the laity, similar to what Luther had in mind when he wrote a preface for each New Testament book when he had finished translating them in 1522.

It is important to note that from the second to the ninth century, virtually every canon (list) of the New Testament's books used in the early churches did not all contain the same books. Moreover, seven books found in today's New Testament were disputed and even rejected in some geographic areas of the Church.

In the mid-second century, the first two canons of the New Testament's books appeared in some early churches. The first list was by Marcion of Sinope[5] (in modern Turkey). Marcion's canon appeared between AD 125 and 145. It contained eleven New Testament books, one of which (Luke's Gospel) he had altered. The next list to appear was the Muratorian Canon in about AD 170. It had twenty-one New Testament books, plus nine New Testament Apocrypha books. It omitted the

Epistles of Hebrews, James, 1 and 2 Peter, and Philemon. Also in about AD 170, the index of the Old Latin Bible listed only twenty-four New Testament books.[6] And around AD 200, the Alexandrian Canon appeared with only twenty-three New Testament books, along with nine New Testament Apocrypha books.

Additional canons appeared in the third and fourth centuries, and one in particular became noteworthy when Athanasius (bishop of Alexandria, Egypt), in AD 367 in his annual Paschal (Easter) letter, listed twenty-seven New Testament books, along with a supplementary list that included the Didache, Shepherd of Hermas, and five Old Testament Apocrypha books. Athanasius's canon was intended only for those under his ecclesiastical jurisdiction in Alexandria, Egypt, and why it later came to be accepted in much of Christendom no historian has thus far been able to explain, because other canons, similar but not identical to this one, still continued to appear at least into the ninth century in different geographical areas. The Syriac Church in the East, for instance, between AD 411–35 used the Peshitta Canon. It contained only twenty-two books of the New Testament.[7] It omitted 2 John, 3 John, 2 Peter, Jude, and Revelation. This canon is still used by Syrian Christians today. Interestingly, by the ninth century, at least thirty different canons existed in different regions of the Church.

HOMOLOGOUMENA AND ANTILEGOMENA BOOKS

Almost one hundred and fifty years before Athanasius's canon appeared in AD 367, the Early Church theologian Origen (in AD 225) listed twenty New Testament books that Christians had universally accepted as written by Christ's apostles. He called them *homologoumena* (universally agreed upon or accepted). Books that were not accepted universally by many early churches he called *antilegomena* (spoken against). Origen listed the latter as 2 and 3 John, 2 Peter, Hebrews, James, Jude, and Revelation. Then in AD 325, Eusebius of Caesarea[8] published a list of the universally accepted books that he, similar to Origen, also called homologoumena, and the books spoken against he also called antilegomena. He also added a third category that he called *notha*, meaning spurious or false. Eusebius's list of homologoumena and antilegomena books were the same as Origen's list. Whether Athanasius knew about Origen's and Eusebius's lists is not known, for his list in AD 367 does not mention this distinction.

HALLMARKS OF LUTHERAN IDENTITY

Books Authored by Christ's Apostles

Just before His crucifixion, Jesus told His disciples, "These things I have spoken to you while I am still with you. But the Helper, the Holy Spirit, whom the Father will send in My name, He will teach you all things and bring to your remembrance all that I have said to you" (John 14:25–26). He further told them, "When the Spirit of truth comes, He will guide you into all the truth" (16:13). Luke, the author of the third Gospel, says the apostles were "eyewitnesses and ministers of the word" (Luke 1:2). And similarly, Jesus (after His resurrection) told Saul (who would later be named Paul) on his way to Damascus, "Rise and stand upon your feet, for I have appeared to you for this purpose, to appoint you as a servant and witness to the things in which you have seen Me and to those in which I will appear to you" (Acts 26:16).

These words that Jesus spoke to the apostles became normative for the Early Church regarding the acceptance or rejection of New Testament books. This norm is mentioned by Irenaeus, who around AD 180 in his work *Against the Heresies* wrote, "This Gospel they [the apostles] first preached orally, but later by God's will they handed it on [*tradiderunt*] to us in the Scriptures, so it would be the foundation and pillar of our faith."[9] Irenaeus also taught that when a New Testament book was written by a scribe under the guidance of an apostle, it, too, was God's inspired Word. Thus, he stated, "Mark, Peter's disciple, handed down to us in writing what was preached by Peter. Luke too, Paul's assistant, set down in a book the Gospel that was preached by Paul."[10] Hence, the Early Church accepted Mark's Gospel as inspired Scripture and similarly, the Gospel of Luke and the Acts of the Apostles. As New Testament canonicity scholar Lee Martin McDonald has stated, "If a writing was believed to have been produced by an apostle, it was eventually accepted as sacred scripture and included in the New Testament canon."[11] If a book was known not to have been authored by an apostle, or if there was serious doubt as to who wrote it, the Early Church did not accept it, and thus it was not included in the New Testament.

Books Authored by False Teachers

History reveals that while the apostles were still alive, but especially after their earthly departure, false teachers appeared in the Early Church, just as the apostle Paul had warned when he said many would "turn away from listening to the truth and wander off into myths" (2 Timothy 4:4). Some false teachers arose and wrote epistles to

Christians, mostly in the second century, after the death of the apostles. Many second or third epistles, several of which are included in the New Testament Apocrypha, claimed to be divinely inspired. In order to give these later works credibility, many were falsely assigned names of some apostles—for instance, the Gospel of Thomas, the Gospel of Philip, the Gospel of Peter, and the Acts of Paul. Some of these books espoused Gnosticism, an early Christian heresy that taught inner, divine knowledge (*gnosis*) could be obtained apart from Holy Scripture, contrary to what Christ's apostles taught and wrote in the four Gospels and in their epistles. The Gnostics also taught that human flesh was evil and that Jesus' resurrection was only a spiritual phenomenon, thus not a real bodily resurrection. Given that these apocryphal epistles circulated rather widely, Christians had to decide which books were or were not written by Christ's apostles so that Christians would not be deceived by false teachings. This concern prompted Christian leaders (usually bishops) to draw up lists of books that would spiritually guide and edify Christians in their Divine Services, as well as in their faith and lives.

LUTHER'S NEW TESTAMENT TRANSLATION AND ITS CANONICITY

When Luther had finished translating the New Testament into the German language in 1522, he did more than translate it. He also wrote prefaces to the New Testament books. Luther knew that of the New Testament's twenty-seven books, seven (Hebrews, James, 2 Peter, 2 and 3 John, James, Jude, and Revelation) from the Church's early early years were not universally accepted as written by Christ's apostles. These books, as noted above, were called antilegomena. Luther, unlike the Ancient Church, doubted only Hebrews, James, Jude, and Revelation, even though all seven still had the status of being noncanonical (noninspired) in his day.

Luther's prefaces in his German New Testament were an important educational aid that helped the laity both to know and to better understand each book's theological emphases, together with learning about its author and its canonical status. These prefaces functioned as an important biblical aid for nearly four centuries after Luther's time. But by the 1890s, German Bibles, published in Germany and in America, no longer included the prefaces. Thus, beginning with the 1900s, Lutheran laity reading German Bibles in Europe or in America were now deprived of knowing that seven books in the New Testament were not accepted as canonical in the Ancient Church and also not by many in Luther's day. Thus, when people read the Bible, they could no longer read the historical prefaces to learn why these disputed books were not accepted as canonical in the Ancient Church.

LUTHER'S VIEW OF NEW TESTAMENT CANONICITY

Martin Luther's strong accent on *sola Scriptura* logically took him back to the Early Church's concern regarding which of the New Testament's books were canonical. Without listing the various and many New Testament canons that appeared in different geographic areas, and at different times, from the second to the ninth century, it is important to note that on some lists 2 and 3 John, 2 Peter, Hebrews, James, Jude, and Revelation did not appear. Or when one or more of these seven books did appear on some lists, they were considered antilegomena (spoken against). Of the seven antilegomena books, Luther accepted 2 and 3 John and also 2 Peter, for he argued they contained no false doctrine and clearly presented the saving Gospel of Jesus Christ. Here he deviated from the Early Church, for it had rejected these three epistles, together with the other four doubted books, because there was insufficient evidence that 2 and 3 John were written by the apostle John, and similarly, the Early Church did not accept 2 Peter because it did not see this book as authored by the apostle Peter. To Luther, a book's Gospel content was highly valued, so he accepted these three epistles despite the Early Church's uncertainty concerning their authorship. In this instance, he departed from the Early Church, for it considered apostolic authorship of a New Testament book as a *sine qua non* (an indispensable condition or requirement). Here it is interesting to note that though the Early Church rejected books on the basis of content, there is no evidence that it ever accepted a book as canonical on the basis of its Gospel content, as Luther did. By Luther's accepting 2 and 3 John and 2 Peter because they preached Christ, he not only deviated from the Early Church's assessment regarding who wrote these three antilegomena epistles, but he thereby also created a canon within the canon. Some have called this "Luther's canon."

Regarding a book's content, Luther stated the Epistle of Hebrews, for example, contained false doctrines in 6:4–6 and in 10:26–27. Both references say if a Christian has willfully sinned, he or she cannot return to his or her former state of grace, thus an argument of content.

Luther also said these references were "contrary to all the gospels and to St. Paul's epistles." He continued, "My opinion is that this is an epistle put together of many pieces, which does not deal systematically with any one subject."[12]

With regard to the Epistle of James, Luther said it contradicted the biblical doctrine that a Christian is saved by faith alone (*sola fide*) in Christ, for it states a person is "justified by works and not by faith alone" (2:24). He called this book "an epistle of straw . . . for it has nothing of the nature of the gospel about it."[13] And he also argued it did "not once mention the Passion, the resurrection, or the Spirit of Christ."[14]

Concerning the content of Jude, Luther said verses 9 and 14 were dubious because they are mentioned nowhere else in the Bible.[15] In regard to the Book of Revelation, he cited a number of reasons for rejecting it. For instance, he did not see it written by an apostle because "the apostles do not deal with visions, but prophesy in clear and plain words, as do Peter and Paul, and Christ in the gospel."[16] This again was an argument from content.

Luther rejected Hebrews, James, Jude, and Revelation on the basis of questionable authorship, along with their dubious content. He said the author of Hebrews was unknown.[17] Here he echoed the third-century Early Church Father Origen. In a statement, now well-known, Origen said: "who wrote Hebrews only God knows." Luther, of course, knew no more than Origen did, nor do we today. Concerning James, he said, "I do not regard it as the writing of an apostle."[18] Regarding the writer of Jude, he stated, "He speaks of the apostles like a disciple who comes along after them."[19] In reference to the Book of Revelation, he reminded readers that "some of the ancient fathers held that it was not the work of St. John, the Apostle."[20]

Luther had no fear that lay Christians' learning that some books in their New Testament had been doubted and not seen as God's Word in the days of the Ancient Church would disturb their faith. Thus, the four books whose canonicity he doubted (Hebrews, James, Jude, and Revelation) he placed at the end of his newly translated German New Testament of 1522. The other twenty-three books Luther accepted preceded the four. He also separated the four from the twenty-three by a space page, and in the index he did not assign a number to any of the four.[21]

Along with Luther's minimizing the importance of these four disputed books by placing them at the end of the New Testament, he also made another change. He omitted the Epistle to the Laodiceans (reputedly authored by St. Paul) that had been in some eighteen German Bibles printed before Luther's translation. This brief epistle was found in "more than one hundred manuscripts of the Latin Vulgate . . . as well as in manuscripts of the early Albigensian, Bohemian, English, and Flemish versions."[22] J. B. Lightfoot, a nineteenth-century British scholar, says that "for more than nine centuries this forged epistle hovered about the doors of the sacred Canon, without either finding admission or being peremptorily excluded."[23]

Interestingly and notably, the English Bible translators at the time of the Reformation—namely, William Tyndale, Myles Coverdale, Oliver Cromwell, Thomas Cranmer, John Rogers, and Richard Taverner, all influenced by Luther—did not assign Hebrews, James, Jude, and Revelation a number in the index of the Bibles they had translated or edited. The Matthews-Tyndale Bible (1537) also had a space page preceding these four books, similar to what Luther did in his German New Testament.[24]

In early 1524, Tyndale crossed the channel to Germany in order to escape persecution for his translating activity. In the city of Worms, he succeeded in secretly publishing the New Testament in English in 1526. While in Germany, did Tyndale visit Luther? Some historians think not. However, F. F. Bruce says Tyndale "spent the best part of a year at Wittenberg."[25] Thus, it would have been highly unlikely that the two men never met in this relatively small town.

Luther's canon was followed for a considerable time in the first Bibles translated into English in England. In 1529, a revised Latin translation was published in Wittenberg that also followed his canon, and in 1740, a Greek New Testament was published in Halle that followed it as well. The first German Bible published in America in 1743 followed it too. And in 1892, "Luther's German Bible," as it was widely known, still placed the four epistles after the New Testament's twenty-three books, but in this edition, they were no longer separated by a space page, and they now were also numbered in the index with the preceding books. The Book of Revelation, however, was still separated in this edition.[26]

The Council of Trent Decrees Antilegomena Books Canonical

From the ninth to the fifteenth century, no known church councils listed any New Testament canons, nor did they make any pronouncements regarding the canonicity of given books. Not listing or citing any canons for six centuries, however, ended when the Council of Florence convened (1439–43). It listed thirty-nine books of the Old Testament, with the Apocrypha books interspersed, plus twenty-seven New Testament books. A hundred years later, the Council of Trent, on April 8, 1546, adopted this same canon with a mere twenty-four yea votes, fifteen nay votes, and sixteen abstentions.[27] Thus, less than half (43.6 percent) of the Catholic bishops voted yea. Still, the council, with less than a majority of the attending bishops, dogmatically decreed the Old Testament Apocrypha and the twenty-seven New Testament books to be canonical. This was the first time in the Church's history that a church council decreed that Christians had to accept the Old Testament Apocrypha and all twenty-seven of the New Testament's books as canonical or be anathematized. Anathema is a designation by a pope or a council of the church, excommunicating a person or denouncing a doctrine or teaching as condemned.

When the Council of Trent issued this decree, it not only annulled the Early Church's historical distinction between the homologoumena and antilegomena books, but it also established another new doctrine in the Roman Church. Trent's decree was firmly rejected by Martin Chemnitz.

Martin Chemnitz Rejects Trent's Decree: Defends Homologoumena-Antilegomena Distinction

In 1565, twenty years after the Council of Trent arbitrarily decreed the seven antilegomena books of

Anathema is a designation by a pope or a council of the church, excommunicating a person or denouncing a doctrine or teaching as condemned.

the New Testament as canonical, Martin Chemnitz wrote the Lutheran response to its autocratic decision. He stated the unqualified acceptance of these seven books ignored "how much harm and neglect and annulment of that most ancient distinction between the canonical books and the apocryphal and spurious, or false, books has brought into the church."[28] He also asked whether the seven antilegomena books could be legitimately declared as "authentic." His answer: "It is evident that [they] can not."[29]

In addition to criticizing Trent for its authoritarian decision, Chemnitz insisted that the difference between the homologoumena and the antilegomena books needed to be observed by Lutheran pastors and theologians when they document given doctrines. "No dogma ought therefore to be drawn out of these [antilegomena] books which does not have reliable and clear foundations and testimonies in other canonical books. Nothing controversial can be proved out these books, unless there are other proofs and confirmations in the canonical books."[30] This meant when Lutherans seek to document given doctrines by citing proof passages from the New Testament, they must only cite passages found in the twenty homologoumena books. If a complementary passage existed in any of the seven antilegomena books, it could only be cited as secondary support.

Chemnitz further contended, "The canonical Scripture has its eminent authority chiefly from this, that it is divinely inspired, 2 Timothy 3:16; that is, it was not brought forth by the will of men but that the men of God, moved by the Holy Spirit, both spoke and wrote."[31] The "men of God" were Christ's apostles, as Chemnitz showed by citing Tertullian, the Early Church Father (d. ca. 225), who wrote, "we establish that a Gospel document has as its authors apostles, to whom this task of promulgating the Gospel was assigned by the Lord Himself."[32] The Old Testament's books, on the other hand, were canonical because they were written by God's prophets, and because Jesus and the four evangelists approved them.[33]

Chemnitz accepted only those books as canonical in the New Testament that were written by Christ's apostles. This stipulation is also found in the Formula of Concord, of which Chemnitz was the chief architect. The Formula states, "We [Lutherans] believe, teach, and confess that the only rule and norm according to which all teachings, together with ‹all› teachers, should be evaluated and judged [2 Timothy 3:15–17] are the prophetic and apostolic Scriptures of the

. . .each New Testament book had to be written by an apostle or by someone under an apostle's direction in order for it to be canonical.

Old and New Testament alone" (FC Ep Summary 1). The words "apostolic Scriptures" echo what Jesus told His disciples; namely, that they would speak and write His words (cited earlier) to His followers after His ascension. Thus, if a book in the New Testament was not written by an apostle, or if its authorship was in doubt, Chemnitz, similar to the Early Church, called it noncanonical.

Therefore, when eight thousand Lutherans signed the Formula of Concord in 1577, they agreed with its authors that each New Testament book had to be written by an apostle or by someone under an apostle's direction in order for it to be canonical. This meant when a book's authorship was in doubt or unknown—for example, the Epistle to the Hebrews—it was not accepted as canonical.

❧❧

Conclusion

To maintain the historic Lutheran position that a New Testament book had to be authored by an apostle in order for it to be canonical is a theologically conservative position. Today, many New Testament scholars, operating with the historical-critical method, do not accept many of the epistles of St. Paul as written by him. They argue that some of his reputed epistles were written and edited in the second century by unknown Christian authors after the death of the apostles. This position rejects apostolic authorship with respect to canonicity and is contrary to what Christ taught; namely, that the Holy Spirit would reveal God's Word to His apostles (John 14:26), and that they would soon convey the Word of God to His people. Thus, from the mid-first century to its last decade, some apostles—notably Paul, Peter, and John—wrote divinely inspired epistles to early Christian assemblies.

The early part of the present chapter stated that informed Lutherans do not accept the Bible in blind faith or hearsay, as Muslims accept the Qur'an and Mormons the Book of Mormon. Rather, Lutheran acceptance of the Bible is linked to the factual, eyewitness accounts recorded by Christ's chosen apostles in the canonical books of the New Testament. These eyewitness accounts, for instance, consistently declare, "For we cannot but speak of what we have seen and heard" (Acts 4:20). Similarly, Luke, a co-worker of the apostle Paul, quoting the apostle Peter, stated, "This Jesus God raised up, and of that we all are witnesses" (Acts 2:32). Luke also declared that Jesus had "presented Himself alive to them after His suffering by many *infallible proofs*, being seen by them [the apostles] during forty days and speaking of the things pertaining to the kingdom of God" (Acts 1:3 NKJV, emphasis added). And as F. F. Bruce has shown, the New Testament's writings are historically accurate and reliable. See his *The New Testament Documents: Are They Reliable?* (1960).

It was these writings of the apostles (epistles/books) that the Early Church with great care and attention selected to comprise the New Testament. Reading and learning from these canonical books enabled Christians to say these are "the words of the Lord." This objective was also what motivated the renowned Lutheran theologians for a hundred years, following Luther, to retain and defend the differences between the homologoumena and antilegomena books in the New Testament.

And it is important to note that some extrabiblical facts provide supplementary support for Christians saying the teachings of the canonical books in the New Testament are "the words of the Lord." In the 1920s, British journalist Frank Morison (pseudonym for Albert Henry Ross, 1881–1950) decided to write a monograph proving that the last seven days of Jesus' life were fictitious and not based on any historical facts. To his great surprise, his research did not support his preconceived hypothesis. He ended up writing a book (*Who Moved the Stone?*) in 1930 defending the historical fact of Christ's bodily resurrection. In addition, numerous archaeological findings continue to corroborate the Bible's containing empirically reliable historical accounts. In regard to the latter, Nelson Glueck, a well-known archaeologist, once remarked, "It may be stated categorically that no archaeological discovery has ever controverted a biblical reference."[34]

Lutheran the-
ology does
not accept
the Bible, or
a given book
between its
covers, on
the basis of
hearsay or
blind faith.

Briefly restated, Lutheran theology does not accept the Bible, or a given book between its covers,
on the basis of hearsay or blind faith. This stance is
another hallmark of Lutheran theology. And as
Lutherans, we want to be informed why a given book
in the Bible is canonically God's inspired Word so we
can defend its teachings when challenged by skep-
tics, remembering the canonical words of the apostle
Peter, to always be "prepared to make a defense to anyone asks you for a reason for the hope that is in you"
(1 Peter 3:15).

1. What does the word *canon* mean in the Greek language?

2. When did the first canon (list) of New Testament books appear in the history of the Church?

3. Why did the Early Church not accept 2 and 3 John, 2 Peter, Hebrews, James, Jude, and Revelation as canonical?

4. In regard to books in the New Testament, what is Bishop Athanasius known for?

5. What does the word *homologoumena* mean?

6. What does the word *antilegomena* mean?

7. In what year did Martin Luther translate the New Testament?

8. How many books are considered antilegomena in the New Testament?

9. What three antilegomena New Testament books did Luther accept as canonical?

10. What prominent Lutheran said we should not use a lone quotation from an antilegomena book in support of a doctrine? Why?

11. Which antilegomena books did Luther not accept as canonical? Why?

12. In what manner did the Council of Trent differ from all previous councils?

CHAPTER 6

New Testament Canonicity

Lutheran Theology after the Council of Trent

*"Concerning the Holy Scriptures, we call only those books
of the Old and New Testaments canonical whose authority
has never been doubted in the church."
—Württembergisches Glaubensbekenntnis, 1552*

Following Luther's questioning the New Testament's canonicity in the early 1520s, prominent Lutheran theologians after him wanted to be sure they could say "This is the Word of Lord" when they quoted from a given New Testament book. Thus, they continued to honor and uphold the historic homologoumena-antilegomena distinction. Similar to Luther, they openly discussed and theologically defended the importance of this distinction in respect to the formation of the New Testament.

Lutheran Defenders of the Homologoumena— Antilegomena Distinction

Below are brief notes of some of the more prominent Lutheran theologians who voiced strong support for this distinction that arose in the Early Church in regard to the canonicity of the New Testament's books. Most of these theologians held teaching positions at German universities.

Johannes Brenz (1499–1570)

A prominent Lutheran reformer in the Duchy of Württemberg and a prolific writer of theological works, Johannes Brenz placed the antilegomena books of the New Testament with the Old Testament Apocrypha and wondered by what right some pastors saw these books as canonical. Similar to Luther, according to Edward Reuss, Brenz argued that "the Epistle of James could not be put in harmony with apostolic doctrine, without the help of forced interpretation."[1] In 1551, Brenz was assigned by ten Lutheran theologians to author and formulate the document *Confessio Württembergica* (*Württembergisches Glaubensbekenntnis*). The first sentence in Article XXVII, as cited at the beginning of this chapter, states, "Concerning the Holy Scriptures, we call only those books of the Old and New Testaments canonical whose authority has never been doubted in the church."[2] This document was published in 1552 and presented to the Council of Trent while it was still in session, but the council refused to consider it.

Martin Chemnitz (1522–86)

Chemnitz, together with Jacob Andreae and Nicholas Selnecker, formulated the Formula of Concord in 1577 (published in 1580). This confessional document united virtually all Lutherans who for thirty years had been bitterly divided into two warring camps, the *Gnesio* Lutherans (Genuine Lutherans) and the Philippists, followers of Philip Melanchthon during the Leipzig Interim (1548–74).

As noted in the preceding chapter, Chemnitz rejected the Council of Trent's decree that had effectively nullified the homologoumena-antilegomena distinction by declaring the New Testament's seven antilegomena books as canonical in 1546. He contended, "The church does not have such power, that it can make true writings out of false, false out of true, out of doubtful and uncertain, certain, canonical, and legitimate, without any certain and firm proofs which, as we have said above, are required for this matter." And, he added, if the church had the authority to declare a book canonical, it could similarly "reject canonical books or declare spurious books canonical."[3]

A book is canonical, said Chemnitz, not because the church declares it, but because "God chose certain definite persons that they should write and adorned them with many miracles and divine testimonies that there should be no doubt that what they wrote was divinely inspired."[4] Thus, the Early Church and its councils did not determine the New Testament's canonicity. Rather, both merely recognized the divinely inspired apostolic content of the homologoumena books because they were written by Christ's chosen apostles. As Bruce M. Metzger, a twentieth-century renowned New Testament scholar, has similarly stated, "Neither individuals nor councils created the canon; instead they came to recognize and acknowledge the self-authenticating quality of these writings, which imposed themselves as canonical upon the church."[5] And regarding Luther's view of the church determining the New Testament's canonicity, Edward Reuss, nineteenth-century French theologian, has stated, "Nothing was further from the thoughts of Luther . . . and [his] illustrious associates."[6]

To contend the church does not determine the canonicity of books in the Bible is a distinctively Lutheran doctrine. It reveals a major difference between Lutheran theology and Roman Catholicism. It is a Lutheran hallmark within the more prominent hallmark of the historical Lutheran concern regarding the New Testament's canonicity.

MATTHIAS HAFENREFFER (1561–1619)

As a Lutheran professor at the University of Tübingen, Hafenreffer taught that the New Testament's seven antilegomena books were permissible for Christians to read but not to be used as dogmatic authority. Hafenreffer called these seven books *Apocryphi Libri* (apocrypha books).[7] During his time, the Lutheran faculty at the University of Wittenberg, in 1619, publicly censured the 1608 catechism of the Socinians (an anti-Trinitarian sect). It accused them "among other heresies with the heresy of effacing the difference between the canonical and apocryphal [antilegomena] books of the New Testament."[8] It was also at this time that the Gustavus Adolphus Bible in Sweden (published in 1618) reflected Luther's view (canon) regarding Hebrews, James, Jude,

> To contend the church does not determine the canonicity of books in the Bible is a distinctively Lutheran doctrine.

and Revelation as noncanonical. This Swedish Bible labeled these four books "apocryphal." This distinction was maintained in Sweden "for nearly a century and a half in a dozen or more printings."[9]

And in 1596, before the Gustavus Adolphus Bible appeared in Sweden, David Wolder, pastor of St. Peter Lutheran Church in Hamburg, had published a triglot Bible (one that includes Greek, Latin, and German). Its table of contents listed Hebrews, James, Jude, and Revelation as "non-canonical."[10] Also in 1596, Jacob Lucius in Hamburg published a German Bible. It named Hebrews, James, Jude, and Revelation as "Apocrypha."[11]

FRIEDRICH BALDUIN (1575–1627)

As a prominent Lutheran theologian, he held several posts before he served on the theological faculty at Wittenberg until his death in 1627. He published numerous books, including a commentary on St. Paul's epistles. On behalf of the Wittenberg faculty, in 1619, he authored the Lutheran criticism of the Socinian Catechism (also known as the Racovian Catechism, published in 1608).[12] In 1626, in one of Balduin's books, he labeled the New Testament's seven antilegomena books as "*Apokryphen*" (apocrypha).[13]

CONRAD DIETERICH (1575–1639)

Dieterich served as a Lutheran pastor and professor who in his publications wrote two expositions—a longer one and a shorter one—of Luther's Small Catechism. The shorter version was translated into German from Latin and widely used, even by many Lutherans in America, including pastors in the Missouri and Wisconsin Synods in the latter part of the 1800s and early 1900s. The larger exposition, initially written in Latin, lists the seven antilegomena books of the New Testament and designates them as "*libros Apocrypha Novi Testamenti*" (Apocrypha books of the New Testament).[14] By this classification, Dieterich equated these seven books with the Apocrypha of the Old Testament, which Lutherans from the time of the Reformation had classified as noncanonical. The large edition of Dieterich's Catechism was widely read by students in German schools and universities.[15]

ANTILEGOMENA BOOKS ELEVATED

When the Council of Trent in 1545 nullified the homologoumena -antilegomena distinction by decreeing the New Testament's seven antilegomena books as canonical, the council turned its back on more than a thousand years of Christian history that reached back to the early third century when Origen first made this important distinction. And prominent Lutheran theologians greatly valued this distinction for a hundred years after Luther. But in 1625, this century-old Lutheran defense suffered a major breach in the wall of this centuries-old theological distinction. The breach was not made by a Catholic or a Reformed theologian, but by a Lutheran dogmatician, Johann Gerhard (1582–1637).

ANTILEGOMENA NAMED SECOND RANK

Born in Saxony, Johann Gerhard later served as a professor of theology at the University of Jena from 1616 until he died in 1637. He belonged to the era known as Lutheran Orthodoxy, which began when Lutherans signed the Formula of Concord in 1577. Among his works was *On the Nature of Theology and on Scripture* (1625). This book has a lengthy chapter titled "On the Canonical Books of the New Testament of the Second Rank." In this chapter, he redefines the historical status of the New Testament's seven antilegomena books by calling them "*secundi ordinis*" (second rank).[16] This was a major departure from the position the Ancient Church held regarding these books, for it did not accept them as canonical, given that their authorship was either uncertain or not known. By redefining them as "second rank," he also departed from Luther's position; even though Luther accepted three of the antilegomena books, he did not accept the remaining four as canonical. And Gerhard especially departed from Chemnitz, Brenz, Balduin, Hafenreffer, Dieterich, the Wittenberg University faculty, and from the *Confessio Württembergica* (1552), noted above. They all considered the antilegomena books as noncanonical, not worthy of even a second-rank status.

By using the term "second rank," Gerhard gave the antilegomena a quasi-canonical status that soon had the effect of making them canonical. This is something the Early Church and its later councils did not see theologically right to do before the Council of Trent disregarded that longstanding tradition. Apparently, none of Gerhard's contemporaries seemed to have criticized his redefining them as second rank. For there appear to be no extant articles or books that questioned his decision, which so clearly departed from the longstanding Lutheran rejection of the antilegomena. This silence is notably puzzling.

Given that Lutheran theology held a century-old opposition to the antilegomena, some Lutherans from Gerhard's time, as Robert Preus (scholar of Lutheran Orthodoxy) noted, "still retained a distinction between antilegomena and homologoumena, but they never doubted the inspiration of the former, only the authorship."[17] This is especially interesting, for if inspiration was now more important than authorship, how did Gerhard and some like-minded Lutherans know these second-rank books, whose authors were not really known, were inspired? For Jesus said (see John 14:26) only His apostles would write God's inspired Word. Moreover, to accept inspiration apart from apostolic authorship ignored the vow Lutheran pastors took in accordance with the Formula of Concord. It states a biblical book is inspired only if authored by a prophet or by an apostle: "We believe, teach, and confess that the only rule and norm according to which all teachings . . . should be evaluated and judged are the prophetic and apostolic Scriptures of Old and New Testament alone" (FC Ep Summary 1).

EFFECTS OF SECOND-RANK STATUS

Robert Preus (1924–1995) also notes that for Lutherans there was now in Gerhard's time, and soon after, "no hesitancy in quoting from the antilegomena. For all practical purposes the antilegomena were canonical."[18] He further indicates that by the mid-1700s some of the Lutheran theologians "do not even mention the distinction between the antilegomena and homologoumena."[19] Similarly, French theologian Edward Reuss, in his monumental work *History of the Canon of the Holy Scriptures in the Christian Church* (1884), states that Lutherans in the eighteenth century no longer had much interest in the antilegomena. And Lutherans who did mention it, merely did so "to defend Luther from the charges made against him on this point; and they make a very expeditious defense by perverting his meaning."[20] Given this context, Werner Elert stated, "Since Chemnitz's time [Lutheran] theologians have become ever more timid in the critical position they take over against the antilegomena."[21]

Preus further notes, "Lutheran theology [since Gerhard's time] greatly oversimplifies the problem of the New Testament canon and fails to be faithful to the historical data."[22] Notably, this oversimplification has since then been accepted by virtually all Lutheran theologians and pastors, most knowing very little about the theological concern that was so vitally important to Lutherans before Gerhard's time. To those pre-Gerhard Lutherans, the homologoumena-antilegomena

HALLMARKS OF LUTHERAN IDENTITY

distinction was highly relevant to the doctrine of *sola Scriptura*, but since Gerhard's day, Lutherans have ironically accepted the Council of Trent's 1546 fiat. Similar to Catholics and non-Lutheran Protestants, they now essentially use the antilegomena books as canonical and thus in effect the New Testament canon is closed. But as Bruce Metzger has shown, no confessional Lutheran documents contain a list of New Testament books, and so theoretically the New Testament canon in Lutheran theology is not closed, but still open. Thus, if two of St. Paul's letters (now lost) that he wrote to the Corinthians (see 1 Corinthians 5:9–11) and another epistle to the Christians in Laodicea (see Colossians 4:16) were found today and authenticated as his, Lutherans would have no theological problem adding both to the New Testament canon, whereas, it would be rather problematic for denominations that now consider the canon closed by their having formally listed the twenty-seven books of the New Testament as a completed act of their canonical history.

No confessional Lutheran documents contain a list of New Testament books, and so theoretically the New Testament canon in Lutheran theology is not closed, but still open.

CANONICITY AND BIBLICAL INSPIRATION

Regarding the New Testament's canonicity, the words of Edward Reuss come to mind. "Everyone understands that the theory of inspiration is very closely related to the conception of the canon."[23] Yet, when Gerhard redefined the antilegomena as second rank, he ignored the Lutheran position that had adhered to the phrase *in codice sunt, non in canone* (they are in the Bible but not in the canon). This phrase meant the antilegomena books were not written by apostles and thus lacked divine inspiration. And by Gerhard giving the antilegomena books second-rank status, he also rejected the *Confessio Württembergica* of 1552 (cited above). It clearly stated that Lutherans only accepted books as canonical that had never been doubted in the Ancient Church. Thus, from Gerhard's time, as Elert has noted, Lutherans took "a retreat along the whole line [of the antilegomena]."[24]

WHY SECOND-RANK STATUS?

Gerhard does not say why he decided to call the antilegomena books second rank. Nor does he provide any information why the Early Church's objections regarding the antilegomena were no longer valid. He also does not say how he came upon the term "second rank." To answer this question, the following possibilities come to mind. One, he may have chosen the term because it had a more positive tone than "antilegomena." The new term no longer conveyed a contrary or doubted status of the seven books, vis-à-vis the twenty accepted books. Two, perhaps he liked Rome's closely related term *deuterocanonical*, a designation Sixtus of Siena (1520–69) gave to the Septuagint's Apocrypha. Three, he may have been influenced by Andreas Osiander the Younger (1562–1617), who shortly before he died, had translated Eusebius's *Ecclesiastical History* (Book III, XXV) and translated Eusebius's concept of homologoumena as *"erster Ordnung"* (first rank) and antilegomena as *"zweiter Ordnung"* (second rank); however, Eusebius did not use these two concepts. That was done by Osiander, and his translation may have influenced Gerhard to choose the concept of second rank, an exact translation of *zweiter Ordnung*.

But what motivated Gerhard to break away from the longstanding Lutheran rejection of the antilegomena? The following seems probable. Theologically and culturally, the Lutheran rejection of the antilegomena in Europe was a minority position, compared to the Roman Catholics, the Reformed Church, and the Church in England. The latter two, without ever having formally admitted it, had accepted Trent's 1546 decision, and thus they did not share the Lutheran rejection of the antilegomena. And given that a majority culture is a powerful phenomenon, it was evidently disconcerting to Gerhard, and some other Lutherans, to maintain the Lutheran rejection of the antilegomena. Thus, a century after Luther, it was easier to conform to the majority's view than to continue teaching contrary to it. As Roman poet Ovid insightfully declared, "Nothing is so powerful as custom" (*Ars Amatoria*, II, 345).

Similar to the likelihood that the majority's culture contributed to Gerhard's discomfort regarding the antilegomena is the observation made by the British theologian Henry H. Howorth. He has argued that Pietism, a sub-cultural movement within the Lutheran Church, influenced Lutherans "to move nearer and nearer to the old accepted Canon of the New Testament, and to base its authority on the perpetual tradition of the Church."[25] If Howorth's point is valid, it sheds some additional light on why Gerhard, though not a Pietist, nevertheless accepted some of Pietism's values by giving the antilegomena books a more ameliorating term. Wilhelm Koepp has shown that Gerhard's close contact with Johann Arndt (1555–1621), "the father of Pietism," significantly influenced him, even years after Arndt, his former pastor, had ministered to Gerhard in his former illness as a young man.[26]

WHAT GERHARD FAILED TO NOTE OR EXPLAIN

In choosing to call the antilegomena books second rank, Gerhard failed to note or explain a number of well-established theological positions. In his book *Theological Commonplaces* (1625), he quotes Irenaeus: "What the apostles first preached they later handed down to us in the Scriptures by God's will."[27] Gerhard, however, fails to note that Irenaeus did not say writings by an unknown author—for instance, the unknown author of the Book of Hebrews—were "Scriptures by God's will." He also failed to note that already in the early third century, Origen had said the author of Hebrews was known only to God. Yet, Gerhard included this epistle as one of the seven doubted books that he renamed second rank.

In addition, he also overlooked the Wittenberg faculty's 1619 published statement that accused the Socinian sect of heresy for effacing the difference between the canonical and the antilegomena books in its Racovian Catechism of 1608.[28] And he failed to make any reference to the Council of Trent's 1546 autocratic fiat that demanded churches accept the seven antilegomena books as canonical or be anathematized.

A BRIEF RETURN OF THE ANTILEGOMENA QUESTION

It is not widely known, but two hundred years after Gerhard renamed the antilegomena as second rank, the question of the antilegomena briefly returned—not in Europe but in America. It returned in some periodicals published by the conservative Missouri Synod.

In 1856, Pastor K. A. W. Roebbelen, a Missouri Synod Lutheran pastor, published a series of articles on the Book of Revelation in the Synod's official periodical *Der Lutheraner*, of which C. F. W. Walther, the Synod's president, was the editor. Roebbelen, in his last article (April 22, 1856), indicated that he, similar to the Early Church and many Church Fathers, could not in good conscience accept the Book of Revelation as canonical. In response, Pastor George Schieferdecker, who had chiliastic[29] leanings and thus liked the Book of Revelation, accused *Der Lutheraner* of casting doubts on the canonicity of the book of Revelation for publishing Roebbelen's article. This prompted Walther to publish an article in which he quoted Chemnitz and other Lutheran theologians in defense of the position that Revelation was an antilegomena book and thus a Lutheran pastor did not have to accept it as canonical. Moreover, given that the Early Church, many Church Fathers, and later also Luther, together with other Lutheran theologians, had serious doubts as to whether this book was written by an apostle, Walther stated that a faithful pastor could rightly see it as noncanonical and not be guilty of false doctrine or heresy (*Ketzer*). He further stated if the Synod were to hold a pastor guilty of false doctrine for denying the canonicity of an antilegomena book, it would be un-Lutheran ("*unlutherisch*").[30] To insist that the antilegomena books be accepted as canonical would be doing what the popes and the Reformed churches ("*Paptisten und Reformierten*") demand.[31] One year later (1857), the Synod met in convention in Fort Wayne, Indiana, and upheld Walther's argument that a Lutheran pastor—for example, Pastor Roebbelen—and the Synod's periodical, *Der Lutheraner*, did not err theologically by publishing an article that questioned the canonicity of the Book of Revelation.[32]

Some sixty years later, in 1924, Francis Pieper, seminary professor and former president of the Missouri Synod, published volume one of a three-volume edition of his *Christliche Dogmatik* (*Christian Dogmatics*). This volume devoted ten pages to the importance of the homologoumena-antilegomena distinction. Later, in 1950, when the three volumes were translated into English, the first volume again included the discussion of the canonicity question. Interestingly, Pieper did not approve of Gerhard's "second rank" redefinition of the seven antilegomena books. He cautioned, "Given that we cannot speak about the doctrine of God of a Godhead in terms of second rank, as the subordinationists do, so too we cannot, without self-contradiction, speak of Holy Scripture as God's inviolable Word, if it has writings of second rank."[33] This pointed criticism of Gerhard's naming the antilegomena books as second rank, however, made no apparent difference to most Missouri Synod pastors. For to them, criticism of Gerhard's accepting the antilegomena as essentially canonical did not arouse renewed interest or move them to rethink their use of these seven books. They saw Pieper's criticism mostly as an academic matter, a perception of the antilegomena that is still prevalent today.

Pieper's three volumes in the English translation are still read by seminary students studying for the Lutheran ministry at the two LCMS seminaries. Hence, most pastors in the Synod have an awareness of the historical antilegomena problem. But how much awareness pastors in the other Lutheran bodies have of this issue is difficult to assess. Nevertheless, Lutheran pastors today (in all Lutheran bodies) on certain Sundays in the Church Year regularly read pericope selections from Hebrews, James, or Revelation. Doing so, they indicate they have unwittingly and ironically accepted the Council of Trent's decree that dictated the acceptance of the antilegomena books as canonical. Reading from antilegomena books in church services is also common in non-Lutheran denominations, including fundamentalist churches. The latter, who especially do not look favorably upon Roman Catholic doctrines, have unequivocally accepted Trent's decree regarding the New Testament's antilegomena books.

It is interesting to note that when Lutheran authors today discuss the authority of Scripture in books or articles, whether it pertains to *sola Scriptura* or some other aspect of God's inspired Word, commonly nothing is said regarding the New Testament's antilegomena books. It is essentially a forgotten concern, and this is not just a recent phenomenon. In 1871, Charles Porterfield Krauth (1823–83), a highly regarded American defender of the Lutheran Reformation's theology, published *The Conservative Reformation and Its Theology*. But Krauth's book does not have one passing reference with respect to the serious theological concerns Luther and later Lutheran theologians had for an entire century regarding the use of the seven antilegomena books.

THE HOMOLOGOUMENA-ANTILEGOMENA DISTINCTION HONORS THE BIBLE

It is important to underscore that this historic distinction does not reflect a disrespectful view of the Bible, as some Christians may initially conclude because they had not previously heard it discussed in Bible classes. For as C. F. W. Walther stated, "The distinction between antilegomena and homologoumena does not indicate a liberal or negative view of the Bible and its canonicity, but rather the opposite."[34] And he also stated, "The thought that it is dangerous to make this distinction known to laypeople can only be true if they from the beginning had never been made aware of it."[35]

Walther knew whereof he spoke, for he did not hesitate to have the antilegomena matter discussed in the Synod's official periodicals, *Der Lutheraner* and *Lehre und Wehre*, where pastors and laity could read and inform themselves regarding the canonicity of the New Testament's books. Even after Walther's time, the antilegomena issue was not hidden from the laity. For in 1896, some congregations in the Synod, together with some churches in the Wisconsin Synod, used Conrad Dieterich's exposition of Luther's Small Catechism. In its foreword, it referred to the epistles of 2 and 3 John, 2 Peter, Hebrews, James, Jude, and Revelation as *"apocryphischen Bücher des N. Test."* (Apocryphal Books of the New Testament).[36]

How the New Testament's books were selected and why some were doubted and even rejected in the Early Church, as previously noted, was prompted by the Christian desire to make certain the selected books were indeed written by Christ's apostles. The Ancient Church knew of Jesus' promise that said His apostles would record for His followers God's revealed Word (John 14:26). It was the awareness of this promise that later prompted Lutheran theologians to follow in the footsteps of the Early Church. They, too, wanted to be certain when they read from a book in the New Testament that they could authentically say, "This is the Word of the Lord." But with respect to the seven antilegomena books before Gerhard, they declined to make that assertion.

As an aside observation, it is interesting to note that when, for example, Missouri Synod Lutheran churches ordain or install pastors, the inductees are asked, "Do you accept the *canonical books* of the Old and New Testaments?" (emphasis added). And given that Lutherans have never listed in any of their confessional documents which books are canonical, this question to informed Lutherans has never theologically meant that the antilegomena books of the New Testament are canonical. It leaves room for inductees to respond "yes" to the question with a clear conscience, while still retaining the Ancient Church's doubts regarding the books of the antilegomena. Here it is helpful to recall what the Lutheran *Confessio Württembergica* of 1552 (noted earlier) said about the status of noncanonical books: namely, books in the New Testament are only canonical if they had never been doubted in the Ancient Church.

Given that all denominations—including both Catholics and Protestants—today accept and use the antilegomena as canonical has recently prompted Lutheran Carl E. Braaten to lament, "This flat, undifferentiated view of the books of the Bible finally triumphed and today survives in Protestant fundamentalism; some Lutherans are located in this group. The canon that was open and flexible in Luther's thinking became closed and rigid in the circles that inherited the doctrine of Scripture in Protestant orthodoxy."[37]

CONCLUSION

This chapter shows the bold effort Lutheran theologians had made to walk with the Early Church, which accepted books as canonical for inclusion in the New Testament only if it was certain that they were authored by Christ's apostles. But after one hundred years of these theologians making such an effort, which had become a hallmark of Lutheran theology and identity, their successors succumbed to what can be called the Council of Trent Effect, a phenomenon that began with Johann Gerhard's redefining the antilegomena books as "second rank." By default, his decision spawned some interesting consequences that, for unknown reasons, have not been consciously recognized.

One, when Lutherans accepted Gerhard's "second rank" definition of the antilegomena books, it soon resulted in pastors using these books as having canonical status. Thus, Lutheran pastors, in effect, had now de facto accepted Trent's 1546 decree that Chemnitz had so vigorously denounced some sixty years earlier.

Two, by using the redefined antilegomena books like those that were canonical also indicated that many Lutheran pastors no longer had a problem with Trent's decree that had ignored apostolic authorship. This helps explain why Gerhard could accept, for instance, the Epistle of Hebrews, whose author has never been known. But for Lutherans to accept books whose authorship was unknown clashed with the Formula of Concord's requirement—and with the Lutheran vow to uphold this requirement—that stated apostolic authorship of New Testament books was a necessary requirement for a book to be canonical. In short, Trent had won, and conquered a noteworthy Lutheran hallmark.

Three, succumbing to Trent's decree was not confined to Lutherans, for though the first British Bible translators from about 1520 to 1550s sided with Luther by not giving Hebrews, James, Jude, and Revelation canonical recognition, their stance had a shorter endurance than it had among Lutherans. For by the time Queen Elizabeth I took the crown in 1558, the English Church, too, had succumbed to Trent's decree that had declared all seven antilegomena books canonical. And given that most Reformed churches had never made much ado about apostolic authorship, they also fell in line with Trent's 1546 decree.

Four, Protestant Christianity is a product of the Reformation that sought to reform the Christian Church, but Rome rejected both. Yet, within a hundred years after the 1546 Council of Trent had departed from all previous church councils by decreeing the seven doubted books as canonical, all Protestant churches had ironically adopted Trent's decision. And interestingly, one cannot find any evidence in Church history of any Protestant church body that has publicly recognized or admitted this major accommodation to Rome.

Five, none of the Protestant churches (Lutheran and non-Lutheran) has ever apparently recognized that, when they accepted Trent's 1546 decree that gave canonical status to the New Testament's seven antilegomena books, they had also accepted (at least implicitly) Rome's doctrine that says the church determines what books are canonical. The latter contradicts the Early Church's position and a basic principle of the Reformation, for the Early Church, and no church council, previous to Trent had ever declared any New Testament antilegomena book as canonical. Similarly, Lutherans also did not declare these disputed books as canonical. The renowned *Württembergische Glaubensbekenntnis* (1522), we recall, specifically stated an antilegomena book was not canonical.

Lutheran skepticism regarding the antilegomena was once a hallmark of more importance in Lutheran theology than it is today. Underlying this hallmark was the commitment to accept only books for inclusion in the New Testament if they were written by Christ's handpicked apostles, His eyewitnesses, as opposed to accepting books whose authorship was dubious and in some instances totally unknown. In short, these *sola Scriptura* Lutherans wanted to be sure when they taught or preached from a book in the New Testament, they could assure their hearers and confidently say, "This is the Word of the Lord."

1. Explain why the authenticity of the Bible is not based on blind faith or hearsay.

2. What name did the Early Church give to the twenty New Testament books that it said were universally accepted as written by Christ's apostles?

3. What name did the Early Church give to the seven New Testament books that it said were not written by apostles and thus not universally accepted by it?

4. What Lutheran theologian said Lutherans were not to cite a proof passage found only in one of doubted seven New Testament books in support of a doctrine? Why?

5. What American Lutheran theologian taught it was "un-Lutheran" to consider a Lutheran person guilty of false doctrine if he or she did not accept one or more of the seven disputed books in the New Testament as canonical?

6. Luther in his Bible wrote a preface to each book in the New Testament indicating its canonical status in the history of the Church. Why do you think Bibles published today no longer have any prefaces to the books of the New Testament, as German Lutheran Bibles did in Germany and in America until the 1890s?

7. Why is the Lutheran concern regarding biblical canonicity a conservative rather than a liberal concern?

8. Why is it unbiblical and un-Lutheran to argue that the Church determined the Bible's canonicity?

9. Why do today's Lutherans, better educated than in the past, know less about the New Testament's seven antilegomena books than they knew in Luther's or Walther's day?

10. What prominent Lutheran theologian renamed the antilegomena as "second rank"? What effect did this have on future generations of Lutherans?

CHAPTER 7

LAW AND GOSPEL

God's Dichotomy

"Without the Law the Gospel is not understood; without
the Gospel the Law benefits us nothing."
—C. F. W. Walther (1811–87)

Another prominent hallmark of Lutheran theology is its strong emphasis on the importance of distinguishing between Law and Gospel in Scripture. When a Lutheran interacts with non-Lutheran Protestants, especially with their clergy, it is not unusual to notice that they see the Law–Gospel paradigm as a distinctive Lutheran teaching. It is a distinction that comes from Luther and reflects his God-given theological insights. As Luther once stated,

> You will not find anything about this distinction between
> the Law and the Gospel in the books of the monks, the can-
> onists, and the recent and ancient theologians. Augustine
> taught and expressed it to some extent. Jerome and others
> like him knew nothing at all about it. In other words, for
> many centuries there has been a remarkable silence about
> this in all the schools and churches.[1]

Clergy in non-Lutheran Protestant churches generally do not talk about Law and Gospel, as Lutheran pastors are known to do. It is not that they deny or reject these theological concepts, but Law and Gospel are not really a part of their theological vocabulary, whereas for most Lutheran pastors, these two concepts have been deeply internalized and thus are frequently heard in their conversations with one another and quite often also with laypeople.

By noting and defining these two biblically based concepts, Luther made a lasting contribution to the Christian Church and its theology. The concepts of Law and Gospel not only help Christians understand the basic intent of God's inspired Scriptures, but they also provide a picture of God Himself. Ignorance of this theological distinction, Luther argued, had "produced a very dangerous condition for consciences; for unless the Gospel is clearly distinguished from the Law, Christian doctrine cannot be kept sound. But when this distinction is recognized, the true meaning of justification is recognized."[2]

LAW AND GOSPEL DEFINED

The Lutheran Formula of Concord states, "The Law is properly a divine doctrine [Romans 7:12]. It teaches what is right and pleasing to God, and it rebukes everything that is sin and contrary to God's will." The article continues, "But the Gospel is properly the kind of teaching that shows what a person who has not kept the Law (and therefore is condemned by it) is to believe. It teaches that Christ has paid for and made satisfaction for all sins (Ep V 3–5). Expressed in another way, "The Law deals with our works, the Gospel with God's works."[3]

The Gospel is revealed and made known only by God's Holy Spirit through the redemptive work of Jesus Christ.

There is also this difference: the Law, which is known to man by nature, at least imperfectly since the fall, differs from the Gospel in that the Gospel is not known to any person by nature. "The natural person does not accept the things of the Spirit of God, for they are folly to him, and he is not able to understand them because they are spiritually discerned" (1 Corinthians 2:14). The Gospel is revealed and made known only by God's Holy Spirit through the redemptive work of Jesus Christ.

The Law also differs from the Gospel in terms of its purposes or functions. This is spelled out in

Luther's Small Catechism (in its Table of Duties), his Large Catechism, and in the Formula of Concord of the Lutheran Confessions. Specifically, the Law has three purposes: (1) It acts as a *curb* on our sinful human behavior. (2) It functions as a *mirror* by showing us our sins. (3) It serves as a *guide* that shows us what God wants us to do. Lutherans call the curbing effect the first use of the Law, the mirroring effect is the second use, and the guiding function is known as the third use of the Law.

During the Reformation in the late 1520s, the third use of the Law was denied by some Lutheran theologians, to Luther's great dismay. They argued that Christians, as redeemed children of God, no longer needed the Law to guide them in their daily lives and activities They were known as Antinomians (anti = against, *nomos* = law). This controversy among Lutherans ended with the signing of the Formula of Concord in 1577. But more recently, some modern-day Lutherans have been contending that the third use of the Law was not part of Luther's theology but derived from the teachings of Philip Melanchthon, Luther's co-worker.[4]

DISTINGUISHING BETWEEN LAW AND GOSPEL

There are several things that need to be noted in regard to the Law and Gospel distinction. First, though Luther brought the concept of Law and Gospel to light during the Reformation, he did not invent it. He only rediscovered it. The apostle Paul already operated with the Law-Gospel dichotomy in his preaching when he said "The letter [the Law] kills, but the Spirit gives life" (2 Corinthians 3:6). Luther saw this passage as a Law-Gospel statement.[5]

Paul also instructed Timothy, "Do your best to present yourself to God as one approved, a worker who does not need be ashamed and who correctly handles the word of truth" (2 Timothy 2:15 NIV). The phrase "correctly handles" (*orthotomounta* in Greek, meaning "cut straight" or "divide correctly") is translated as "rightly dividing" in the New King James version. Similarly, Luther, in his German translation of the Bible, renders *orthotomounta* as *"recht teile"* ("correctly dividing"). Thus, Luther saw Paul's words to Timothy, similar to 2 Corinthians 3:6, as the foundation of the Law-Gospel distinction. These Pauline words, said Luther, "teach that you apply Gospel and Law rightly, lift up, make alive, and set the conscience free through the Gospel and not suppress or burden it with the Law or works and sins."[6]

Following Luther's insights and his teachings, the distinction between Law and Gospel according to Lutheran theologians and pastors contends that teaching and preaching in conformity with Law and Gospel is not merely an option but a vital necessity in declaring God's Word to His people. To a great extent, Lutherans define themselves by this doctrine. It is a distinctive hallmark of their theological identity.

THE IMPORTANCE OF DISTINGUISHING BETWEEN LAW AND GOSPEL

Lutheran theology insists it is absolutely necessary to distinguish between the Law and the Gospel. Why? For one, if only the Law is preached, the hearers may despair, for given what we have just seen, "the letter kills, but the Spirit gives life" (2 Corinthians 3:6). Second, if hearers do not despair, they may become self-righteous and spiritually smug about their own efforts and thus not see any need to repent and ask for God's gracious forgiveness in Jesus Christ. Third, not distinguishing between the Law and the Gospel threatens to destroy the Gospel of Jesus Christ. In this regard, Luther said, "For unless the Gospel is clearly distinguished from the Law, Christian doctrine cannot be kept sound."[7] Again, concerning those who confuse Law and Gospel, he stated, "Because they confuse Law with the Gospel, it is inevitable that they subvert the Gospel."[8] In order to preserve the Gospel, he insisted, "God's promises and threats must not be intermingled."[9]

Although Luther consistently taught that Law and Gospel must be clearly distinguished from each other, he never said it was an easy task. "Therefore whoever knows well how to distinguish the Gospel from the Law should give thanks to God and know that he is a real theologian." He then added, "I admit that in the time of temptation I myself do not know how to do this as I should."[10] C. F. W. Walther, the first president of The Lutheran Church—Missouri Synod, in

Teaching and preaching in conformity with Law and Gospel is not merely an option but a vital necessity in declaring God's Word to His people.

HALLMARKS OF LUTHERAN IDENTITY

his book *The Proper Distinction between Law and Gospel*, echoed Luther's words by saying that for Christians, "the proper distinction between Law and Gospel is the highest and most difficult art."[11]

When the distinction between Law and Gospel is not properly made, it is also possible for some individuals to see the Bible as contradicting itself. Walther cites two such perceived contradictions. In one place, he says, the Bible offers the forgiveness of sins to all sinners, but in another place it withholds forgiveness. Or, in one passage the free gift of eternal life is extended to all men, while in another biblical reference individuals are directed to save themselves. According to Walther, "This riddle is solved when we reflect that there are in the Scriptures two entirely different doctrines, the doctrine of the Law and the doctrine of the Gospel."[12] In a similar vein, Siegbert W. Becker, a Wisconsin Synod New Testament professor, said that when "a few of the seemingly contradictory statements of law and gospel [are taken] to the foot of the cross in faith," we then see "how perfectly they are joined."[13]

CONFUSING LAW AND GOSPEL

Not properly distinguishing between Law and Gospel invariably also results in confusing the two, as well as confusing Christians. Following are a few examples of how Law and Gospel are confused, many of which are extrapolated from Walther's work just cited.

1. The Law, rather than the Gospel, is used to motivate Christians to do good works.

2. Christians are told they are saved on *account of* their faith rather than *through* faith.

3. Small sins are presented as really being no sins.

4. Christians are told that God is pleased when they do the best they can.

5. Christians are led to believe that they must have a lot of faith in order to be saved.

6. A contrite Christian is presented with more Law instead of being comforted by the Gospel.

7. The Gospel is preached without any Law.

8. The Law is preached without any Gospel.

9. Christians are taught that their faith justifies them before God, rather than faith being the *hand* that receives God's promises in the Gospel.

10. Christians are taught to trust their emotions rather than God's Word in order to be certain they are justified before God.

11. God is presented only as a God of love, devoid of any wrath or anger over people's sin.

12. Christians are told that a Christian is always happy and joyful.

13. A given act or behavior is declared sinful when it is not.

14. Christians are led to believe they must *feel* that they are saved.

15. Christians are led to believe they are saved by faith together with their good works, as the 1547 Council of Trent declared in its statement on justification. Its Canon 9 states, "If any-one shall say that by faith alone the sinner is justified, so as to understand that nothing else is required to cooperate in the attainment of the grace of justification, and that it is in no way necessary that he be prepared and disposed by the action of his own will: let him be anathema."[14]

This Catholic dogma may in part explain why, as Avery Dulles (Jesuit Catholic theologian and later a cardinal) has said, the Law and Gospel distinction is not found "in modern Catholic systematics."[15] This observation provides added evidence that the Lutheran accent on Law and Gospel is an important hallmark of Lutheran theology and identity.

PREACHING AND TEACHING LAW AND GOSPEL

It has been a distinctive characteristic of Lutheran theology, ever since Luther's time, to urge pastors to preach Law and Gospel in every sermon. So deeply have most Lutheran pastors internalized the necessity of preaching both Law and Gospel in every sermon that there is probably no greater criticism a faithful Lutheran pastor can receive than being told a given sermon of his contained little or no Gospel. Similarly, to be told that he confused Law and Gospel is equally devastating to conscientious Lutheran pastors.

Faithful Lutheran pastors heed the following old advice: Preach the Law so that those who are spiritually comfortable will become uncomfortable, and preach the Gospel so that those who are spiritually uncomfortable will become comfortable.

Law and Gospel: The Bible's Two Main Doctrines

"If you divide all Scripture," said Luther, "it contains two topics: promises and threats or benefits and punishments."[16] This view is consistent with Luther's belief that the Bible was the cradle of Christ (discussed in chapter 1), and that without Christ the Bible was a meaningless book theologically. To say Law and Gospel are the Bible's two main doctrines is another way of arguing that God chose and inspired holy men of God to write the Bible in order to make its readers or hearers "wise for salvation through faith in Christ Jesus" (2 Timothy 3:15).

To assert that Law and Gospel are the two doctrines in Scripture is not to say there are no other doctrines taught in the Bible. Nor does it mean there is no important information regarding geographical, historical, and cultural information in the Bible. These are all, in varying degrees, important regarding the many different events and incidents recorded in the Bible, but they are largely ancillary to God's purpose of communicating the message of salvation to His people.

Law and Gospel in Classic Lutheran Hymns

The Law-Gospel motif is also found in countless classic Lutheran hymns, many of which are sometimes known as Lutheran chorales. These Christian hymns underscore how all have fallen short of God's Holy Law, but that there is forgiveness, life, and salvation for all who have faith in the redemptive work of Jesus Christ.

Suffice it to say, many of these hymns were penned by Martin Luther, Johann Crüger, Martin Rinckart, Paul Gerhardt, Philipp Nicolai, Johann Olearius, Nicholas Selnecker, and Johann Heermann. These men all understood the importance of Law and Gospel, and their hymns reflected this theological awareness. It is an awareness that we Lutherans want to keep in mind when we sing Christ-centered hymns in church or in the context of informal gatherings or in devotions.

However, given that people, including many Christians, are often attracted more to the tunes or melodies of hymns than to their words or lyrics, the Law-Gospel content of the traditional Lutheran hymns is not always fully grasped or appreciated by all Lutherans today. Many modern hymns—and there are scores of them—have very appealing tunes, but they often fall short in their Law-Gospel content. Many of these hymns often accent the subjective or emotional feelings of singers in the pew. They may even be considered spiritually edifying, but they must not weaken or preempt the Law-Gospel message.

CONCLUSION

Understanding and believing with Luther that Law and Gospel are the Bible's two main doctrines has a salutary function. It reminds us Christians that the Bible was not written to predict specific future apocalyptic or millennial-like events and happenings, as is sometimes incorrectly believed by some Christians. As already noted, the Bible was written to make us "wise for salvation," rather than tell us when a presumed Battle of Armageddon will take place. Ruminations about future events, supposedly foretold in the Bible, appeal to "itching ears," to use St. Paul's expression in 2 Timothy 4:3. Moreover, they are fraught with the danger of losing sight of why God revealed His inspired Word in the first place, and more specifically, why He sent Jesus Christ to redeem sinful people in a sin-ridden world. Seeing the Bible in the light of Law and Gospel helps keep Christians from becoming sidetracked by peripheral matters and keeps their eyes focused on Christ's redemptive work, accomplished on the cross and the open tomb.

Finally, why is the distinction of Law and Gospel in Lutheran theology so important? Regarding this question, John Warwick Montgomery says, "Simply because the whole message of salvation turns on it."[17] This is a well-stated answer, for as the apostle John has written, "For the law was given through Moses; grace and truth came through Jesus Christ" (John 1:17). With these words, the apostle underscored Law and Gospel, God's sacred dichotomy, which is not only biblical but also a noteworthy hallmark of Lutheran theology and identity.

CHAPTER 7 DISCUSSION QUESTIONS

1. How does the Law differ from the Gospel?

2. What are the first, second, and third uses of the Law?

3. Why should a good sermon contain both Law and Gospel?

4. Is it the Law or the Gospel that motivates Christians to do God-pleasing acts? Why?

5. When non-Christians contribute to charity, are they motivated by Law or Gospel? Why or why not?

6. How can the Law sometimes get Christians to do the right thing for the wrong reason?

7. Why do Christians, redeemed though they are, still need the third use of the Law?

8. Why should sermons not preach only the Law?

9. As a faithful parishioner, how can you tell which parts of your pastor's sermons are Law and which are Gospel?

10. How can the Law-Gospel distinction be used in everyday family life?

CHAPTER 8

WORD AND SACRAMENT

Two Means of Grace

"The Word of God and the use of the Sacraments are the
proper, genuine, and infallible marks of the Church."
—Johann Gerhard (1582–1637)

There are not many Lutherans, if any, who have not heard the expression "Word and Sacrament." Lutheran pastors utter these three words rather frequently, and they usually say Sacrament (singular), rather than plural, as Luther did. The expression "Word and Sacrament" is really not heard in non-Lutheran circles. It is a hallmark of Lutheran theology.

Similarly, the phrase "Means of Grace" is also not a common term in non-Lutheran circles. Most non-Lutheran Protestants do not use this phrase, largely as a result of having adopted the theological views of the radical reformers in the 1520s who denied that Baptism or the Lord's Supper was a Means of Grace conveying the forgiveness of sins to repentant Christians.

Lutheran pastors are known to use the phrase "Word and Sacrament" in sermons, Bible classes, and informal contexts. Given its frequent use, the phrase to some may sound like a Lutheran cliché; such a conclusion, however, would miss the mark, because the phrase is packed with theological significance.

THE WORD

There are several meanings in the Lutheran usage of "Word" in the phrase "Word and Sacrament." One meaning says it is only through God's Word, the Bible, read or heard by an individual, or faithfully paraphrased by someone else, that the Holy Spirit creates saving faith in a person, thus making him or her a Christian, a member of the household of faith. This Lutheran teaching is based on a number of biblical references, but the most pertinent passage is Romans 10:17: "So faith comes from hearing, and hearing through the word of Christ." It is on the basis of this passage and similar ones that Luther, in his explanation of the Third Article of the Apostles' Creed, says,

> I believe that I cannot by my own reason or strength believe in Jesus Christ, my Lord, or come to Him. But the Holy Spirit has called me by the Gospel, enlightened me with His gifts, sanctified and kept me in true faith. In the same way He calls, gathers, enlightens, and sanctifies the whole Christian Church on earth and keeps it with Jesus Christ in the one true faith. In this Christian Church He daily and richly forgives all my sins, and the sins of all believers. On the Last Day He will raise up me and all the dead and will give eternal life to me and to all believers in Christ. This is most certainly true. (Small Catechism)

It is only through God's Word that a person by God's grace comes to believe in Jesus Christ.

These words by Luther underscore that it is only through God's Word that a person by God's grace comes to believe in Jesus Christ. Thus, in Lutheran theology, the Word, whether read or heard, is a Means of Grace.

Given that it is only through God's Word that individuals are brought to faith in Christ, Lutherans have always rejected the faulty belief that someone can become a Christian apart from the Word of God. The proponents of this false teaching in Luther's day, such as Ulrich Zwingli, Andreas Carlstadt, and Thomas Münzer, taught that God converts individuals apart from His Word, read or preached. Lutherans called these proponents and others like them *Schwärmer* ("Enthusiasts" in English), meaning they believed that they obtained God's grace and salvation apart from any means or channels such as the Word, Baptism, or the Lord's Supper. In response, the Lutheran Confessions state, "We also reject and condemn the error of the Enthusiasts. They imagine that God without means, without the hearing of God's Word, and also without the use of the holy Sacraments, draws people to Himself and enlightens, justifies, and saves them" (FC Ep II 13).

Lutheran theology also teaches that God creates faith not only in adults through their hearing the Word but also in infants in the Rite of Baptism. Luther stated it well in his answer to the Small Catechism's question "How can water do such great things?" He said,

> It is not the water indeed that does them, but the Word of God, which is in and with the water, and faith, which trusts this Word of God in the water. For without the Word of God the water is simple water and no Baptism. But with the Word of God it is a Baptism, that is, a gracious water of life and a washing of regeneration in the Holy Spirit. (Small Catechism, Baptism, Third Part)

Another meaning of "Word" in Lutheran theology says it is only through the Word that Christians are kept and sustained in their faith. That is why Christians must not neglect the Word of God. They need to read it regularly in devotions at home, hear it

It is only through the Word that Christians are kept and sustained in their faith.

preached in church, and study it with fellow Christians in Bible classes or similar settings. Here the words of Jesus are pertinent: "If you abide in My word, you are truly My disciples, and you will know the truth, and the truth will set you free" (John 8:31–32).

Lutheran pastors also use "Word" in the broad sense, referring to both Law and Gospel. That is what St. Paul meant when he told Timothy to "preach the word; be ready in season and out of season; reprove, rebuke, and exhort, with complete patience and teaching" (2 Timothy 4:2).

But most often, pastors use the narrower meaning of "Word"; namely, the Gospel that promises God's forgiveness, eternal life, and salvation in Jesus Christ. In the narrower sense, pastors try to accomplish a couple of things. One, they try to remind their parishioners to be mindful that "the Word," the Gospel, gives them the assurance of the forgiveness of sins and the promise of eternal life. Two, it is only the Gospel that can give them the proper motivation to deport themselves as Christians. It is the Gospel that motivates Christians to do the right thing for the right reason.

"The Word" also provides guidance in the lives of Christians. As King David so poignantly proclaimed, "Your word is a lamp to my feet and a light to my path" (Psalm 119:105).

It also helpful to note that there are a few instances in the New Testament where Jesus is referred to as "the Word," or *Logos* in the Greek text. We find this example in the Gospel of John. "The Word [*Logos*] became flesh and dwelt among us, and we have seen His glory, the glory as of the only Son from the Father, full of grace and truth" (1:14). Equating the Word with Jesus Christ is also found in John 1:1–2, where we read, "In the beginning was the Word [*Logos*], and the Word was with God, and the Word was God. He was in the beginning with God." Seeing Christ as the Word [*Logos*] is also found in Revelation 19:13: "He is clothed in a robe dipped in blood, and the name by which He is called is The Word of God."

"The Word of God," as Siegbert W. Becker has noted, must not be seen as "primarily a designation for the only begotten Son of God."[1] This view, he says, is often held by those (even by some erring Lutherans) who have problems with the doctrine of verbal inspiration and the divine authority of Scripture. Hence, Becker further states that anyone who argues that the Word of God refers only to Jesus Christ "either has not read the Bible with close attention or is deliberately falsifying the evidence. Almost invariably, as used in Scripture, the Word of God is a word that is spoken, a word that is heard, a word that is written in a book."[2]

SACRAMENT AND SACRAMENTS

The word *sacrament* is derived from the Latin *sacramentum*. In Roman society, this referred to a solemn and sacred engagement a Roman soldier affirmed by taking an oath to be loyal to his military commander(s). Christians, by the end of the second century, took the word *sacrament* and applied it to Baptism and the Lord's Supper, thus indicating that both were sacred engagements to God. Later, in the Middle Ages, the Church added another five sacraments, bringing the number to seven. Roman Catholic and Eastern Orthodox churches still hold to seven sacraments: Baptism, Lord's Supper, Ordination, Confirmation, Marriage, Penitence (Absolution), and Extreme Unction (Last Rites).

Luther, however, argued there was no biblical basis for seven sacraments. Initially, he reduced the number to three: Baptism, Penitence, and the Lord's Supper. In the beginning of his tract *The Babylonian Captivity of the Church* (1520), he still mentioned penitence as a sacrament, but toward the end of this tract he wrote, "There are, strictly speaking, but two sacraments in the church of God—baptism and the bread [Lord's Supper]."[3] Yet, it is interesting to note that the Apology of the Augsburg Confession, written by Philip Melanchthon in 1531 and officially accepted as a Lutheran-confessional document in 1537, still cited penitence as a sacrament. Thus, it states, "Baptism, the Lord's Supper, and Absolution (which is the Sacrament of Repentance) are truly Sacraments" (XIII [VII] 4).

Given that Lutherans in the early years of Reformation saw penitence as a sacrament, the question is sometimes asked: Why do Lutheran pastors and the Small Catechism no longer teach it as a sacrament? The answer lies in what Luther said in the latter part *The Babylonian Captivity of the Church*, and also what he wrote in his Large Catechism (1529). In the latter, he speaks of penitence, saying, "It is really nothing other than Baptism" (V 74). And between 1530 and 1532, when he produced his commentary on the Gospel of John, he discussed the sacraments but listed only Baptism and the Lord's Supper.[4]

Although these three references by Luther preceded the formal acceptance of the Apology of the Augsburg Confession in 1537, Lutherans have followed what Luther said in his classic treatise *The Babylonian Captivity of the Church*, the Large Catechism, and his commentary on the Gospel of John regarding penitence. Thus, the Formula of Concord (1580) does not mention penitence as a sacrament.

In part, Lutherans also hold to only two sacraments instead of three or seven because of St. Augustine's (d. 430) influence. He saw a sacrament as "God's visible Word."[5] In Baptism, it is the visible water connected with the Word of God; in the Lord's Supper, there are the visible elements of bread and wine connected with the God's Word. Only Baptism and the Lord's Supper have visible elements connected with God's Word. Moreover, only these two rites have been instituted by Christ Himself. Hence, Lutherans accept only these two as biblically based sacraments.

> Only Baptism and the Lord's Supper have visible elements connected with God's Word.

Lutherans also teach that a sacrament is a Means of Grace; that is, it conveys the forgiveness of sins to penitent sinners. Thus, Lutheran theology teaches a sacrament requires three criteria: (1) it is instituted by Jesus Christ; (2) it contains visible (external) elements; (3) it conveys forgiveness of sins. In light of the first two criteria, the five rites (penitence, ordination, confirmation, marriage, and extreme unction) do not qualify as sacraments.

THE SACRAMENT OF BAPTISM

Although the ministry of Jesus began with His Baptism by John the Baptizer (Mark 1:9–11), the Sacrament of Baptism was not formally instituted until Jesus, at the end of His ministry, commissioned His disciples to "make disciples of all nations, baptizing them in the name of the Father and of the Son and of the Holy Spirit" (Matthew 28:19). These words became (and still are) Christianity's baptismal formula.

Given Christ's words regarding Baptism, Luther notes in his Small Catechism, "Baptism is not simple water only, but it is the water included in God's command and connected with God's Word" (Holy Baptism, First Part).

Although Baptism for many Christians is an initiation rite by which individuals, including infants, enter the Christian Church, it is more than an initiation rite. It is also, as most Lutheran catechumens have learned in confirmation class, a Means of Grace through which the Holy Spirit, with water connected to the Word, creates faith—for example, in the hearts of baptized infants. Here the words of St. Paul apply: "For in Christ Jesus you are all sons of God, through faith. For as many of you as were baptized into Christ have put on Christ" (Galatians 3:26–27).

From the Church's very beginning, Christians believed these words included infants and young children, as appears evident in the Book of Acts, where we read that Lydia "and her household as well" were baptized (16:15). And since households in that era were relatively large (including servants and their children), her household most likely included young children. In 1 Corinthians 1:16, St. Paul says he also baptized an entire household; namely, that of Stephanus. It is examples such as these and similar Early Church accounts that led Luther to say that "baptism of infants is right, and . . . they are thereby received into God's grace and into Christendom."[6] Luther seemed to have the household Baptisms of Lydia and Stephanus in mind when he said, "The apostles baptized entire households."[7] Here it is worthy of note that up to the time of the Reformation—for a period of fifteen hundred years—infant Baptism was universally accepted in the Church. During these preceding fifteen centuries, not even prominent heretics questioned the validity of infant Baptism. The first notable rejection of infant Baptism among Christians occurred in the 1520s with the rise of the Anabaptists, and since then this false teaching has characterized a number of Protestant denominations (e.g., Baptists, Pentecostals, Disciples of Christ, and Mennonites).

As a Means of Grace, Baptism serves as an instrument of God's forgiveness. That is what the apostle Peter meant when he told his audience in his sermon on the Church's first Pentecost Day, fifty days after Christ had risen from the dead, "Repent and be baptized every one of you in the name of Jesus Christ for the forgiveness of your sins" (Acts 2:38). In a similar manner, St. Paul, right after his dramatic conversion, was told by Ananias, "Rise and be baptized and wash away your sins"

Baptism is a Means of Grace that forgives sins and regenerates the repentant Christian.

(22:16). And later, St. Paul assured his co-worker Titus that Baptism is "the washing of regeneration" (Titus 3:5). Given this biblical evidence, Lutherans believe, teach, and confess "baptismal regeneration," meaning Baptism is a Means of Grace that forgives sins and regenerates the repentant Christian.

The forgiveness of sins is not just a one-time phenomenon but a divine promise in which God offers and assures every repentant Christian that his or her sins are daily forgiven—in fact, forgiven many times each day. Baptized Christians live in baptismal grace as they daily drown their sinful nature in the water of Baptism, just as St. Paul told the Christians in Rome, "Do you not know that all of us who have been baptized into Christ Jesus were baptized into His death?" And he continues, "We were buried therefore with Him by baptism into death, in order that, just as Christ was raised from the dead by the glory of the Father, we too might walk in newness of life" (Romans 6:3–4). These baptismal words we Lutheran Christians want to remember each and every day of our lives, especially when we feel spiritually glum and dejected. They are words for spiritual renewal.

The biblical teaching that Baptism forgives the sins of every baptized Christian who repents and believes in God's gracious promises in Jesus Christ is not, however, believed by many Christians. This is especially true of those who call themselves Baptists; but it is also true of some other Protestant denominations, many who in American culture today are referred to as "Evangelicals." These groups reject this God-given gift in Baptism despite God's clearly stated words in Acts 2:38; 22:16; and Titus 3:5, cited above.

Here, for instance, is an official statement that portrays the Southern Baptist position: "Christian baptism is the immersion of a believer in water in the name of the Father, the Son, and the Holy Spirit. The act is a symbol of our faith in the crucified, buried, and risen Saviour."[8] Note the statement makes no mention of Baptism as a Means of Grace through which repentant Christians receive the forgiveness of sins. Hence, Southern Baptists do not believe in baptismal regeneration. To them, Baptism merely symbolizes that someone is a Christian. That particular understanding of Baptism, of course, has no basis in Holy Scripture.

As Lutherans, we want to pray that we will never be tempted to forget or even to minimize what God does for us in Baptism. We need to remember the words St. Paul wrote to the Christians in Ephesus, "Christ loved the church and gave Himself up for her, that He might sanctify her, having cleansed her by the washing of water with the word" (Ephesians 5:25–26). Similarly assuring are the words of St. Peter: "There is also an antitype which now saves us—baptism" (1 Peter 3:21 NKJV). And equally assuring and comforting are the words the apostle Paul wrote to the Corinthians, "But you were washed, you were sanctified, you were justified in the name of the Lord Jesus Christ and by the Spirit of our God" (1 Corinthians 6:11).

Finally, we Lutherans also want to remember the importance of emergency Baptism. Thus, if an unbaptized infant, or an unbaptized person who is older, is on the brink of death, he or she may be baptized by a lay Christian. This practice goes back at least to the Synod of Elvira in Spain (ca. AD 305 or 306). In Canon 38, this Synod stated that lay Christians could baptize infants or catechumens who were at the point of death. When such Baptisms are performed with water in the name of the Father, the Son, and the Holy Spirit, they are truly valid Baptisms. It is helpful to note that most non-Lutheran Protestant denominations do not practice emergency Baptisms, mostly because they do not accept Baptism is a Means of Grace that imparts faith and the forgiveness of sins.

THE SACRAMENT OF THE LORD'S SUPPER

There are two very distinctive accents in Lutheran theology regarding the Lord's Supper. One, in this sacrament Christ's body and blood are supernaturally truly present. Two, it is another Means of Grace through which God conveys the forgiveness of sins to repentant Christians as they partake in this Holy Meal. This spiritual benefit, for instance, is clearly spelled out in Matthew's Gospel, where Christ told His disciples at the Last Supper in the Upper Room, "Drink of it, all of you, for this is My blood of the covenant, which is poured out for many for the forgiveness of sins" (26:27–28).

At the Last
Supper,
Christ prom-
ised the for-
giveness of
sins not only
to His disci-
ples but also
to all repen-
tant com-
municants
whenever
they partake
of this Holy
Meal.

At the Last Supper, Christ promised the forgiveness of sins not only to His disciples but also to all
repentant communicants whenever they partake of
this Holy Meal. To receive the forgiveness of sins has
an ancillary effect. It strengthens the participant's
faith, for receiving the assurance one's sins are forgiven strengthens the Christian's faith.

The benefits of the Lord's Supper, however, are
not received by communicants who come to the
Lord's Supper without repentance and without faith
in what this Supper offers. Partaking of Christ's body
and blood in an idle-minded or insincere manner by
merely going through the motions, so to speak, offers no spiritual benefit(s). In fact, such participation
is spiritually harmful to the individual, for as Paul
told the Corinthians, "Whoever, therefore, eats the
bread or drinks the cup of the Lord in an unworthy
manner will be guilty concerning the body and blood
of the Lord" (1 Corinthians 11:27).

When taking part in the Lord's Supper, it is helpful to recall the words of St. Augustine. He said the
Lord's Supper, similar to Baptism, is "God's Word
made visible."

CONCLUSION

The Lutheran concept of Word and Sacrament
underscores how God's grace is given to all His children who believe in the atoning merits of His Son,
Jesus Christ. For us Lutherans, it is important to
remember that Word and Sacrament are God's divinely ordained means through which He creates
and sustains us in the true faith as baptized members
of His kingdom. Thus, we would do well to make a
deliberate and conscious effort—to make it a habit—
of verbally using this salutary expression, "Word and
Sacrament," in our conversations with fellow Lutherans and also in the context of our family devotions.

To do so is another way of reminding ourselves of God's grace in Jesus Christ.

And all Lutherans would do well to remember that when a Lutheran person decides to leave the Lutheran Church to join a non-Lutheran Protestant church, he or she has at that point thrown out, so to speak, the biblical teaching that Baptism and the Lord's Supper are two means of God's grace. For as noted above, non-Lutheran Protestant churches deny this clear biblical teaching.

Finally, when talking about Word and Sacrament, it is also important to remember the words of the renowned Lutheran Hermann Sasse. "Without the sacraments," he said, "the call of the Gospel would be swallowed up and disappear like a voice in the wind. Perhaps there would be a brief echo, but that would be all. Therefore the sacraments must accompany the preached Word."[9] Sasse's words help us recall that the Lutheran expression "Word and Sacrament" is a distinctive, comforting hallmark of Lutheran theology and identity.

The next chapter provides a more detailed discussion of the Lord's Supper.

1. How do Lutherans define "Means of Grace"?

2. How many Means of Grace are there? What are they?

3. If one denies that Baptism forgives sins, as some Christians do, is it still a Means of Grace? Why or why not?

4. How do Baptism and the Lord's Supper (each a Means of Grace) differ from the Word as a Means of Grace?

5. Explain why no one can become a Christian without at least one of the Means of Grace.

6. What was the original meaning of the word *sacrament*?

7. How does Lutheran theology define *sacrament*?

8. Roman Catholics teach there are how many sacraments? What are they?

9. Is the word *sacrament* Law or Gospel? Why?

10. Why should we teach catechumens in confirmation classes the importance of emergency Baptism?

11. Why do you think the Early Church saw it important to practice emergency Baptism?

12. What does official Baptist theology say about Baptism?

13. Why is the Lord's Supper a Means of Grace?

14. Do unbelievers receive the body and blood in the Lord's Supper? Why or why not?

CHAPTER 9

THE LORD'S SUPPER

Christ's Supernatural Bodily Presence

"Bread and wine are received by the mouth immediately
and naturally; the body and blood of Christ are received
mediately and supernaturally."
—David Hollaz (1648–1713)

Another distinctive hallmark that distinguishes Lutheran theology from the theology of non-Lutheran Protestants is the doctrine of the supernaturally bodily presence of Christ in the Lord's Supper. When Christ instituted the Lord's Supper in the Upper Room in Jerusalem, He gave bread to the disciples and said, "Take, eat; this is My body" (Matthew 26:26). Then He took a cup of wine and said, "Drink of it, all of you, for this is My blood of the covenant, which is poured out for many for the forgiveness of sins" (vv. 27–28).

These words of Christ should be enough to persuade us that His body is truly present in His Holy Supper. And there is even more evidence. St. Paul told the Corinthian Christians if any of them ate and drank this holy meal unworthily, they would be "guilty of profaning the body and blood of the Lord" (1 Corinthians 11:27 RSV). This statement makes it clear that Christ is bodily present in His Supper, for how could any of the Corinthian Christians be guilty of profaning the body and blood of Christ if His body and blood were not present in this Supper?

That Christ's body and blood are truly present in the Lord's Supper was unequivocally stated by Lutherans at the Diet of Augsburg in 1530 when they presented the Augsburg Confession to Emperor Charles V and to the territorial princes. This document declares, "The body and blood of Christ are truly present and distributed to those who eat the Lord's Supper" (X 1).

In teaching the doctrine of Christ's bodily presence in the Lord's Supper, Lutherans do not teach that Christ's body and blood are physically or materially present in the Lord's Supper. Rather, they are present supernaturally. David Hollaz, a well-known Lutheran theologian (cited above), said the bread and wine are received in the communicant's mouth and pass into the stomach, where they are digested and eliminated, but the body and blood of Christ, which are also received through the mouth, are not digested and eliminated in a natural way.[1]

Thus, contrary to some false accusations made against Lutherans, the doctrine of Christ's bodily presence in this sacrament does not mean that "the body of Christ is literally eaten, therefore masticated by the teeth."[2] This point is also underscored in the Lutheran Formula of Concord, which in reference to Christ's words "eat and drink," states, "This command clearly cannot be understood as anything other than oral eating and drinking. However, this is not in a crude, carnal, Capernaitic[3] way, but in a supernatural way, beyond understanding" (SD VII 64). The diagram below illustrates the biblically based Lutheran doctrine.

WHAT IS RECEIVED IN THE LORD'S SUPPER

VISIBLE ELEMENTS	INVISIBLE ELEMENTS
(Received in a natural way)	(Received in a supernatural way)
Bread	Body
Wine	Blood

The doctrine of Christ's bodily presence in the Lord's Supper is a major difference between Lutherans and other Protestant groups who commonly deny Christ's real bodily presence in His Supper. Those who deny Christ's bodily presence do so in two different ways.

One group teaches that the Lord's Supper is only a memorial eating and drinking of bread and wine (or bread and grape juice) in which Christ is only figuratively or symbolically present. Hence, it is observed only in memory of Christ's suffering and death, and, unlike in Lutheran theology, the Supper is not seen as a Means of Grace that offers forgiveness of sins to penitent communicants. This false teaching

HALLMARKS OF LUTHERAN IDENTITY

is largely derived from Swiss reformer Ulrich Zwingli (1484–1531), who strenuously opposed Luther's defense of Christ's bodily presence in the Lord's Supper at the Marburg Colloquy in 1529.

The other non-Lutheran Protestant teaching of the Lord's Supper comes mostly from John Calvin (1509–64), whose influence is most prominent in Presbyterian-related churches and some other Reformed groups. Calvin's position is sometimes a little confusing to Lutherans, for he tried to find a middle ground between Luther and Zwingli. So he spoke of Christ being *spiritually* present in the Lord's Supper. He argued, "We do not deny that God himself is present in his institution [Lord's Supper] by the very-present power of his Spirit."[4] But he strongly denied Christ's bodily presence in the Sacrament, saying, "It is not, therefore, the chief function of the Sacrament simply and without higher consideration to extend to us the body of Christ."[5] In response to saying Christ's body is present in the Holy Supper, he critically asked, "What sort of madness, then, is it to mingle heaven with earth rather than give up trying to drag Christ's body from the heavenly sanctuary?"[6] And Calvin also denied Christ's real presence in the Supper on the basis of his belief that *"finitum non est capax infiniti"* (the finite is not capable of the infinite). Thus, if he had been consistent in this belief, he also would have had to deny Christ's incarnation, for when the infinite God became man, He took upon Himself the finite body of a man in a finite world.

Thus, while there were some differences between Calvin and Zwingli, both agreed and argued that Christ's body was in heaven and therefore could not be present in the Lord's Supper. The latter is still commonly taught and believed in non-Lutheran Protestant churches.

Two comments seem in order regarding Calvin's teaching that says Christ is only spiritually present in the Sacrament. First, while it is permissible to say that Christ is spiritually present in the Lord's Supper, it is only partially correct, for Christ is also bodily present. His body and blood are received orally (*manducatio oralis* in Latin) by every communicant. This point, as we have seen, Calvin refused to accept. Second, it is also important for Lutherans not to confuse Christ's spiritual presence with His body and blood being supernaturally present. Christ's spiritual presence and His bodily presence are categorically different. Spiritual presence does not mean Christ's body and blood are truly present, whereas His supernatural bodily presence does also include His spiritual presence.

Luther took
Christ at His
Word. He did
not permit
himself to
rationalize
what did not
make sense
to human
reason.

Luther took Christ at His Word. He did not permit himself to rationalize what did not make sense to human reason. By conforming mostly to reason, contrary to Scripture, Zwingli and Calvin both argued that Christ's human body, according to its human nature, must always be visible and occupy given space. It could not be omnipresent. Whereas, Luther and the formulators of the Lutheran Confessions firmly held to the position that Christ is omnipresent, even in His human nature. The Calvinistic/Reformed denial of Christ's bodily presence in the Lord's Supper is premised on the belief that His human body is "a merely human body, but not of the body united with the Logos."[7]

The doctrine of Christ's bodily presence in the Lord's Supper was to Luther and the theologians who followed him a miracle, the miracle of the Gospel. It was not just a memorial meal. Hence, it is important for us Lutherans to remember that even though non-Lutheran-Protestant churches may repeat Christ's words "This is My body" and "This is My blood" when they give their members Communion, they do not take these words at face value. To them, these words are only symbolic; that is, the Lord's Supper is merely a memorial meal, and thus it is also not a Means of Grace.

THE BENEFITS OF THE LORD'S SUPPER

As noted in the previous chapter, when we Lutherans, as Christians, repent and in faith partake of Christ's body and blood in this Sacrament, we receive the forgiveness of sins. This is what Christ meant when He instituted His Supper, saying, "Drink from it all of you. This is My blood of the covenant, which is poured out for many for the forgiveness of sins" (Matthew 26:27–28). Receiving the forgiveness of sins in the Lord's Supper, as Luther says, also provides the "food of souls, which nourishes and strengthens the new man" (LC V 23). Hence, in addition to providing

HALLMARKS OF LUTHERAN IDENTITY

the forgiveness of sins in the Lord's Supper, it also strengthens the repentant recipient's faith. Both are Gospel-based reasons, in addition to Christ's command, for Lutherans to partake of this Holy Meal.

Regarding communicants receiving benefits from Christ's Holy Meal, Roman Catholicism teaches "that the sacraments act *ex opere operato* (literally: 'by the very fact of the action's being performed')."[8] Expressed in another way, it means that the Sacrament operates by virtue of a power within itself. In this regard, as Roland H. Bainton (Luther and Reformation scholar, Yale University) has stated, "In Luther's eyes such a view made the sacrament mechanical and magical."[9] This also means Catholic participants need not have faith or understand what is offered in the Sacrament in order to benefit spiritually. Mere participation in a spiritual rite of the Church is sufficient. Lutheran theology teaches participation without repentance and faith bestows no spiritual benefit. Instead, to receive the Sacrament in this manner may even harm the person. For 1 Corinthians 11:28–29 states, "Let a person examine himself, then, and so eat of the bread and drink of the cup. For anyone who eats and drinks without discerning the body eats and drinks judgment on himself."

Lutheran theology teaches participation without repentance and faith bestows no spiritual benefit.

Also contrary to Roman Catholicism, Lutheran theology teaches the Lord's Supper is neither an *opus bonum* (a good work) on part of communicants nor is it a *sacrificium* (a sacrifice) made by the pastor when he consecrates the elements. Instead, the Lord's Supper is a Means of Grace for Christians who in repentance and faith believe that in receiving Christ's body and blood they receive the forgiveness of sins.

THE BODILY PRESENCE IS NOT TRANSUBSTANTIATION

Although the Roman Catholic Church, similar to the Lutheran Church, believes and teaches the doctrine of Christ's bodily presence in the Lord's Supper, it differs greatly from the biblical doctrine taught by Lutherans. Rome teaches that when the priest speaks the Words of Institution or Consecration, those words change the bread and wine into the body and blood of Christ. This doctrine, known as transubstantiation, states that after the bread and wine are consecrated, bread and wine are no longer present; they only appear as such. Transubstantiation is contrary to the Lutheran biblical position, which asserts that though Christ is truly present bodily in the Sacrament, the bread is still bread, and the wine is still wine.

Regarding the Roman Catholic doctrine of transubstantiation, Hermann Sasse said, "What we object to in the doctrine of transubstantiation as Lutheran theologians is that it is a wrong philosophical explanation or description of a miracle which defies all human attempts to explain or describe it."[10] It is also helpful to know the doctrine of transubstantiation was "unknown during the first 1,000 years of the church."[11] It became official Catholic teaching at the Lateran Council in 1215.

Lutheran theology does not explain how Christ's bodily presence in the bread and wine of His Holy Supper takes place. Hence, Sasse states, "As to the *how* of the Presence of the whole Christ, of His body and blood, of His human and divine nature, there is no dogma in the Lutheran church because the Holy Scripture does not answer this question."[12] Neither does Scripture explain *when* Christ's real presence occurs.[13] This means Lutheran theology does not engage in speculation, even though it does say without the words of consecration Christ would not be bodily present in the bread and wine. "Luther and the early Lutheran church avoided forming any theory about the 'moment' when the Real Presence begins, and the 'moment' when it ceases."[14] Summing up the matter, Sasse states, "Not the *way* in which the Real Presence may be understood is decisive, but the *fact* that it is acknowledged."[15]

THE BODILY PRESENCE IS NOT CONSUBSTANTIATION

Although Lutheran theology, similar to the Roman Catholic Church, holds to the real presence of Christ's body and blood in the Lord's Supper (as noted above), it differs from Catholic doctrine, for it does not accept its doctrine of transubstantiation. This, however, has not prevented some non-Lutheran Protestants from erroneously referring to the Lutheran doctrine of the real presence as consubstantiation, a concept that superficially appears similar to transubstantiation.

Consubstantiation, however, means the bread and wine are mixed or commingled with the body and blood into one substance. This is a wrong understanding of what Lutheran theology teaches about Christ's bodily presence in the Lord's Supper. The faulty label of consubstantiation seems to come from a wrong understanding of the Lutheran explanation that says Christ's body and blood are present "in, with, and under" the bread and wine. But the word *under* does not permit one to say there is a mixing or commingling of the bread and wine; hence no consubstantiation. When a substance is under something, it must be separate from that which it is under, and thus it cannot be mixed or commingled with another element. In refuting the notion that the Lutheran doctrine of the real presence is consubstantiation, Sasse rightly states, "the Lutheran church has never accepted it."[16] Orthodox Lutheran theology has always taught that in the Lord's Supper the bread remains bread, and the wine remains wine, even though Christ's body and blood are supernaturally present with both elements. (See the table below on p. 126.)

THE BODILY PRESENCE IS NOT IMPANATION

Besides those who say Lutherans believe in consubstantiation, some, also mistakenly, use the concept of impanation to describe the Lutheran doctrine of Christ's bodily presence in the Supper. Impanation means that Christ's body and blood are embedded or enclosed in the bread and wine; analogous, for example, to the contents in a sandwich. This concept is even more incorrect than consubstantiation. As in the case of consubstantiation, the word *under* does not allow for the concept of impanation. Hence, whether some erroneously see the Lutheran doctrine of the real presence as impanation or consubstantiation, it is well to remember the words of theologian Johann Gerhard, who said, "We [Lutherans] do not believe in impanation, nor in consubstantiation."[17]

The following table gives a visual portrayal of what is taught by Lutherans, Roman Catholics, and non-Lutheran Protestants regarding the bodily presence of Christ in the Lord's Supper.

DENOMINATIONAL TEACHINGS REGARDING THE REAL PRESENCE IN THE LORD'S SUPPER

DENOMINATION	BREAD PRESENT	WINE PRESENT	CHRIST'S BODY IS PRESENT	CHRIST'S BLOOD IS PRESENT
Lutheran	Yes	Yes	Yes	Yes
Roman Catholic	No	No	Yes	Yes
Non-Lutheran Protestants	Yes	Yes	No	No

WORDS OF INSTITUTION

There is another significant difference between Lutherans and non-Lutheran Protestants. It pertains to Christ's Words of Institution or consecration of the bread and wine. Non-Lutheran Protestant churches commonly reject the idea that the elements of bread and wine are to be consecrated by reciting the very words Christ spoke to His disciples when He instituted the Lord's Supper. Sasse says that "none of the classical liturgies of the Reformed churches contains a consecration in the proper sense. The Words of Institution are rather understood as a historical narrative addressed to the people."[18] Not using the Words of Institution or consecration reflects the Reformed or generic Protestant churches' denial of Christ's bodily presence in the Supper.

Although, as already indicated, Lutheran theology does not speculate at what moment the bread and wine become the body and blood of Christ, it does, however, not see the Lord's Supper as valid if the Words of Institution (consecration) are not spoken. Thus, when Lutherans speak of Christ's bodily presence in the Sacrament, they have in mind the consecrated bread and wine, together with both being received by the communicants. Here it is also important to remember that the words of consecration not only give validity to the Lord's Supper but also honor what Christ said and did. Moreover, they are words that declare God's message of forgiveness. They are Gospel-based words, reminding us that the Lord's Supper is one hundred percent Gospel.

CONCLUSION

Some critics have at times accused Luther of retaining the doctrine of the real presence because, in their opinion, he was unable to shed all of his former Catholic beliefs. In response to this accusation, Sasse says, "Luther retained the Real Presence, not because he could not get rid of the orthodox Catholic tradition, but because he was convinced that the Real Presence was deeply rooted in Holy Scripture."[19] That is why at the Marburg Colloquy (1529), he refused to see Christ's words, "This is My body" (*hoc est corpus meum* in Latin) in a figurative or symbolic sense, as Zwingli had maintained. For Luther to think as Zwingli did would not only have been unfaithful to what Christ literally said and taught, but it would also have compromised the very Gospel of Jesus Christ for him. Luther's firm conviction regarding Christ's real bodily presence in the Lord's Supper is important for us Lutherans to remember and to retain in today's multi-denominational environment that makes it tempting and easy to minimize doctrinal differences, including those that pertain to what the Lord's Supper is and what it does for faithful, repentant Christians.

Although Lutheran catechetical materials rightly teach that Christ's body and blood are truly present in the Lord's Supper, they often tend not to state that Christ's body and blood are present in a *supernatural manner*. The term *supernatural* is also rarely found in print or heard when the real presence of Christ's body and blood is mentioned in sermons or in Bible classes. If this term were used more frequently in discussions or sermons pertaining to the Lord's Supper, it would likely give many Lutherans a better understanding of this important biblical doctrine.

Finally, many informed non-Lutherans, both Catholics and Protestants, know that Lutherans believe in the real presence of Christ's body and blood in the Lord's Supper. Hence, it is proper to say that they recognize this doctrine is a hallmark of Lutheran theology and identity.

1. What is meant by the Catholic doctrine of transubstantiation?

2. Why is it incorrect to say Lutherans teach consubstantiation?

3. How do consubstantiation and impanation differ?

4. Although Zwingli and Calvin differed somewhat in their views on the Lord's Supper, in what way(s) did their views agree?

5. If a pastor forgot to say the Words of Institution (consecration) and then distributed the bread and wine to the communicants, would that be a biblically valid Lord's Supper? Why or why not?

6. Why do non-Lutheran Protestants reject the doctrine of Christ's real bodily presence in the Lord's Supper?

7. Why does Lutheran theology decline to say exactly *when* and *how* the real presence of Christ takes place during the consecration of the bread and wine in the Lord's Supper?

8. Why does Lutheran theology say the Lord's Supper is a Means of Grace?

9. Do you think most Lutherans know that non-Lutheran Protestant churches do not believe in Christ's real presence in the Lord's Supper? Explain.

10. If more Lutherans understood the radically different beliefs non-Lutheran Protestants teach concerning the Lord's Supper, do you think they would be more concerned about their son or daughter marrying or becoming a Methodist, Presbyterian, Baptist, etc.? Why or why not?

11. Why does Lutheran theology call the Lord's Supper a Means of Grace?

12. In Lutheran theology, how do Baptism and the Lord's Supper differ?

CHAPTER 10

LUTHER'S SMALL CATECHISM

The Laity's Bible

"Yonder sun has not seen, next to the Holy Scriptures,
a better book than the Catechism of Luther."
—Andreas Fabricius (1528–77)

A noteworthy hallmark that distinguishes Lutherans from other Christians is their centuries-long use of Luther's Small Catechism. Many, if not most, Lutherans have studied and memorized much of the Small Catechism when they were catechumens in junior confirmation classes, commonly when they were thirteen or fourteen years of age.

Catechisms of many other church denominations have come and gone, but Luther's Small Catechism, first published in 1529, has endured the ravages of time. Writing in the 1950s, Erwin L. Lueker said it is "the oldest catechism of the Church still in use."[1] Even now, in the second decade of the twenty-first century, it appears the majority of Lutheran congregations still use the Small Catechism in junior confirmation classes.

Several years before Luther wrote the Small Catechism in 1529, he had asked two of his co-worker pastors, Johann Agricola and Justus Jonas, to write a catechism that would instruct laypeople in the basic Christian doctrines. They did not get it done. Then in 1528, after Luther had visited a number of congregations in Saxony (known as the Saxon

Visitation), he discovered an alarmingly high degree of ignorance regarding basic Christian doctrine among lay members and even among many priests (pastors) who had joined the Reformation. He wrote,

> The common person, especially in the villages, has no knowledge whatever of Christian doctrine. And unfortunately, many pastors are completely unable and unqualified to teach. ‹This is so much so, that one is ashamed to speak of it.› Yet, everyone says they are Christians, have been baptized, and received the holy Sacraments, even though they cannot even recite the Lord's Prayer or the Creed or the Ten Commandments. They live like dumb brutes and irrational hogs. Now that the Gospel has come they have nicely learned to abuse all freedom like experts. (SC Preface 2–3).

Luther's findings prompted him to write the Small Catechism himself, and by January 1529 it appeared, containing three chief parts with explanations; two more parts were soon printed thereafter.[2] The first printing appeared on large poster sheets of paper, but by May 1529, the catechism was published in book form.[3] Luther called it *Der kleine Katechismus fur die gemeine Pfarherr und Prediger* (The Small Catechism for the Common Pastors and Preachers).

The word *catechism* comes from the Greek *katechaeo*, meaning "to make heard." *Katechaeo* in the Early Church referred to oral instruction given to those who desired to join the Christian Church. In many regions, catechetical instruction took two to three years before converts were baptized as adult members of the church. Later in the Middle Ages, not all catechetical instruction was confined entirely to oral instruction. In some regions, catechesis also included written explanations of the Apostles' Creed and the Lord's Prayer, along with written lists of mortal sins.[4] Although some catechetical materials appeared in written form in the Middle Ages, scholars believe Luther's Small Catechism was the first printed catechetical work called "Catechism" when he in German used the name *Der kleine Katechismus*.[5]

Although Luther wrote the Small Catechism in 1529, he had done a considerable amount of preparatory work before he wrote it. As early as 1520, he "had collected the results of his previous catechetical labors."[6] These consisted of a number of catechetical sermons he had preached in the early 1520s. Even when writing his *Deutsche Messe*

HALLMARKS OF LUTHERAN IDENTITY

(German Mass), which he finished in 1526, he had asked his assistants to include catechetical materials that could be used in Divine Services.[7]

THE ENCHIRIDION, PLUS

The Small Catechism of 1529 was often referred to as the "Enchiridion," meaning handbook. Initially, it contained only the following five chief parts: the Ten Commandments, the Apostles' Creed, the Lord's Prayer, the Sacrament of Baptism, and the Sacrament of the Lord's Supper. Its present sixth chief part, Confession, was added in 1531 by Andreas Osiander (1498–1552), a Lutheran pastor in Nuremberg.[8] Thus, this part of the Small Catechism is technically not Luther's contribution. The Table of Duties, which addresses the obligations a Christian father has in his household, was also not a part of the original catechism in 1529.[9]

Once the Small Catechism was printed in 1529, it became

> an immediate success in terms of circulation. Evangelical [Lutheran] pastors preached from it; city councils adopted it as the basic school textbook; schoolmasters drilled it; parents instructed out of it; and at least some children learned it by heart. Religious leaders, even some who detested Luther, admired it and allowed it to influence their own attempts at writing catechisms.[10]

The Enchiridion of 1529 did not have the biblical proof-texts that Luther's Small Catechisms now have and of which many generations of Lutheran catechumens have memorized. These biblical texts, together with accompanying questions and explanations, were added by different Lutheran editors. Catechism proof-texting began between 1531 and 1542.[11] Later, other individuals also wrote editions with proof-texts and explanations. The following are some of the better-known editors: Conrad Dieterich (d. 1639) in Germany, Wilhelm Loehe (d. 1872) in Germany, Joseph Stump (d. 1935) in the United Lutheran Church in America, J. Michael Reu (d. 1943) of the Iowa Synod, Carl Gauswitz (d. 1928) of the Wisconsin Synod, and Jacob A. Dell (d. 1953) of the American Lutheran Church. In The Lutheran Church—Missouri Synod, the edition by Heinrich C. Schwan was popular from the late 1890s to 1943.

SOME CREATIVE INNOVATIONS

Luther made a number of creative innovations in his little gem, the Small Catechism. All of them were designed to enhance the learning process of the catechumens so they would grow in knowledge, wisdom, and assurance regarding God's love and grace in Jesus Christ.

LOCATION OF THE TEN COMMANDMENTS

Luther placed the Ten Commandments between his Preface and the Apostles' Creed. This is an important location of the Ten Commandments, for it means Christians not only would know how God wants them to live and know how they as sinners fall short of God's Law, but so that they can also appreciate God's Good News (the Gospel) that immediately came after the Commandments in the form of the Apostles' Creed. The Creed contains only Gospel, no Law. By placing the Commandments before the Creed, the Small Catechism reflected Luther's strong Law-Gospel orientation. He believed the Gospel could only be appreciated by Christians after they recognize they have broken God's Commandments and thus needed to repent and receive God's forgiveness conveyed by the Gospel.

> By placing the Commandments before the Creed, the Small Catechism reflected Luther's strong Law-Gospel orientation.

THREE ARTICLES OF THE APOSTLES' CREED

Another creative act was Luther's dividing the Apostles' Creed into three parts (articles) instead of twelve separate sentences that once had been the church's traditional way of teaching this creed. For the creed not only had been named in honor of the twelve apostles, but it was once incorrectly believed that each of the twelve apostles had written a portion of the creed. Luther no longer held to that view.

Luther's threefold division of the creed highlighted the work of the three persons in the Trinity. The first article focused on God the Father, creator of heaven and earth. The second article confessed the person and work of Jesus Christ, God's only-begotten Son. The third article concentrated on the work of the Holy Spirit, the Christian Church, the communion of saints, and the Christian's belief in a future resurrection of the body after death.

"This Is Most Certainly True"

The catechism gives a detailed, thoroughly biblical explanation for each of the three articles. And most interestingly, at the end of each of the three explanations, which describe the articles' teachings, Luther unequivocally states, "This is most certainly true." This affirmative proclamation is a hallmark within the Small Catechism, which is itself one of the most prominent hallmarks of Lutheran theology.

"Was ist Das?" ("What Does This Mean?")

After each of the Ten Commandments, as well as after each of the three articles of the Apostles' Creed, and after each of the seven petitions of the Lord's Prayer, the catechism asks: "Was ist das?" ("What is this?"). This German question is translated in English as "What does this mean?" In reality, however, the translation, as Timothy Wengert has shown, "implies that something is unclear, that there is some deeper, hidden meaning behind the words. [But] Luther's question was simpler by far . . . his question was an invitation to paraphrase." A better translation of Luther's question, according to Wengert, would be "That is to say?" or "In other words?" [12]

Although the question "Was ist das?" really calls for paraphrased responses, the catechism does, however, provide a biblically based answer for each question. And whether the question is asked in German or in the English translation, it is another hallmark within the more prominent Lutheran hallmark of the Small Catechism.

Seven Petitions of the Lord's Prayer

Another feature of the catechism is Luther's division of the Lord's Prayer into seven petitions. Most people, even when they have learned the Small Catechism by memory, are not really cognizant that when Christ taught His disciples this prayer, He gave the prayer seven specific petitions or requests. In each petition, the catechism again asks the catechumens, "Was ist das?" ("What does this mean?")

Portraying the Lord's Prayer in this manner is an example of Luther's pedagogical (teaching) concerns. In his little essay *A Simple Way to Pray*, Luther characterized the Lord's Prayer as "the greatest martyr on earth" because "nearly everyone mistreats it and abuses it. Only a few are comforted by it and find joy in its correct use."[13] The catechism's questions and explanations pertaining to the petitions are designed to minimize idle speaking of this Christ-given prayer. The pedagogical value of Luther's Small Catechism sheds light on why it has outranked and outlived other catechisms, including many written after his time.

LUTHER'S MORNING AND EVENING PRAYERS

As a man of prayer, Luther penned two short prayers in the Small Catechism, one to be prayed in the morning and the other when retiring at night. With regard to the Morning Prayer, his preface instructs, "In the morning, when you rise, you shall bless yourself with the holy cross and say, 'In the name of God the Father, Son, and Holy Spirit.'" Similarly, making the sign of the cross and calling upon the triune God is repeated by the person before he or she prays the catechism's Evening Prayer.

Instructing Christians to make the sign of the cross was Luther's way of reminding them that they were redeemed children of God as a result of Christ's suffering and death on the cross. Although Luther criticized and changed many practices that were abused and misused in the Catholic Church, he never found fault with making the sign of the cross. To him, making the sign of the cross was not "Catholic," but Christian. After all, Christ did die on a cross. Thus, it has been unfortunate that some American editions of Luther's Small Catechism omit Luther's instruction preceding his Morning and Evening Prayers to "bless yourself with the holy cross."

J. Michael Reu (d. 1943), a well-known Lutheran professor in the Iowa Synod (later the American Lutheran Church) who is often called an expert on Luther's Small Catechism, omitted Luther's instruction to make the sign of the cross in his 1904 edition of the Small Catechism, immediately preceding both the Morning and Evening Prayers.[14] This instruction of Luther's was also omitted in the Small Catechism edited by Joseph Stump and published by the General Council of the Evangelical Church in North America in 1907. And the most recent catechism published in

> Instructing Christians to make the sign of the cross was Luther's way of reminding them that they were redeemed children of God.

HALLMARKS OF LUTHERAN IDENTITY

1998 by the Wisconsin Evangelical Lutheran Synod (WELS) also omits Luther's instructing Christians to make the sign of the cross preceding his Morning and Evening Prayers.[15]

Along with editors in some Lutheran bodies who omitted Luther's instructions on making the sign of the cross, there were also many Lutheran pastors who in confirmation classes skipped over these words by Luther, even when the catechism they used contained them. In both instances, it resulted in countless Lutheran confirmands never having learned that Luther wanted Christians to make the sign of the "holy cross," as he phrased it. This teaching of his has always been (and still is) an integral part of his Small Catechism.

Why do some present-day Small Catechisms still omit Luther's instruction of making the sign of the cross when they pray his Morning and Evening Prayers? A couple of probable answers come to mind. One, it undoubtedly reveals an overreaction to Roman Catholicism. For it is well-known that Catholics customarily make the sign of the cross when they pray.

Two, in North America, Lutherans have always been a religious minority in the presence of Baptists, Congregationalists, Methodists, and Presbyterians. These denominations, for the most part, never valued the cross as a visual symbol, especially not in terms of signing oneself with it. They saw it as "Catholic." Thus, Lutherans, residing in this predominant Protestant culture, absorbed this negative view of making the sign the cross.

When Luther advocated making the sign of the cross, he reflected what Christians had already been doing in the Ancient Church. The Early Church Father Tertullian in northern Africa, in about AD 195, wrote, "At every forward step and movement, at every going in and out, when we put on our clothes and shoes, when we bathe, when we sit at table, when we light the lamps, on couch, on seat, in all the ordinary actions of daily life, we trace upon the forehead the sign [of the cross]."[16]

Immediately following Luther's instruction to make the sign of the cross, before praying his Morning and Evening Prayers, each prayer begins the same way: "I thank You, my heavenly Father, through Jesus Christ, Your dear Son . . ." Praying in this manner was an example of Luther's firm conviction that God only hears prayers that are voiced in the name of God's Son. It is another example of his strong belief

To Luther,
it was un-
thinkable
that a Chris-
tian would
pray without
addressing
Jesus Christ.

in *solus Christus*, noted in chapter 1. To Luther, it was unthinkable that a Christian would pray without addressing Jesus Christ, for he firmly believed that "God will hear and acknowledge only what is presented in the name of Christ."[17] He would have been appalled to hear some Christians praying (often in ignorance) without invoking the name of Jesus Christ. The latter (to repeat, as noted in chapter 1) sometimes happens when a Christian is asked to say a prayer, for instance, at a civic gathering, and the prayer often ends, "Dear God, we ask this in Your name." The word *God* is not His name; it is a generic term. Such a prayer fails to mention Jesus Christ. Luther would never have prayed that kind of prayer. Neither should any Christian today say a prayer in that manner.

The Morning and Evening Prayers in the catechism are two unique features of this little book. And these two prayers, similar to Luther's unique assertion, "This is most certainly true," are, to say it again, a hallmark within the Small Catechism, which is the better-known Lutheran hallmark.

RHYTHM AND CADENCE

Another noteworthy quality of the Small Catechism is its rhythm and cadence, both in the German edition and in the English translation. For instance, notice Luther's explanation of the First Article of the Apostles' Creed. After saying "I believe that God has made me and all creatures," his explanation states:

> He has given me my body and soul, eyes, ears, and all my limbs, my reason, and all my senses, and still preserves them. In addition, He has given me clothing and shoes, meat and drink, house and home, wife and children, fields, cattle, and all my goods. . . . He does all this out of pure, fatherly, divine goodness and mercy, without any merit or worthiness in me.

For all this I out to thank Him, praise Him, serve Him, and obey Him. This is most certainly true.

The cadence and rhythm are strikingly beautiful and harmonious. They greatly facilitate memorization. The cadence and rhythm in the explanation of the Second Article are equally well-crafted. In part, the explanation reads:

> I believe that Jesus Christ, true God, begotten of the Father from eternity, and also true man, born of the Virgin Mary, is my Lord. He has redeemed me, a lost and condemned creature, purchased and won me from all sins, from death, and from the power of the devil. He did this not with gold or silver, but with His holy, precious blood and with His innocent suffering and death, that I may be His own, live under Him in His kingdom, and serve Him in everlasting righteousness, innocence, and blessedness, just as He is risen from the dead, lives and reigns to all eternity. This is most certainly true.

This same cadence is also present in the Third Article's explanation that confidently speaks for every pious, devout Christian:

> I believe that I cannot by my own reason or strength believe in Jesus Christ, my Lord, or come to Him. But the Holy Spirit has called me by the Gospel, enlightened me with His gifts, sanctified and kept me in the true faith. In the same way He calls, gathers, enlightens, and sanctifies the whole Christian Church on earth and keeps it with Jesus Christ in the one true faith. In this Christian Church He daily and richly forgives all my sins and the sins of all believers. This is most certainly true.

Was it accidental that the cadence and rhythm of the words just cited appeared as they did in Luther's Small Catechism? No, not at all. One can argue that the rhythmic cadence of these words was the result of Luther's deliberate intent and design, prompted most likely for three reasons. One, it would facilitate the memorization of his explanations. Two, Luther was a gifted musician; he recognized the value of rhythm and cadence. Three, Luther had received a classical education.

"FEAR AND LOVE GOD"

Another important aspect of the catechism is the response Luther gives to "What does this mean?" at the end of each commandment, where it enjoins, "We should fear and love God so that . . . ." Then, at the close of the Commandments, the following directive is underscored: "God threatens to punish all who sin against these commandments. Therefore, we should fear His wrath and not act contrary to these commandments. But he promises grace and every blessing to all who keep these commandments. Therefore, we should also love and trust in Him and gladly do what He commands."

To say we Christians are to "fear and love God" sounds strange to many today, perhaps even to some Lutherans. Our secular culture has led many to believe that because they have heard "God is love" He is not one whom they should ever fear. But this modern belief is not in accord with God's Word, which asserts, "The fear of the LORD is the beginning of knowledge" (Proverbs 1:7), or "Let all the earth fear the LORD" (Psalm 33:8). Moreover, should we not fear God's anger because of our many sins? "For we daily sin much and surely deserve nothing but punishment" (SC, Explanation of the Fifth Petition). May we Lutherans remember that our need to fear God—taught in the catechism—does not nullify our love for Him, given that our love is the result of His Son having first loved us (1 John 4:19).

> May we Lutherans remember that our need to fear God—taught in the catechism—does not nullify our love for Him.

NOT JUST FOR CHILDREN

It is well-known that many Lutherans think of the Small Catechism as a book primarily for children in junior confirmation classes. This belief overlooks what the catechism says in its preface; namely, that it was intended to be used by the father to teach all members of his household, as both the German and Latin editions indicate. Preceding the Ten Commandments, the Creed, the Lord's Prayer, the

Sacrament of Holy Baptism, and the Sacrament of the Altar, the Small Catechism, for each of these five parts, states, "As the head of the family should teach it in a simple way to his household." The German edition says *Hausvater* (father of the household), and the Latin has *paterfamilias*, rather than "head of the family," as in the English translation. Nevertheless, the point is clear—the catechism was not written just for children. Rather, it was written for the entire household: children, adults, domestic workers, and whoever resided in the home. And Luther expected the father to teach these individuals the Christian basics of the catechism.

The catechism was not written just for children.

Given that many Lutherans think the Small Catechism is only for children probably helps explain why many Lutheran pastors do not use it in adult instruction classes for individuals who want to become members of the Lutheran Church. Viewing the Small Catechism primarily for children overlooks that Luther himself prayed and studied it every day. He once said, "Like a child who is being instructed in the Catechism, I too recite, read, and speak it word for word each morning, and when I have time, I also say the Lord's Prayer, the Ten Commandments, the Creed, Psalms, etc. . . . For I must remain a child and student of the Catechism, and I do so gladly."[18] Luther's daily use of the catechism is a good example for us Lutherans to imitate. We, too, should recite and study it daily. Leopold von Ranke, a nineteenth-century German church historian, said of the catechism, "Blessed is he that nourishes his soul with it [and] holds fast to it!"[19]

PREACHING THE CATECHISM

That the Small Catechism is not only for children is also evident from records that show Luther preached the catechism to adults in church. Even before the Small and Large Catechisms were published in early 1529, Luther preached three series of sermons on parts of the catechisms (Large and Small); the series consisted of thirty-one sermons he preached between May and December of 1528. The day before the First Sunday in Advent, when he began to preach his third series, he announced that sermons on the catechisms were going to be preached in Wittenberg's St. Mary's Church four days per week (at two o'clock in the afternoon) for two weeks each quarter of each year.[20] As he made this announcement, he also admonished the hearers not to neglect attending these catechism sermons.[21] Briefly stated, Luther's sermons were not mere devotional treatises; they were also notably didactic.

Sometimes Luther also read a portion from the catechism to the congregation after he had preached the sermon.[22] And he was not the only one who preached the catechism, for in 1542, Johann Bugenhagen, close friend of Luther's and pastor of St. Mary's Church in Wittenberg, indicated that he personally had preached on the catechism some fifty times.[23]

The Laity's Bible

The Small Catechism has been called the layman's Bible, a designation that began with Luther, who called it *der Laien Biblia* (the layman's Bible). It contains everything a person needs to know for his or her salvation. As one observer has stated, "Luther's Small Catechism is a little Bible, and like the Bible itself, it has in it an element that is timeless, something that lifts it above the historic conditions and circumstances of a particular time in which it originated and to which it belongs."[24] This observer also said, "No other church has anything that can equal it."[25] Also extolling the Small Catechism, renowned German historian Leopold von Ranke wrote, "Blessed is he who clings to it and nurtures his soul with it."[26] Briefly put, this little book is the Bible in a nutshell.

Seeing it as the layman's Bible prompted Johannes Campanius to work as a missionary on the lower shores of the Delaware River among the Lenape Indians. Campanius, a Swedish Lutheran pastor, had migrated in 1643 to the Colony of New Sweden in America, an area that included today's Delaware, New Jersey, and eastern Pennsylvania. In 1646, he started to translate Luther's Small Catechism into their Algonquian language.[27] In 1648, he returned to Sweden for health reasons. While back in Sweden, he completed his translation and dedicated it to King Karl X Gustav with the hope it would be published. But when Sweden had surrendered its New Sweden territory to the Dutch in 1655, it resulted in the Swedes largely losing interest in missionary work among the Indians in America. Several decades later, a renewed Swedish interest in missionary efforts among the Lenape Indians resulted in the catechism being published in 1696, thirteen years after Campanius had died.[28] In part, the translation was also the result of the high regard Sweden had for Luther's catechism. For already in the 1630s it was considered to be Sweden's unofficial Bible.[29]

Reasons to Celebrate

The Small Catechism's succinct, brief summaries of basic biblical doctrines and its continued use for almost five hundred years has given it an unequaled reputation. And many commentators have added to its reputation by noting that the catechism can be prayed, a practice that Luther himself did on a daily basis. Justus Jonas, a co-worker of Luther's and whom Luther initially had asked to write a catechism with Johann Agricola, believed the Holy Spirit inspired Luther to write it. Polycarp Leyser (1552–1610), once a professor at the University of Wittenberg, said,

> I can truthfully affirm that this very small book contains such a wealth of so many and so great things that, if all faithful preachers of the Gospel during their entire lives would do nothing else in their sermons than explain aright to the common people the secret wisdom of God comprised in those few words, and set forth from the divine Scriptures the solid ground upon which each word is built, they could never exhaust this immense abyss.[30]

The Small Catechism has also been hailed for its irenic tone. Although Luther often engaged in a great deal of vociferous polemics against the false teachings of the pope, the Zwinglians, and the Anabaptists, his Small Catechism contains not a single polemical word. It only accents the positive. One observer has said, "The Catechism is permeated with one thought, that of justification by faith."[31]

As already noted, the catechism is also a prayer book. All Lutherans would do themselves a spiritual favor if they were to use it in their daily devotions, as Luther did. It has been rightly said that the Small Catechism is not just a book of Christian instruction but also a devotional book. Luther prayed the catechism daily. Each day, he would recite (out loud) the Ten Commandments, the Creed, the Lord's Prayer, and renew his memory of God's free grace in Baptism and the Lord's Supper. He once stated, "Like a child, I still read and speak the Catechism, word for word, every morning, and when I have enough time, I also recite out loud the Lord's Prayer, the Ten Commandments, the Creed, and a Psalm, etc."[32]

It is interesting to note that in the sixteenth century, "Lutheran thought turned increasingly to the Small Catechism as the banner of its faith."[33] Ever since then, though small in size, the catechism has functioned in this manner for committed Lutherans, strengthening their faith and guiding their lives.

The amazing qualities of the Small Catechism called for celebration, and that is just what many Lutherans, mostly from the Missouri Synod, did in 1929 when they honored the catechism's four hundredth anniversary. Special services were held in various parts of the United States. Some sixty thousand Lutherans gathered in Soldiers' Field in Chicago on July 23, 1929, to thank God for their having been taught Luther's Small Catechism. On October 13, 1929, some forty-five thousand Missouri Synod Lutherans, with a choir of thirteen hundred singers, packed the State Fair Grounds Coliseum in Birmingham, suburban Detroit, Michigan. In St. Louis, Missouri, twenty-five thousand seats were filled in the city's arena, where thirty-five hundred children sang in a celebratory service. Other celebratory services were also held in Cincinnati, Milwaukee, San Francisco, and other American cities. Even small towns in North Dakota, Kansas, Nebraska, Wisconsin, and other states saw Lutherans honor the Small Catechism. In the small town of Corvallis, Oregon, Lutheran children celebrated the catechism's four hundredth birthday in a special service by orally reciting its Ten Commandments and the Three Articles of the Apostles' Creed. And in Calgary, Alberta, the catechism was honored by a large gathering of Canadian Lutherans, accompanied by a children's choir of two-hundred voices.

However, in 1979, when the Small Catechism attained its 450th anniversary, Lutherans held no noteworthy celebratory services to thank God for this theological masterpiece. One cannot help but ask, why not? What happened in the fifty years since 1929? Did the forces of secularism and multiculturalism negatively affect American Lutherans so that they no longer saw the Small Catechism as a hallmark of their theology and identity? Most likely, these two forces contributed to the absent services for the Small Catechism's 450th anniversary in 1979. But there seems to have been another variable that contributed to the lack of interest. In 1929, the majority of Lutherans had been confirmed in junior confirmation classes that required them to study and memorize much of the catechism. Thus, they were quite familiar with it. But by 1979, many had joined the Lutheran Church from non-Lutheran backgrounds in the 1950s, 60s, and 70s as adults who commonly were not required to study the catechism in order to join the church. Many were briefly instructed with other materials, and so numerous Lutherans by 1979 did not know of the edifying Christian teachings that the catechism contains. Furthermore, by 1979 educational progressivism had so influenced even many Lutheran day schools that traditional memorization had been supplanted by child-centered "discovery" learning and other methods antithetical to historically Lutheran, content-based catechesis.

Conclusion

Luther was theologically serious about the importance of the Small Catechism in every Christian's life. In one of his sermons, he said, "Whoever does not know it [the catechism] cannot be numbered among the Christians. For if he does not know these things, it is evident that God and Christ mean nothing to him."[34]

These words of Luther may sound rather strong, perhaps even legalistic, as some Lutherans may think today. They are, however, instructive, especially in our age of low expectations and high permissiveness. Although Luther was firmly Gospel-oriented, he had clear parameters in mind regarding what qualified someone to be called a Christian. To him, anyone not knowing the Small Catechism's teachings was outside the circle of Christianity.

As Lutherans today, we often do not value the Small Catechism as we should. When this happens, it would be well to remember that Luther never lost sight of this little book's value. Given the many volumes and letters he wrote in his lifetime, he once said there were only two books by which he would like to be remembered. One was his book *The Bondage of Will* (1525), written to counter the learned Erasmus's faulty theological arguments. The other book was his Small Catechism. It is truly an outstanding God-given hallmark of Lutheran theology and identity.

1. What experience in 1528 prompted Luther to write the Small Catechism?

2. Although it is known today that the twelve apostles did not write the Apostles' Creed, how did the Church for a long time try to honor the apostles in regard to this creed?

3. What instruction, preceding Luther's Morning and Evening Prayer in the Small Catechism, has often been ignored or omitted? Why?

4. Christians signing themselves with the sign of the cross goes back to when in the Church's history?

5. What technique did Luther use in the Small Catechism that shows his pedagogical (teaching) concerns?

6. Why has Luther's Small Catechism often been called "the layman's Bible"?

7. Why do you think Luther's Small Catechism is frequently not used in adult instruction classes, especially in light of the fact that it was not written just for children?

8. Who did Luther say was to teach the Small Catechism in a family household?

9. What evidence is there in the Small Catechism that it was not just intended for children?

10. What do you think prompted so many Lutherans in the United States in 1929 to celebrate the Small Catechism's four hundredth anniversary in special services?

11. Why do you think the Small Catechism is today not used as it was in the past?

12. How might we help motivate fellow Lutherans to make better use of Luther's Small Catechism in their homes, for instance, in family devotions?

CHAPTER 11

LUTHER'S LARGE CATECHISM

A Teachers' Manual

"But as for you, continue in what you have learned and
have firmly believed, knowing from whom you learned it."
—St. Paul; 2 Timothy 3:14

While most Lutherans know about the Small Catechism, many do not seem to know much about Luther's other catechism, the Large Catechism. This book by Martin Luther is another Lutheran hallmark, distinguishing the Lutheran Church from the other Christian denominations. Both the Small and Large Catechism appeared in 1529.[1] The Large Catechism initially had the title of *Deutsch Katechismus* (German Catechism). But later in Luther's preface to the Small Catechism, he refers to the *Deutsch Katechismus* as the "Large Catechism" because it was longer than the Small Catechism. And it is also interesting to know Luther's Large Catechism "was published as a companion to the *German Mass*."[2]

THE LARGE CATECHISM'S ACCENTS

Luther wrote the Small Catechism for lay Christians, both children and adults. The Large Catechism, on the other hand, was written for pastors and teachers as a guide or handbook to help them in their teaching.[3] Regarding its intended use for pastors, Lutheran pastor and professor Friedrich Bente says, "The Large Catechism was to enable the less educated pastors in the villages and in the country to do justice to their sacred duty."[4]

The Large Catechism has two prefaces; one is relatively long and the other is quite brief. In the longer preface, Luther addresses all Christians, but especially pastors and teachers. He commands pastors and teachers not to "think of themselves as doctors [teachers] too soon and imagine that they know everything . . . [but that] they should guard with all care and diligence against the poisonous infection of contentment and vain imagination, but steadily keep on reading, teaching, learning, pondering, and meditating on the catechism" (LC Longer Preface 19). In his urging pastors and teachers to keep on studying the catechism, he also told them, and chidingly so,

> I am also a doctor and preacher; yes, as learned and experienced as all the people who have such assumptions and contentment. Yet I act as a child who is being taught the catechism. Every morning—and whenever I have time—I read and say, word for word, the Ten Commandments, the Creed, the Lord's Prayer, the Psalms, and such. I must still read and study them daily. Yet I cannot master the catechism as I wish. But I must remain a child and pupil of the catechism, and am glad to remain so. (LC Longer Preface 7–8).

I must remain a child and pupil of the catechism, and am glad to remain so.

Luther also criticized the superficial thinking of many pastors who thought one reading of the Small Catechism was sufficient. So he wrote, "These dainty, fastidious fellows would quickly, with one reading, become doctors above all doctors [teachers], to know all there is to be known. Well, this, too, is a sure sign that they despise both their office and the people's souls, yes, even God and his Word."[5]

In the shorter preface of the Large Catechism, similar to what Luther once said in one of his sermons, he contends that the Small Catechism "teaches what every Christian must know. So a person who does not know the catechism could not be counted as a Christian. . . . Therefore, we must have the young learn well and fluently the parts of the catechism" (LC Short Preface 2–3).

THE TEN COMMANDMENTS

The Ten Commandments are presented differently in the Large Catechism than in the Small Catechism. The discussion of each commandment is also considerably longer, and to highlight given points, the Large Catechism cites many examples from Scripture, history, and also from people's lives and culture at the time of Luther. Unlike the Small Catechism, the pedagogical question of *"Was ist das?"* ("What does this mean?") is not asked in this book.

The Ninth and Tenth Commandments are discussed together. As in the Small Catechism, the Large Catechism also has a conclusion to the Ten Commandments. The Small Catechism's conclusion to the Ten Commandments cites Exodus 20:5–6, "I the LORD your God am a jealous God, visiting the iniquity of the fathers on the children to the third and fourth generation of those hate Me, but showing steadfast love to thousands of those who love Me and keep My commandments."   In the Large Catechism's conclusion to the Ten Commandments, Luther briefly summarizes them.

THE APOSTLES' CREED

Unlike the Small Catechism, the Large Catechism has a brief introduction to the Apostles' Creed. In this introduction, Luther informs readers that this creed once was divided into twelve articles. But he does not say that each apostle penned one part, as was once erroneously thought as far back as approximately AD 400. Luther knew the old assumption was historically wrong.

Similar to the Small Catechism, Luther's presentation of the Apostles' Creed is exclusively Gospel-oriented. But unlike the Small Catechism, his explanations of the three articles are not intended to be memorized, nor are they written in a rhythmic or cadence-like manner.

THE LORD'S PRAYER

Luther's discussion of the Lord's Prayer in his Large Catechism is preceded by a lengthy introduction, really a plea for Christians to take seriously man's need and God's command to pray. Then, as in the Small Catechism, the Lord's Prayer is divided into seven petitions. The explanations of each petition are not intended to be memorized. Instead, they are intended to help pastors and teachers in their teaching. At the end of the Seventh Petition, Luther reminds the reader that when a Christian prays the Lord's Prayer, or any prayer, it is important to conclude this praying with "Amen." This small word, according to Luther, is to be spoken with a strong conviction that "our prayer is surely heard and that what we pray shall be done," and he adds, "where there is no such faith, there cannot be true prayer either" (LC III 119–20).

When one reads Luther's numerous volumes of writing, commonly known as "Luther's Works," there is hardly a volume in which he does not extol the Lord's Prayer. He highlights each of the prayer's seven petitions with insights that are often not readily perceived by us when we pray this "perfect prayer," to use Luther's assessment. For instance, he indicates that when we utter the prayer's petition "give us our daily bread," our request does indeed include everything (not just bread) that we need for the present day and that we should not be overly concerned about tomorrow's bread. Similarly, when we pray "Thy will be done," God wants us not only to pray these words but to also trust that His will indeed will take place. Numerous other edifying insights regarding this prayer are found in Luther's writings.

The Large Catechism underscores the Gospel embedded in Baptism.

SACRAMENT OF BAPTISM

As in the Small Catechism, the Large Catechism underscores the Gospel embedded in Baptism. "For no one is baptized in order that he may become a prince, but, as the words say, that he 'be saved.' We know that to be saved is nothing other than to be delivered from sin, death, and the devil" (LC IV 24, 25).

Unlike the Small Catechism, the Large Catechism's treatise on Baptism devotes a section to the defense of infant Baptism. Given that the Large Catechism was written primarily as a manual for pastors and teachers, Luther included this section on infant Baptism to help pastors and teachers counter the Anabaptists of his day who spurned the baptizing of infants. And it is interesting to note that this rejection of infant Baptism, which began with the Anabaptists in the early 1520s, has endured to the present day, for their religious descendants and similarly like-minded Christian groups have continued not to accept infant Baptism. They received the name Anabaptists (rebaptizers in Latin) because they rebaptized all adults who had been baptized as infants.

Although today's Baptists and Pentecostals also reject infant Baptism and rebaptize those who were baptized as infants, they are, however, not necessarily descendants of the sixteenth-century Anabaptists. Most descendants of Anabaptists today are usually found in various Mennonite groups.

SACRAMENT OF THE ALTAR

Similar to the Small Catechism, the Large Catechism underscores the real presence of Christ's body and blood in the Lord's Supper, and that it is also a Means of Grace. Comparing the Lord's Supper to Baptism, Luther states that just as Baptism is not mere water, so the Lord's Supper is "not mere bread and wine, such as are ordinarily served at the table [1 Corinthians 10:16–17]. Rather, bread and wine are included in, and connected with, God's Word" (LC V 9.) Luther calls it "a food of souls, which nourishes and strengthens the new man" (LC V 23).

The Small Catechism's relatively brief treatment of the Lord's Supper does not discuss the matter of how frequently Christians should attend the Lord's Supper, but the Large Catechism does. Christians, says Luther, are not left free to neglect (he calls it despising) the Lord's Supper. It is evident he saw the words "do this" (Luke 22:19) in Christ's instituting the Lord's Supper as a commandment. Thus, Luther said, "If you want to be a Christian, you must from time to time fulfill and obey this commandment" (LC V 49).

In some editions of the Large Catechism, there is a relatively long section in the treatise on the Lord's Supper titled, "A Brief Exhortation to Confession." In that treatise, Luther notes that confessing sins must be part of every Christians' life, but legalistically requiring Christians to make formal confession he saw as a papal error, not consistent with the Gospel. He believed that Christians, alive in Christ, will confess their sins both in formal settings as well as informally to their fellow Christians, be it husband, wife, brother, sister, children, or Christian friends.

CONCLUSION

Since Luther primarily wrote the Large Catechism as an instructor's manual for pastors and teachers in the church, it is somewhat understandable—but still unfortunate—that this valuable book is not well-known by many Lutheran laypeople today. Although Luther wrote it to bolster the knowledge of pastors and teachers, many of whom in the early days of the Reformation lacked the basics of Christian doctrine, he never intended to keep laypeople from using it for their Christian growth and edification. Hence, all Lutherans today would do well to read and study the Large Catechism. This would enhance their understanding of some basic Lutheran doctrines, and also help them grow in faith and knowledge, making them more conscious of another Lutheran hallmark.

1. Explain why Luther wrote the Large Catechism.

2. Cite some differences between the Large Catechism and the Small Catechism.

3. How can some of the Large Catechism's teachings enhance our understanding of the teachings in the Small Catechism?

4. How does the Large Catechism differ pedagogically from the Small Catechism?

5. Why do you think so many members of the Lutheran Church do not know about the Large Catechism?

6. What does the Large Catechism teach about Baptism that the Small Catechism does not?

7. What does the Large Catechism teach about the Lord's Supper that the Small Catechism does not?

8. Why were the Anabaptists in the sixteenth century given that name?

9. Who, for the most part, are the Anabaptists today?

10. What significance can be given to the fact that until the Reformation era no one, not even any of the heretics, denied infant Baptism?

11. What does Luther say in the Large Catechism regarding required formal confession of sins?

12. What did Luther mean by the phrase "food of souls"?

CHAPTER 12

SINNER AND SAINT AT THE SAME TIME

"We are sinners and at the same time righteous."
—Martin Luther

When Luther discovered the Gospel, he saw that Christians are not only sinners but at the same time also saints; that is, people holy in God's sight because of their faith in Jesus Christ. This theological insight is a distinctively Lutheran hallmark.

Although numerous accounts in Holy Scripture show many individuals as both sinners and saints, this biblical truth had largely been forgotten in the Middle Ages and remained forgotten until the time of Martin Luther. Even today, one hears very little about this comforting doctrine among Christians outside the Lutheran Church.

During much of the Middle Ages, only dead Christian martyrs or heroes were considered saints. Ordinary Christians had virtually no idea that they, too, were saints. Pictures from the Church's early years showed Christ as the Good Shepherd, often with a lamb draped over His shoulders. This told penitent Christians they were not just sinners but also saints, whom the Good Shepherd retrieved. But by the Middle Ages, such pictures had largely disappeared, leaving primarily the understanding that Christians were only sinners. In addition, numerous portraits of Christ, from the Middle Ages to the time of the Reformation, showed Christ as a stern judge, conveying the notion that God only punished sinners, overlooking that He also forgave all sinners who repented. Roland H. Bainton's biography of Luther, *Here I Stand,* captures this mindset so prevalent in Middle Ages and in Luther's time by depicting a portrait of Christ as the formidable judge sitting on a rainbow. Before Luther had discovered the Gospel, Bainton says, "Luther had seen pictures such as these and testified that he was utterly terror-stricken at the sight of Christ the Judge."[1]

SINNERS AND SAINTS IN THE BIBLE

Luther's teaching that Christians are simultaneously sinners and saints was not an idea he concocted on his own, but one he found throughout Holy Scripture. He discovered that Abraham, Jacob, Moses, Aaron, Elijah, David, and others in the Old Testament were not only sinners but also saints because they repented of their sinful deeds.[2] For instance, Moses recognized his sinfulness, saying to God, "You have set our iniquities before You, our secret sins in the light of Your presence" (Psalm 90:8). David, both an adulterer and murderer, when confronted by the prophet Nathan, repented over his grievous sins. He confessed and said, "For I know my transgressions, and my sin is ever before me" (Psalm 51:3).

Similarly, in the New Testament, Luther found that Paul, though a Christian (hence a saint), confessed being a sinner when he declared, "Christ Jesus came into the world to save sinners, of whom I am the foremost" (1 Timothy 1:15). The New Testament depicts Peter, a cocky and brash disciple of Christ, as a noteworthy sinner but also as a repentant saint. On the night before Jesus' crucifixion, Peter boasted to Him about his loyalty, saying he would go to prison and even die for Him (Luke 22:23). Not long after his boasting, a woman asked Peter whether he was a friend of Jesus, and he answered, "I do not know what you are talking about" (22:60). He denied Christ three times, proving he was a sinner. But right after his third denial, a rooster crowed, which reminded him what Jesus had told him earlier—namely, that he would deny Him three times before the rooster would crow. After hearing the rooster crow, Peter then "went out and wept bitterly" (22:62). His sorrowful repentance unmistakably demonstrated that he was not just a sinner but also a saint, someone who is holy and righteous in God's sight through his faith in Christ.

Sinner and Saint Underscores the Gravity of Sin

As already noted, Christians in the Middle Ages had no doubt that they were sinners. In contrast, today we live in a very different world, one in which the recognition and awareness of sin are almost nonexistent. Hermann Sasse has rightly noted, "The church today lives in a world that has lost the sense of sin and guilt in an appalling way."[3] And along with today's loss of the sense of sin, the world, of course, sees no need for God's grace.

The doctrine of sinner and saint runs counter to today's sin-denying world, for it underscores the gravity of sinfulness inherent in every human being. That is why St. Paul confessed, "I know that nothing good dwells in me, that is, in my flesh" (Romans 7:18). These words were followed by his lamenting, "Wretched man that I am! Who will deliver me from this body of death?" (Romans 7:24). The gravity of sinfulness was also recognized by the terrified Philippian jailer who fearfully asked Paul and Silas, as their shackles were miraculously unfastened, "Sirs, what must I do to be saved?" (Acts 16:30). In the Old Testament, David declared, "Behold, I was brought forth in iniquity, and in sin did my mother conceive me" (Psalm 51:5). After the flood, long before David and Paul, God reminded Noah that "the intention of man's heart is evil from his youth" (Genesis 8:21).

The sinner side of the doctrine of sinner-and-saint does indeed underscore the gravity of sin, for it tells us that not only are we born in sin but we are also guilty of sins in thoughts, words, and deeds that we daily commit and omit. "Surely there is not a righteous man on earth who does good and never sins" (Ecclesiastes 7:20). This knowledge is frightening, all the more so, when we remember God wants us to be perfect, for Christ said, "You therefore must be perfect, as your heavenly Father is perfect" (Matthew 5:48). People may seek to deny or minimize the gravity of sin, but God does not.

Along with today's loss of the sense of sin, the world, of course, sees no perceived need for God's grace.

Sinner and Saint Underscores God's Grace

People may seek to deny or minimize the gravity of sin, but God does not.

Were it not for the saint side of the sinner-and-saint doctrine, the gravity of sin would indeed be cause for us to despair. But knowing that by repentance and faith in Christ we are recipients of God's gracious forgiveness (Ephesians 2:8–9), we are no longer condemned sinners but His saints, for as St. Paul assured the Corinthians—and us as well—God does not hold our sins against us (2 Corinthians 5:19). Similarly, Isaiah said, "though your sins are like scarlet, they shall be as white as snow; though they are red like crimson, they shall become like wool" (Isaiah 1:18). Like Isaiah, the apostle John also understood the forgiveness of sin when he declared, "The blood of Jesus His Son cleanses us from all sin" (1 John 1:7), and following up on these words, he further said, "If we confess our sins, He is faithful and just to forgive us our sins and to cleanse us from all unrighteousness" (1:9). In short, it is the saint side of the sinner-saint concept that so magnanimously underscores God's abundant grace that only repentant Christians can understand.

The saint side of the sinner-saint doctrine makes Christians aware that they have a gracious God. In the words of Luther, "The saints are always aware of their sin and seek righteousness from God in accord with His mercy, for this very reason they are always regarded as righteous by God." Luther continues, "Thus in their own sight and in truth they are unrighteous, but before God they are righteous because He reckons them so because of their confession of sin. They are actually sinners, but they are righteous by the imputation of a merciful God."[4]

The Sinner-Saint Doctrine Nullifies Self-Righteousness

The informed Christian, knowing he or she is both sinner and saint, knows that this doctrine does not leave room for self-righteousness, for as Luther said, "A godly man [a saint] feels sin more than grace, wrath more than favor, judgment more than redemption." On the other hand, "An ungodly man feels almost no wrath," Luther noted, "but is smug as though there were no wrath anywhere, as though there were no God anywhere who vindicates His righteousness."[5]

Luther also warned, "A slip in faith is easy. So Moses, Aaron, David, Peter, all the apostles, Jerome, Augustine, and others fell. There has always been some remnant of the flesh in the saints, as we see from 1 Corinthians 10:12. Therefore, let no one be presumptuous."[6] These words of Luther remind us there is no room for even a scintilla of self-righteousness. "A Christian," said Luther, "is not someone who has no sin or feels no sin; he is someone to whom, because of his faith in Christ, God does not impute his sin."[7]

Thus, Christians who truly believe and recognize they are both sinners and saints can never, biblically speaking, adopt the self-righteous attitude that they can attain perfection in life; that is, reach a point in life where they no longer sin. Unfortunately, there are some misguided Christians in "holiness bodies" who mistakenly believe they can through much prayer, church attendance, and spiritual discipline attain a perfectly sinless life here on earth.

To believe that one can become free of sin not only denies the sinner side of the doctrine of sinner and saint, but it also spurns Christ's redemptive work on the cross and open tomb. Anyone who believes he or she has reached spiritual perfection has, of course, either rejected or forgotten God's words: "If we say we have no sin, we deceive ourselves, and the truth is not in us" (1 John 1:8).

ROMAN CATHOLICISM AND THE DOCTRINE OF *SIMUL JUSTUS ET PECCATOR*

Ever since the Council of Trent (1545–63), the Roman Catholic Church has rejected the teaching that Christians are simultaneously both sinners and saints. The Catholic theologian Robert A. Sungenis, in his book *Not By Faith Alone*, which has the church's imprimatur, states, "Catholicism denied the '*simul justus et peccator*' on the basis that the residual effects of original sin, e.g., the inclination to sin, must be understood not as sin but as *concupiscence* [sic]."[8] For in Roman Catholic theology, inclination to sin (concupiscence) is not sin. It only becomes sin when an individual makes a "deliberate attempt to act on his sinful inclinations."[9] In Lutheran theology—and in Scripture as well—the inclination to sin (concupiscence) is definitely sin, for the inclination to sin is the consequence of original sin. As St. Paul stated, "For I delight in the Law of God, in my inner being, but I see in my members another law waging war against the law of my mind and making me captive to the law of sin that dwells in my members" (Romans 7:22–23).

Regarding the nature of original sin, the Augsburg Confession states, "Our churches teach that since the fall of Adam [Romans 5:12], all who are naturally born are born with sin [Psalm 51:5], that is, without the fear of God, without trust in God, and with the inclination to sin, called concupiscence. Concupiscence is a disease and original vice that is truly sin" (II 1–2).

As just seen, Roman Catholic theology does not consider concupiscence as sin. It teaches that "Baptism, by imparting the life of Christ's grace, erases original sin and turns a man back toward God."[10] Lutheran theology, on the other hand, teaches that Baptism does not erase original sin, but that baptized Christians through repentance and faith in Christ merely have the guilt of original sin daily removed. This position was also held by St. Augustine (354–430), who taught, "Sin is remitted in Baptism, not in such a manner that it no longer exists, but so that it is not imputed."[11] Although the Christian is a saint through faith in Christ, original sin unfortunately remains with every Christian throughout his or her entire life.

One prominent reason why the Roman Church rejects the sinner-and-saint doctrine in Lutheran theology is that it runs counter to its practice of canonizing selected deceased individuals, a practice popes began in the tenth century. Ever since then, Rome only uses the word *saint* (spelled with a capital "S") for those who have been canonized. It does not use the word *saint* for Christians who are still alive, as St. Paul did in his epistles. For instance, to the Christians in Philippi he wrote, "All the saints greet you, especially those of Caesar's household" (Philippians 4:22).

CONCLUSION

The sinner-and-saint (*simul justus et peccator*) doctrine can only be understood by baptized Christians, informed by God's Word. It is in Baptism that Christians have received the promise of the forgiveness of sins (Acts 2:38; 22:16), and therefore, according to Luther, they are

God's saints. It is a doctrine that accents the gravity of sin, but it also accents the magnanimous grace of God's love in Jesus Christ. It is a doctrine that, on one hand, serves as an antidote to spiritual despair, and, on the other, nullifies any pretense of self-righteousness.

Finally, it is a doctrine that strongly underscores the doctrine of justification by faith in Christ alone. In the words of Luther, "A Christian man is righteous and a sinner at the same time, holy and profane, an enemy of God and a child of God. None of the sophists will admit this paradox because they do not understand the true meaning of justification."[12] This doctrine is a highly significant Gospel-oriented hallmark of Lutheran theology and identity.

> A Christian man is righteous and a sinner at the same time, holy and profane, an enemy of God and a child of God.

1. Who were some notable individuals in the Bible who were both sinners and saints?

2. How does the sinner-saint doctrine highlight the gravity of sin?

3. How does the sinner-saint doctrine highlight the grace of God?

4. Why does the sinner-saint doctrine not leave any room for self-righteousness?

5. Why did Christians in the Middle Ages not know they were both sinners and saints?

6. What does Roman Catholicism mean by concupiscence?

7. How does Lutheran theology differ from Roman Catholic theology in terms of the concept of concupiscence?

8. How does Lutheran theology differ from Catholic theology in regard to original sin?

9. How does the Augsburg Confession's definition of original sin in Article II (cited in this chapter) exclude Jesus Christ from having been born with original sin?

10. What relevance does the doctrine of sinner and saint have in regard to self-righteousness?

CHAPTER 13

LUTHERAN CHURCH

The Singing Church

"Music is well said to be the speech of angels."
—Thomas Carlyle (1795–1881)

When Martin Luther nailed his Ninety-Five Theses to the door of the Castle Church in Wittenberg on October 31, 1517, or when he stood accused before the emperor and princes at the Diet of Worms in 1521, he surely did not think that in a few short years he would introduce major changes in the church's music. Changes in church music began in 1524, when he not only wrote a number of hymns but also motivated others to write hymns that would laud and praise God for the free gift of salvation that was the hymn singers' by their faith in Jesus Christ.

Luther revealed his interest and talent in music when still a teenage student in Eisenach, where he participated in the boys' choir at St. George's Church and where people loved to hear him sing.[1] Much of his singing was Christ-centered, as is evident from his singing the words of Luke 23:46, words Jesus spoke on the cross, "Father into Your hands I commit My spirit." He sang these words "almost every day for much of his life."[2] He also liked to sing after an evening meal.[3] Given his love for music, "He never ceased to wonder at its profound effects on him as a performer and listener, and he was certain that the finest music he had heard in this life would be surpassed in the life to come."[4]

EARLY BURST OF LUTHERAN HYMNS

The first and oldest collection of Lutheran hymns was compiled and published in 1524, titled *Etlich Cristlich lider Lobgesang und Psalm* (A Few Christian Songs, Canticles, and Psalms). It contained eight songs, four of which were by Luther. This collection is also known as the *Achtliederbuch* (The Eight-Song-Book),[5] a publication of broadsheets rather than a bound book. Interestingly, its cover stated the hymns were based on "*dem rainen wort Gottes*" (the pure word of God). The claim that this publication is the first and oldest collection of Lutheran hymns has also been made by some for the *Erfurt Enchiridion*, published in 1524.

The year 1524 was an especially productive year for evangelical hymns by Luther and others.

Research reveals "more than two-thirds of Luther's hymns were written between the late fall of 1523 and summer of 1524."[6] The year 1524 was an especially productive year for evangelical hymns by Luther and others. It was in 1524 that Johann Walter (*Hofkapellmeister* from the court of Frederick the Wise), at Luther's request and encouragement, compiled *Eyn Geystlich Gesangk Buchleyn* (*A Booklet of Spiritual Songs*), also known as *Choralgesangbuch* (Choir Book).[7] It contained forty-three polyphonic hymns, twenty-four from Luther's quill. It went through many editions, adding new songs in German and Latin, and for years it served as a model for many Lutheran hymn collections.[8] Still more hymns appeared in another publication, the *Erfurt Enchiridion*, also published in 1524. It was a handbook of hymns printed by two different publishers at the same time; one contained twenty-six hymns and fifteen tunes, while the other had twenty-five. Each had eighteen hymns by Luther.

One year later, in 1525, Luther requested Johann Walter (sometimes spelled Walther) and Conrad Rupsch to help him prepare suitable music for his *Deutsche Messe* (German Mass), a work he completed one year later.[9] It was the German version of the Latin *Formula Missae*, Luther's 1523 revision of Rome's

Canon of the Mass that he made theologically compatible with the doctrine of justification by faith in Christ's atoning work.

These early musical contributions by Luther showed his interest and ability in incorporating Christ's redemptive message into music that Christians could sing in their native tongue during their church's Divine Services. His focus on producing church music far exceeded his love and talent for playing the lute in relaxed social settings, given that he also wrote and translated at least forty hymns in his ministerial career.[10]

Music: Living Voice of the Gospel (Viva Vox Evangelii)

Luther not only loved music and had many musically talented associates, but he also saw music as a gift from God that enhanced conveying the Gospel of Jesus Christ to people. He ranked music next to theology, saying, "except for theology there is no art that could be put on the same level with music, since [music] alone produces what otherwise only theology can do; namely, a calm and joyful disposition." And he further remarked, "The devil, the creator of saddening cares and disquieting worries, takes flight at the sound of music almost as he takes flight at the word of theology."[11] Luther wrote these words in 1530 to the court musician Ludwig Senfl, while holed up in the Coburg Castle during the Diet of Augsburg, which he for safety reasons was advised not to attend. Senfl was considered "one of the German masters of the sixteenth century polyphonic hymn and song."[12] He wrote two motets for Luther, even though he never formally left the Roman church.

Lutheran Chorales

Seeing music as the living voice of the Gospel prompted Luther to introduce the chorale in the mid-1520s. (The German word *choral* originally meant singing in unison and unaccompanied, as in the Gregorian chant). According to music professor and Bach scholar Robin A. Leaver, the chorale became "the defining feature of Lutheran church music [and] a fundamental development of the Lutheran Reformation of the sixteenth century."[13] It also became a hallmark of Lutheran identity. This was especially true in comparison to the notably different Reformed church services of Zwingli and Calvin. Lutheran theology considered chorales and church music as a divine, God-pleasing art, whereas Zwingli and Calvin did not.[14] "To the extent that music was a

Lutheran theology considered chorales and church music as a divine, God-pleasing art.

cultivated art," both contended, "it had no place in the church [and] to the extent it had a place in the church, it was to be 'uncultivated' and unlettered."[15] Thus, they clung to the Psalter as the only acceptable musical vehicle to praise God. They rejected the chorales which, as influential British musicologist Charles Terry says, "Consequently condemned their communities to musical infertility."[16] And in the words of American musicologist and critic Richard Taruskin, "Nowhere do the differences [between] the Reformed [and the Lutheran] churches show up more clearly than in their attitudes toward music."[17]

Early Lutheran chorales were sung like the Gregorian chants. Their "melodies were in fact developed from specific chants."[18] The church music of some chorales at this time "was essentially limited to vocal polyphony, Gregorian chant, and Latin and vernacular hymnody."[19] Gregorian music was impersonal and objective. It tried to present the Word rather than interpret it. Interpretation was largely subjective and personal and not desired. Similarly, the Lutheran chorales presented the objective Word of God in music. "Luther's hymns were not meant to create a mood, but to carry a message. They were a confession of faith, not of personal feelings."[20] This, of course, was Luther's intent, but it did not mean his hymns did not reveal any personal or emotional feelings. Indeed, they did. Martin Bertheau, in his book *400 Jahre Kirchenlied* (*400 Years Hymns*), says that some of Luther's hymns clearly reveal his emotional feelings. For instance, when "A Mighty Fortress Is Our God" is sung, one can sense (*spürt*) Luther's feelings in every stanza ("*in jedem Verse*").[21]

A mighty fortress is our God,
    A trusty shield and weapon;
He helps us free from ev'ry need
    That hath us now o'ertaken.
The old evil foe
Now means deadly woe;
    Deep guile and great might
    Are his dread arms in fight;
On earth is not his equal.

With might of ours can naught be done,
    Soon were our loss effected;
But for us fights the valiant One,
    Whom God Himself elected.
Ask ye, Who is this?
Jesus Christ it is,
    Of Sabaoth Lord,
    And there's none other God;
He holds the field forever.

Though devils all the world should fill,
    All eager to devour us,
We tremble not, we fear no ill;
    They shall not overpow'r us.
This world's prince may still
Scowl fierce as he will,
    He can harm us none.
    He's judged; the deed is done;
One little word can fell him.

The Word they still shall let remain
    Nor any thanks have for it;
He's by our side upon the plain
    With His good gifts and Spirit.
And take they our life,
Goods, fame, child, and wife,
    Though these all be gone,
    Our vict'ry has been won;
The Kingdom ours remaineth. (*LSB* 656)

Concerning the objective aspect of music in hymns, it is appropriate to note that in contrast to many Christians who today want "contemporary services" and their complementary songs, the chorales were not sung to please listeners by seeking to appeal to their emotions, as many contemporary service hymns do. Nor did they contain pious clichés, implying they are biblically derived. Regarding the latter, and as an example, one thinks of Robert Lowry's Gospel song "Shall We Gather at the River?" Responding to this subjective, nonbiblically based hymn, Lutherans, with the mindset of Luther, would say, "As Christians, we gather at the altar, not at an imaginary river." Thus, in contrast to "Shall We Gather at the River?" the Lutheran chorale "is the biblical Word itself, not its substitute; it is an essential part of the liturgy, not its appendage."[22]

Theodore Hoelty-Nickel, a defender of Lutheran chorales, has argued,

> The modern Gospel song [in contrast to chorales] is no more than the expression of a subjective, egocentric experience. Completely missing is a consciousness of the disparity between our ego and the level of the Godhead. We [Lutherans] must be unwilling to be restricted to egocentric expression.[23]

Hoelty-Nickel did not, however, want Christians to be passive listeners in Divine Services, without emotions, as though they were attending a concert. He continues, "From the role which the hymn has played in the Church's history it is perfectly clear that songs were never sung for the purpose of creating beauty but in order to express the emotions of the soul."[24] Luther's hymns, and those by many other Lutheran hymn composers and writers, such as Heinrich Schütz, Johann Crüger, Nicolaus Herman, Martin Rinckart, Johann Heermann, Paul Gerhardt, and Johann Sebastian Bach also operated with this theological understanding of church music, as shown below.

CONGREGATIONAL SINGING

When Luther introduced and promoted congregational singing in the 1520s, he really revived the singing of Christian laity that extended back at least to the fourth century in Milan, Italy. It was there in 386 that Bishop Ambrose (339?–97) had his Christians barricade themselves in the Portian basilica (located in the outskirts of Milan) to prevent the imperial army and the Arians from taking possession of the church. As the Christian laity barred the Arians from entering the church, Ambrose divided the Christians into two groups, having each group sing stanzas alternately, singing psalms and religious hymns. (Here we find the origin of antiphonal singing.) By having the laity sing, Ambrose ignored the ban on congregational singing that had already been decreed by the Council of Laodicea in 367. This council set the precedent that for centuries "church music was almost exclusively the province of the choir and clergy."[25] Thus, when in 1526 Luther in his *Deutsche Messe* (German Mass) specified "the whole congregation sings a German hymn,"[26] he desired to restore congregational singing that harked back not only to Ambrose but also to St. Paul, who had urged Christians in Colossae and Ephesus to sing psalms and hymns. Luther's advocacy took hold. By 1545, even outside of Wittenberg, "it had become customary to sing German hymns during the distribution of Communion, as Luther had requested it in the *Formula Missae*."[27]

Despite the noteworthy phenomenon of Lutheran congregational singing, Joseph Herl, a Lutheran music historian, has found it took some time for Lutheran congregational singing to become firmly established. "It was only in the eighteenth century, with the introduction of organ accompaniment and official congregational hymnals, that the song of the people came to resemble what is familiar to us today."[28] That said, it is not an exaggeration to say the singing of hymns by laity in congregations received its first impetus from Luther. After he had introduced the first German Mass in St. Mary's Church in Wittenberg on October 29, 1525, "he constructed a completely sung worship service that incorporated the congregation. The congregation sang an opening hymn, the Kyrie, a hymn between the readings, the Creed and hymns during the distribution of the

It is not an exaggeration to say the singing of hymns by laity in congregations received its first impetus from Luther.

Lord's Supper."[29] The German Mass was published in 1526. And with its publication, congregational singing became a hallmark of Lutheran theology and identity.

Given that today's Christians in most denominations take congregational singing for granted, it is fitting to call Luther the "Ambrose of the Reformation." And it is also fitting to note that Luther's most well-known hymn, "A Mighty Fortress Is Our God," a hallmark of Lutheran identity, is now widely sung across the denominational spectrum.

Biblically speaking, Lutheran theology teaches there are two facets present in a congregation's Divine Service: one is sacramental and the other is sacrificial. In the sacramental part, God is serving His people by declaring what He has done for them in the suffering, death, and resurrection of His Son, Jesus Christ. This includes reading the Scriptures (an Old Testament, an Epistle, and a Gospel reading), pronouncing the Absolution, administrating the Lord's Supper, preaching the sermon, and pronouncing the Benediction. The sacrificial parts of the service include speaking the Invocation; participating in Corporate Confession; singing the Kyrie, Gloria Patri, Gloria in Excelsis, and Nunc Dimittis; confessing the creed; praising; praying; and giving thanks. Thus, when Lutheran congregations sing chorales, they are not passive but active, a vital part of the "living voice of the Gospel."

The sacramental activities are why Lutherans prefer to say "Divine Service" rather than "worship service." The term "Divine Service" accents what God does as He serves His people with His Word and Sacrament, whereas "worship service" puts the emphasis on the human activities. In the English dictionary, the word *worship* only refers to what humans do for some deity or God. Thus, the sacramental role of God in the service is absent.

It is also not in accord with confessional Lutheran theology for pastors, unlike Reformed clergy, to say, when they mention the number of people who attend church on Sunday mornings, "We worship about 200 people most Sundays." Similarly, Lutheran pastors do well not to say to their parishioners that given information is in their "worship bulletin." And finally, Lutheran pastors also do well not to use the expression "Call to Worship," commonly heard in many Reformed and Evangelical churches. It clashes with Lutheran theology, but this expression can be seen in some Lutheran church bulletins today.

The hymns written in Wittenberg in the 1520s, meant to be sung by the congregation, were known as *Katechismuslieder* (catechism hymns). These hymns did not accent "Christian experience," which as a twenty-first-century phenomenon, according to Robin Leaver, contain "almost nothing about the essential catechesis of hymnody."[30] On the other hand, catechetical hymns accented the biblical doctrine that by God's grace Christians are justified by faith in Christ's redemptive work. A prominent example of a catechetical hymn is Luther's *"Aus tiefer Not schrei ich zu dir"* ("From Depths of Woe I Cry to Thee"), penned in 1523. Another hymn of this kind is Luther's 1524 *"Wir glauben All an einen Gott"* ("We All Believe in One True God").

Richard Taruskin, in *The Oxford History of Western Music*, says, "The effects of the Reformation were felt very keenly in the musical sphere."[31] Indeed, even Roman Catholics, who had confined singing in church to choirs and clergy, felt these effects of the Reformation. Reflecting Rome's negative view of congregational singing by the laity, Adam Conzenius (a Jesuit) in 1620 scathingly declared, "Luther has damned more people with his hymns than with his writings and sermons" (*"Hymni Lutheri animas plures quam scripta et declamationes occiderunt"*).[32] This remark came a hundred years after Luther had written his first hymns in the 1520s for Christian laity to sing in church. Conzenius, like many other Catholics, did not think kindly of the Lutheran Church being "the singing church." Rome disliked congregational singing because its *cantus firmus* (fixed song) was the chanting of its clergy choir, but now in the Lutheran Church, the *cantus firmus* was the singing of chorales by the congregation.

In the words of Luther D. Reed, American Lutheran hymnist and theologian, it was Martin Luther who "taught the German nation to sing in church."[33] To Catholics, this was a drastic, unwelcome change, and a pronounced dislike of this prominent Lutheran hallmark.

CHURCH MUSIC: THE CENTURY AFTER LUTHER

As already indicated, laity singing chorales in church largely began with Luther's *Deutsche Messe* (German Mass), and it continued into the seventeenth century, the century after Luther. It was a century that provided Lutheran churches with exceptionally talented hymnwriters and composers who gave prominence to people singing the Word of grace to one another, along with personal, emotional effects fostered by their compositions. For want of space in this chapter, I discuss only a few of those highly talented musicians and their salutary contributions.

NICOLAUS HERMAN (CA. 1480–1561)

A resident of Joachimsthal, a silver-mining town in Bohemia just over the mountains of Saxony, Nicolaus Herman was a talented teacher and a writer of German hymns who also set his own tunes. He embraced Lutheran theology early in the Reformation and corresponded with Luther. In 1525, he introduced Luther's hymns in his town's schools and church, first using Johann Walter's 1524 *Geystliche Gesangbüchlein* ("Sacred Hymnbook") music.[34] Under Herman's leadership,

> Lutheran music also found a central place in each of the most important pedagogical institutions of Joachimsthal: the church, the schools, and above all the home. In each of these spheres, Lutheran music was intended to inculcate Lutheran doctrine and to equip the laity at every level of society with a knowledge of Scripture sufficient to allow them to minister to their own religious needs.[35]

According to Christopher Boyd Brown, the German Lutheran hymns, including some of Herman's own, became part of the town's lay culture.[36] And people also sang his Christ-centered hymns in their homes "with an alacrity that surprised even their pastors."[37] Being the staunch Lutheran that he was, Herman successfully used Lutheran hymns to counter Catholic teachings. One example being that departed saints do not make intercession for people with God, for that role belongs solely to Christ.

Lutheran music with its doctrinal accents in Joachimsthal produced stalwart Lutherans, in spite of the Catholic opposition that had made its presence in this mining town in the 1530s. But it became more

Herman successfully used Lutheran hymns to counter Catholic teachings.

intense as time wore on, especially in the 1650s, when Rome's Counter-Reformation expurgated many Lutheran hymns and forced other Catholic practices on the people in this devoted Lutheran town. And in 1662, Lutherans "emigrated *en masse* to Saxony,"[38] a distance of approximately eighty kilometers to the northwest.

Herman's Lutheran hymns were primarily written for students, both boys and girls, to sing in school to supplant profane songs. Many of his hymns soon became a part of Sunday church services. He also wrote hymns for housefathers and housemothers in Joachimsthal, and even for miners working in the silver mines.[39] Herman's use of Lutheran hymns, including his own, greatly contributed to the Lutheran Church as a singing church that sang the Gospel. Thus, not surprisingly, a century after his death, this influential, talented, Lutheran musician, schoolmaster, and layman was honored by Johann Sebastian Bach, who used three of his hymns in his cantatas.

Philipp Nicolai (1556–1608)

Philipp Nicolai was born in Mengeringhausen, a small village in Germany's federal state of Hesse. Early in his adult life, Nicolai became a Lutheran pastor and was soon revered as a gifted preacher, resulting in his being called the "Second Chrysostom" in honor of the eloquent Greek Church Father John of Antioch (d. 407), known as *Chrysostomos* ("golden mouth" in Greek). But Nicolai was also a highly talented musician. He titled his first hymn "Wake, Awake, for Night Is Flying," and unlike many other hymnwriters, he also composed this hymn's tune. His second hymn was "O Morning Star, How Fair and Bright." The first hymn is sometimes called "King of Chorales" and the second as "Queen of Chorales."

Some music critics contend that Lutheran hymns in the sixteenth century, especially after the publication of the Formula of Concord in 1580, stressed the objective, doctrinal aspects of Christian theology but ignored the subjective and devotional needs for Christian living. But Nicolai's hymns, written after 1580, do not fit this criticism, for they clearly provide subjective consolation to Christians in times of suffering and distress. In 1597, when a plague killed thirteen hundred of his parishioners, he penned several meditations titled *"Freudenspiegel des ewigen Lebens"* ("The Mirror of Joyful Life in Eternity"), and to these he appended the two hymns just cited above.[40]

HEINRICH SCHÜTZ (1585–1672)

Music historians consider Schütz to have been the most important composer before Johann Sebastian Bach. He composed motets, concertos, and oratorios in German—one of the latter is his Easter oratorio, "Resurrection History" (1623). He also wrote Passions that were performed *a cappella*. He spent most of his musical career in the court of the Elector of Saxony in Dresden. Modern-day Lutherans commemorate him and his many contributions on July 28.

> Music historians consider Schütz to have been the most important composer before Johann Sebastian Bach.

Compared to many Reformation-era hymnwriters in the sixteenth century, Schütz, as a composer, "preferred to illustrate text segments, to express emotions, and to interpret."[41] This personal or emotional element (often referred to as "mystical") had also received some expression in some of Luther's hymns, as noted below. But for the most part, the music of Schütz accented personal or emotional qualities, as did the hymns of Martin Rinckart, Johann Heermann, and Paul Gerhardt, and also many of Bach's chorales.[42]

JOHANN CRÜGER (1598–1662)

This highly talented musician was born in Gross-Breesen, near Guben in Brandenburg, close to the Polish border. He first studied theology at Wittenberg but left early to pursue his musical talents when in 1622 he was called as cantor to St. Nicholas Church in Berlin, where he remained active glorifying God with music until his death in 1662. He was not a poet, and thus he wrote no lyrics for hymns. Instead, he composed melodies for those who wrote poetry so Christians could sing the lyrics of their poems. In all, he composed seventy-one edifying chorale melodies.[43] The following are only a few examples: "O Lord, How Shall I Meet You"; "All My Heart Rejoices"; "Now Thank We All Our God." The tune of the latter hymn provides ample proof why he became known as "*der Melodienschöpfer*" (the melody creator).

In 1644, Crüger published *Praxis pietatis melica* (*Practice of Piety in Song*), a hymnal widely used in the seventeenth century that later went through many editions. In his long tenure at St. Nicholas, Crüger also set music to some sacred poems by Martin Rinckart, Johann Heermann, and Paul Gerhardt. Some of these tunes became widely known, bestowing great honor on these three highly talented, devout Lutherans for their sacred poems, many of which became hymns sung in Lutheran churches.

MARTIN RINCKART (1586–1649)

Born in Leipzig and educated in Lutheran theology at the University of Leipzig, Rinckart became Arch *diaconus* (pastor) at St. Nicholas Church in Eilenburg in 1617. This was on the eve of the Thirty Years' War, which erupted the following year. Along with his devout theological convictions and strong pastoral orientation, he was also a highly talented musician and a prolific writer. Many of his hymns, however, are no longer extant.

Rinckart's hymn "Now Thank We All Our God," initially written as a table prayer, was set to music by Johann Crüger in about 1647, roughly ten years after it was written. Its precise date of origin is not known, but it seems fairly certain that he wrote it during the horrors and tragedies of the war that struck Eilenburg in the mid- to the latter-1630s. It was a time when many were tempted to curse God rather than thank Him, given that the town was ravaged three times by invading soldiers. In addition to the brutality of the war, the town was stricken by famines and pestilences, resulting in the death of some eight thousand individuals, many of whom were strangers and refugees who sought shelter in this walled community. There were times Rinckart found it difficult to find food for his family. And after he was left as the only pastor, he sometimes buried forty to fifty bodies a day. In two years, he had buried nearly five thousand, one of whom was his wife, who died in 1637, and at whose funeral he preached.[44]

Historians have often noted Rinckart's majestic hymn is based on Sirach 50:22–23 (an Old Testament apocryphal book). This, however, is only true for the first two stanzas, for the third stanza is really based on the ancient Gloria Patri. This remarkable hymn has been called the Lutheran *Te Deum*. Bach included it in some of his cantatas. It has been sung, and continues to be sung, at weddings, at national festivals, on special occasions, on Thanksgiving Day, and at dedications—for example, when Germany dedicated its beautiful Cologne Cathedral in 1880. But even earlier, during the Seven Years' War (1756–63), after the successful Battle of Leuthen on December 5, 1757, an unknown Prussian soldier, standing near Frederick the Great (the commander), began singing "Now Thank We All Our God," and soon 25,000 soldiers joined in the singing.[45] Since then, many Germans call this hymn "*das Leuthen Choral.*"

JOHANN HEERMANN (1585–1647)

He was born in Germany's province of Silesia, which in the 1630s became a war-torn territory of the Thirty Years' War. Before this treacherous war, Heermann, a gifted poet, had been crowned poet laureate in 1608 for his Latin poetry.[46] His poems were mostly sacred renditions based on the Gospels. In 1611, he became the Lutheran pastor in Köben, Silesia (now in Poland), on the banks of the Oder River. In 1616, a fire swept through the town; the next year his wife died. In 1618, the Thirty Years' War began. In 1623, ill health struck him and severely infected his nose and throat, making breathing difficult, an ailment from which he never really recovered. Between 1629 and 1634, Catholic troops sacked the town four times, resulting in his losing all his movable possessions—twice he had to flee for safety and once he hid for seventeen weeks as a fugitive. Yet, despite his many afflictions, he wrote numerous sacred poems (hymns). In the midst of the war's painful tragedies, one of his best-known hymns, "O God, Thou Faithful God" (*O Gott, du frommer Gott*) was included in his 1630 publication *Music for a Devout Heart* (*Devoti Musica Cordi*).[47] In 1634, his preaching days came to an end because of his failing health. Following his physician's advice, he moved in 1638 to Leszno, Poland, where he died in 1647. Given his numerous misfortunes and afflictions, German Christians call him "*der schlesische Hiob*" (the Silesian Job).

Some music historians say Heermann's hymns mark the transition from the more objective hymns of the Reformation in the sixteenth century to the more personal, experiential aspects of a Christian's relationship with God. His hymns convey the Christian's submission to God's will and compassion. This emphasis, says Friedrich Blume, a German music historian and critic, argues that Heermann's hymns leaned toward Pietism.[48] This is not, however, an entirely correct assessment, for it ignores that Luther's hymns, as indicated earlier, are not really devoid of the subjective, personal relationship between Christian hymn singers and God. Heermann's hymns were not the first to include the personal element in Lutheran hymns. Moreover, given that Heermann's hymns accent personal, faith-focused expressions does not make them Pietistic, at least not according to what Pietism became in the latter half of the seventeenth century when it promoted and practiced Philipp Spener's more radical teachings espoused in his book *Pia Desideria* (*Pious Desires*, 1675). For it was Spener's teachings that largely made Pietism a protest movement within the Lutheran Church, in contrast to the earlier, milder teachings of Johann Arndt (1555–1621), espoused in his work *Four Books of True Christianity*.

That Arndt's teachings influenced Heermann's hymns and sacred poems cannot be denied, for he was well acquainted with his writings. He was also influenced by reading the devotional books of Martin Moller (1547–1606), a Lutheran pastor and a contemporary of Arndt, who also advocated greater personal piety among Lutherans.[49]

As an aside, it is interesting to note that Arndt also influenced Johann Gerhard (1582–1637), the renowned Lutheran dogmatician. When Gerhard was gravely ill at age fifteen, Arndt, his pastor, ministered to him. Then, eight years later in 1605, Arndt published his *First Book of True Christianity* (*Erstes Buch vom wahren Christentum*),[50] a book that encouraged Lutherans to live pious, devotional lives. One year later, in 1606, Gerhard published his own devotional manual, *Sacred Meditations* (*Meditationes Sacrae*). It reflected accents similar to Arndt's book. But neither Heermann nor Gerhard can rightly be considered seasoned Pietists because they taught Christians to live sanctified lives and to find personal consolation in Christ's suffering pertaining to their personal experiences.

PAUL GERHARDT (1607–76)

Music historians rank Johann Heermann and Paul Gerhardt as the two most renowned Lutheran musicians of the seventeenth century; many rank Gerhardt first of the two. Gerhardt was born in Gräfenhainichen, a small village near and south of Wittenberg. After the death of his parents, he attended secondary school in Grimma, where Lutheran theology, Latin, and music were emphasized. In 1628, he enrolled at Wittenberg's university, "where he developed his poetic skills, most likely under August Buchner (1591–1661), and his use of hymnody as a tool for religious instruction and pastoral care under Paul Röber (1587–1651)."[51] He remained in Wittenberg until the early 1640s, for in 1641 his name appears as godfather on a baptismal record in the town's

St. Mary's Church,[52] the church Luther and his family attended one hundred years earlier.

Before he moved to Berlin in the early 1640s, he had lived through the horrors of the Thirty Years' War, an experience that greatly influenced his poetry (hymn) writing, in addition to the influence that Johann Arndt ("the Father of Pietism") left on him. For as Elke Axmacher has argued, "Paul Gerhardt's work cannot be understood apart from Johann Arndt."[53]

Upon graduating from the University of Wittenberg, he served as a private tutor in the home of Berlin's Chancellor-Advocate, Andreas Barthold, whose daughter he later married.[54] And it was in Berlin that he came to the attention of Johann Crüger, the cantor, organist, and composer at St. Nicholas Church there, resulting in Crüger's adding eighteen of Gerhardt's hymns to Crüger's hymnal *Practice of Piety in Song* (*Praxis pietatis melica*) in the 1647 edition.[55] It has been noted that had Crüger not discovered Gerhardt and his superb talent for writing sacred poems that beckoned to be set to music, the world would likely never have heard of him, much less have experienced the joy of singing his spiritually edifying hymns.

Some years after arriving in Berlin, Gerhardt finally attained a permanent position in 1651, at the age of forty-four, when he became *diaconus* (pastor) in Mittenwalde, a small town near Berlin. It was in this rural parish, where he served as a faithful pastor, that he wrote most of his hymns.[56] Then in 1657, he received a call to become assistant pastor at St. Nicholas Church in Berlin, where he enjoyed nine years of trouble-free service that sadly ended in 1666 when the Elector of Brandenburg and Duke of Prussia, Friedrich Wilhelm (a staunch Calvinist), deposed him from his pastorate for not accepting his edict that forbade Lutherans from preaching or teaching against Calvinistic (Reformed) teachings. The elector's goal was to get Lutherans, who vastly outnumbered the Reformed, to unite with them theologically. Although Gerhardt was a mild-mannered individual, he could not in good conscience accept this royal edict. He felt if he conformed to the elector's edict, he would be violating his ordination vow to teach and preach in conformity with the Formula of Concord.

The next two years, he and his family were essentially wandering exiles. It was also during this time that his wife and son died, adding to his sorrow of having lost three children earlier. In all, he experienced a rather sorrow-ridden life, but his faith in Christ never faltered, for during this time he even wrote the hymn "Commit Thou All Thy Griefs."

In 1668, he received a call to a church in Lubben, outside the Prussian elector's boundaries. Here he could, as arch deacon, once again preach freely until he died in 1676, leaving behind a legacy of 139 German hymns and devotional poems. Many of his well-known hymns—for example, "O Sacred Head, Now Wounded," "Now Rest beneath Night's Shadow," "Why Should Cross and Trial Grieve Me"—are sung by Lutherans and many other Christians to the present day. As Frank Senn has correctly stated, "With Gerhardt we reach the high point of classical Lutheran hymnody."[57]

JOHANN SEBASTIAN BACH (1685–1750)

A century and a half after Luther's death, Johann Sebastian Bach was born in Eisenach, Saxony, into an already well-known musical family. For some time, especially since Felix Mendelssohn (1809–47), Bach has been recognized as one of the most gifted musicians the world has ever known. He has been called the "'composer's composer,' whose analytical mind, belief in God, and melodic genius led him to create some of the greatest religious music we have."[58] He also has been referred to as "the Fifth Evangelist."

Unlike Heermann and Gerhardt, known for their hymns and sacred poems, Bach's musical contributions added to the Lutheran Church's reputation as the singing church by his many settings of chorales and other musical compositions, all of which reflected his strong theological convictions. Throughout his life, he faithfully read and studied the Bible, along with other Christian writings. At his death, his private library contained "some eighty books, Luther and Lutheran pillars of the seventeenth and eighteenth centuries."[59]

His Lutheran convictions are evident in his oratorios, such as the St. Matthew Passion and the St. John

Bach has been recognized as one of the most gifted musicians the world has ever known.

Passion and in the titles of some cantatas. For instance, "Christ Lay in Death's Bands" (*Christ lag in Todesbanden*); "Lord Jesus Christ True Man and God" (*Herr Jesus Christ, wahr' Mensch und Gott*); "He Who Believes and Is Baptized" (*Wer da glaubet und getauft wird*). His composition "Before Thy Throne I Appear" (*Vor deinen Thron tret' ich hiermit*) was his last, and reportedly, he was virtually blind and his hands paralyzed when he dictated it one week before he died.[60]

Before writing a musical composition (as noted in chapter 1), Bach often wrote the initials "J. J." (*Jesu Juva*: Help Me Jesus) or "I. N. J." (*In nomine Jesu*: In the Name of Jesus). At the end of each composition, he would write "S. D. G." (*Soli Deo Gloria*: To God Alone All Glory). American composer and conductor Patrick Kavanaugh says, "To Bach these [notations] were not trite religious slogans but sincere expressions of personal devotion."[61] He composed chorales, preludes to chorales, chamber sonatas, concertos, oratorios, toccatas, music for orchestras, fugues, and numerous cantatas. The majority of his cantatas (two hundred plus) were sacred compositions; only a minority were secular.[62] His church cantatas were spiritually reflective rather than dramatic, as in opera. They were largely musical sermons that reinforced the pastor's preaching in church. In Leipzig, Bach performed cantatas in the main Divine Service (*Hauptgottesdienst*). Some cantatas "were divided into halves, with the first half performed before the main sermon and second half after it (or sometimes during the communion)."[63] Bach's *Christmas Oratorio* consisted of six cantatas.[64] His cantatas in Leipzig were usually performed in two of the city's five churches: St. Thomas and St. Nicholas.[65]

Musicians have assigned some of Bach's tunes and settings to some Lutheran hymns, thus further adding to his contribution to the Lutheran Church as "the singing church." Some of these hymn tunes and settings are still found in Lutheran hymnals of today. His contributions include incorporating into his sacred cantatas some hymns by Johann Heermann, Paul Gerhardt, and some other noteworthy Lutheran hymnwriters. His contributions are also found in his St. Matthew Passion, where he incorporated some stanzas from Heermann's hymns—for instance, "Ah, Holy Jesus How Hast Thou Offended"—and also in his Matthew Passion he incorporated some stanzas from Gerhardt's hymn "O Sacred Head, Now Wounded." Similarly, in his St. John Passion, he incorporated some stanzas from some hymns by Heermann and Gerhardt. In light of these musical contributions, the assessment of

Robin A. Leaver comes to mind, "Bach represents the high point of the Lutheran tradition of church music."[66]

CONCLUSION

This chapter focused on some of the more prominent Lutheran musicians. Numerous others could have been cited, for to a large degree, the Lutheran Church became "the singing church," beginning with Luther. God blessed this church with so many talented musicians who not only left their imprint on the Lutheran Church but also through their musical contributions enriched the musical life of Christians in many non-Lutheran churches. In summary, the musicians noted in this chapter, along with their many Christ-centered hymns, can without exaggeration be rightly credited as major contributors to the Lutheran Church's reputation as the singing church, a noteworthy hallmark of Lutheran theology and identity.

CHAPTER 13 DISCUSSION QUESTIONS

1. Luther was musically talented. Do you think God perhaps gave him this talent so he could use music as a means of voicing the Gospel of Jesus Christ? Why or why not?

2. Why do Lutheran hymnwriters so consistently pen hymns that include the Gospel?

3. What was the original meaning and nature of the word *choral* (chorale)?

4. What is meant by what Lutherans call "objective" versus "subjective" nature of hymns?

5. When Luther introduced congregational singing by the laity, how did this differ from the singing that commonly took place in church services previously?

6. How did Luther's theology motivate him to have the laity, not just choirs, sing hymns in church?

7. Lutheran theology commonly distinguishes between "Divine Service" and "worship service." Explain the difference.

8. Why did prominent Roman Catholics in Luther's day not take kindly to Lutheran laity singing in church?

9. What specific label did the Catholics use to show their disgust with Lutheran laity singing?

10. Have you, as a Lutheran, ever thought that congregational singing is a hallmark of Lutheran theology and identity? Why or why not?

11. Most Lutheran hymns teach specific doctrines; for example, Law and Gospel. Do you think most Lutherans perceive this when they sing hymns in church? Why or why not?

12. When you sing a given hymn in church, do you think it would be spiritually beneficial if you were to look at the small print on the hymn's page to see who wrote the text and tune and wonder what motivated the hymnist to write the hymn? Why or why not?

13. The present chapter discusses a number of prominent Lutheran hymnwriters. Do you think it would be spiritually beneficial to Lutherans in the pews to have their pastor in his sermons sometimes give a brief spiritual biography of these Lutheran hymnists? Explain.

14. Many Lutherans know that Martin Luther wrote "A Mighty Fortress Is Our God." Do you think it would be good if more of us also knew and remembered who, for instance, penned some of the following well-known hymns? Why or why not?
    "O God, Thou Faithful God"
    "Now Thank We All Our God"
    "Now Rest beneath Night's Shadow"
    "O Sacred Head, Now Wounded"

15. Cite some evidence why Johann Sebastian Bach has been called "the Fifth Evangelist."

CHAPTER 14

THE DIVINE LITURGY TEACHES THE FAITH

*"The music of the church, if it is to serve its right function,
must be inspired by the church's liturgy."*
—J. F. Ohl (1850–1941)

The Lutheran Church, along with the Roman Catholic, Episcopalian (Anglican), and Eastern Orthodox churches, is known as a liturgical church. Its orders of Divine Service have commonly included historic liturgical components, some dating back to the early centuries of the Christian Church. This ancient heritage was one reason why Luther "prized the historical dimension of the liturgy [because it] preserved the continuity with the faithful of all ages."[1] For instance, the Sanctus was already part of the Christian Church's Divine Service as early as AD 96, as shown in *I Clement* 34, a letter written by Clement of Rome (d. AD 99) to the Christians in Corinth.[2]

Although the Lutheran Church is a liturgical church, many Lutherans seem to know very little about the traditional liturgy or why their church uses it, especially when they compare it to the many non-Lutheran Protestant churches who largely abandoned the liturgy at the time of the Reformation. Those churches thought the liturgy was "too Catholic." But Luther, a conservative reformer, continued to use the liturgy. In 1526, he revised and translated the Latin Mass into German, known as *Deutsche Messe*, making some doctrinal corrections in it.

Liturgy Defined

The term *liturgy* is derived from the Greek word *leitourgia*. The first half of the Greek word, *leitos*, refers to people or the public; the word's latter half, *ergon*, means work. In some instances, *leitourgia* among the ancient Greeks referred to work *of* or *by* the people. But some ancient Greek literature also uses the term *leitourgia* to refer to work done *for* the people; for example, the legislative work that citizen assemblies did for the populace in ancient Athens. Some Greek literature also uses *leitourgia* in terms of service that slaves provided for their masters and the service rendered by a father to his sons.[3]

Writing to the Christians in Rome, St. Paul called himself "a minister [*leitourgos*] of Christ Jesus to the Gentiles" (Romans 15:16). Here the emphasis is on what he did *for* the people as their servant. On another occasion, regarding a collection taken for the poor in Jerusalem, Paul said the collection was a service (*leitourgias*) for the people (2 Corinthians 9:12–13). In Hebrews 8:1–6, Christ is called a *leitourgos*, a minister or servant who performs priestly work *for* Christians. This is similar to the position of the Lutheran Church's Apology of the Augsburg Confession, which says, "The term *leitourgia* agrees well with the ministry" (Ap XXIV [XII] 81). And according to Lutheran liturgical scholar Frank C. Senn,

> In Hebrews 8:1–6, Christ is called a *leitourgos*, a minister or servant who performs priestly work for Christians.

> The fundamental meaning of liturgy is that it is the public work of the church in which the gospel of Jesus Christ is publicly proclaimed; adoration, praise, and thanksgiving are offered to God the Father along with petitions and supplications for the life of the world; and the Lord's Supper is celebrated in anticipation of the banquet of the kingdom of God.[4]

Contrary to what some Christians say who do not understand or like the liturgy and prefer what is today often called "contemporary services," the Church's liturgy is not an antiquated ritual that no longer has any meaning or relevance. Nor does the liturgy refer to "a collective term for everything that is not important in a service."[5] To Lutherans who believe Christ's body and blood are supernaturally present in the Lord's Supper, the traditional components of the liturgy are highly relevant and are not to be minimized or abandoned. For to minimize or ignore the liturgy is to minimize or ignore the Lord's Supper, as Hermann Sasse has noted: "It is out of the Lord's Supper that the liturgy grew."[6]

When the Lord's Supper is administered apart from the historic liturgy, as often happens in many contemporary services, it becomes a mere appendix, at best an isolated event, for these services usually no longer contain the complementary liturgical parts such as the Gloria Patri, Gloria in Excelsis, Sanctus, Agnus Dei, Nunc Dimittis, and Pax Domini, many of which date back to the earliest centuries of the Church.

Contemporary services, commonly devoid of the liturgy's historical components, have made inroads into many Lutheran churches apparently because many pastors and parishioners do not understand the liturgy's theological role and function. This is evident when the question is sometimes asked negatively, "What is the liturgy?"

In this context, the words of renowned Lutheran scholar Kurt Marquart are helpful and relevant. He explains the liturgy "is much more than forms and ceremonies, which are in themselves indifferent. It is first and foremost a firm theological content; namely, the holy Gospel and sacraments of God."[7] And it is also important to note that most of the traditional liturgy's content is drawn from Scripture; in numerous instances, verses from Scripture are quoted and sung verbatim. Briefly stated, the historic liturgy proclaims the Gospel, and thus it teaches the faith.

The historic liturgy proclaims the Gospel, and thus it teaches the faith.

Liturgical Components

While there have been different liturgies in the Christian Church over the span of time, historically the main liturgy has usually included most of the following components, though not always in the same order. Traditionally, already at the time of the Lutheran Reformation, the components usually consisted of the Invocation, Introit, Gloria Patri, Kyrie, Gloria in Excelsis, Salutation, Collect, Epistle Reading, Gradual and Alleluia, Gospel Reading, *Credo* (the Creed), Sermon, Lord's Prayer, Sanctus, Preface, Proper Preface, Words of Institution, Agnus Dei, Distribution of the Elements, Pax Domini, General Prayer, and Benediction. Some of these components comprised part of Luther's *Deutsche Messe* of 1526. Many of these liturgical components became parts of liturgies in different geographic areas. One such example was the liturgy of the Lutheran Church in Amsterdam, which later became the liturgy of St. Mary's of Savoy (a German Lutheran chapel in London) in 1694.[8] In 1748, this liturgy was largely adopted by German Lutherans in the Pennsylvania Ministerium, led by Henry Melchior Muhlenberg.[9] It appeared only as an outline in handwritten form; "it was never printed."[10] Some incomplete and varying copies have been found.

Trinitarian Invocation

The trinitarian Invocation, "In the name of the Father and of the Son and of the Holy Spirit," is derived from Matthew 28:19, where Christ commands these words as the formula for Baptism. The Invocation, as renowned Lutheran liturgical scholar Luther D. Reed (1873–1972) says, "is addressed to God and not to the congregation."[11] And as Lutheran music professor James Brauer notes, when we hear the Invocation, "we are reminded of our becoming Christians, of receiving new birth and of the renewal of the Holy Spirit."[12]

Historically, when the Invocation was spoken, it was accompanied by making the sign of the cross.[13] Given that the Invocation is directed to God, the pastor faces the altar. In liturgical decorum, facing the altar symbolizes the pastor is speaking to God on behalf of the congregation. And when the pastor faces the congregation, it symbolizes God is speaking to the people.

The symbolism of the pastor's role at the altar, facing it and then facing the congregation, has important spiritual value. It distinguishes the pastor's activities from, say, those of a theatrical stage performer.

The pastor and the congregation during the Divine Service in the church are, as the prophet Habakkuk said, in the Lord's "holy temple" (Habakkuk 2:20). If Lutherans remember and internalize the meaning of this liturgical symbolism, attending Divine Services on Sundays will be a different experience than attending a church service where there is no altar, no cross, and no trinitarian Invocation.

CONFESSION OF SINS

To be a Christian is to confess one's sins and sinfulness. King David said, "I will confess my transgressions to the LORD" (Psalm 32:5). The apostle John told Christians of his day, "If we say we have no sin, we deceive ourselves, and the truth is not in us. If we confess our sins, He is faithful and just to forgive us our sins and to cleanse us from all unrighteousness" (1 John 1:8–9). Following this biblical advice, the early Christians told one another when they assembled on Sunday, "On the Lord's own day, when you come together, break bread and have the Eucharist after confessing your transgressions" (Didache 14).[14] This reference in the Didache, an early Christian manual (written about AD 100), shows confession of sins was one of the Early Church's first activities in a Divine Service. This practice has been followed rather faithfully by Lutherans when they (in their Divine Services) publicly confess their sins, usually right after the Invocation is spoken.

The Confession of Sins must always reflect a true, penitent heart, for it is not a confession when one is not penitent. That is why a Lutheran pastor from the altar faces the congregation and, for example, says, "Beloved in the Lord! Let us draw near with a true heart and confess our sins unto God our Father, beseeching Him in the name of our Lord Jesus Christ to grant us forgiveness." Following these words, the pastor turns to face the altar and says, "Our help is in the name of the Lord," to which the congregation

The Confession of Sins must always reflect a true, penitent heart.

responds, "who made heaven and earth." The pastor further states, "I said, I will confess my transgressions unto the Lord," and the congregation adds, "and You forgave the iniquity of my sin."[15]

In this format, the pastor implores God, saying, "O almighty God, merciful Father." Following this phrase, each parishioner audibly confesses:

> I, a poor, miserable sinner, confess unto you all my sins and iniquities with which I have ever offended you and justly deserved your temporal and eternal punishment. But I am heartily sorry for them and sincerely repent of them, and I pray You of Your boundless mercy and for the sake of the holy, innocent, bitter sufferings and death of Your beloved Son, Jesus Christ, to be gracious and merciful to me, a poor, sinful being.[16]

As noted in the Introduction, the phrases "I, a poor, sinful being" and "We are by nature sinful and unclean" are distinctively Lutheran, found only in Lutheran liturgies.[17] The British Book of Common Prayer has a more ameliorated confession: "There is no health in us." Thus, this Lutheran confession is a hallmark of Lutheran theology and identity.

THE ABSOLUTION

Immediately following the congregation confessing its sins, many Lutheran pastors use one of two formats to announce forgiveness. One is the Authoritative Absolution. In this format, the pastor, after the public confession of sins, says, "Upon this your confession, I, by virtue of my office, as a called and ordained servant of the Word, announce the grace of God unto all of you, and in the stead and by the command of my Lord Jesus Christ I forgive you all your sins in the name of the Father and of the Son and of the Holy Spirit. Amen."[18]

The other format is known as the General Absolution. Some see this format as "less Catholic." The following is an example spoken by the pastor after the congregation's confession. "Almighty God, our heavenly Father, has had mercy upon us and has given His only Son to die for us and for His sake forgives us all our sins. To those who believe on His name He gives power to become the children of God and has promised them His Holy Spirit. He that believes and is baptized shall be saved. Grant this, Lord, unto us all."[19] It is a less-personalized absolution.

HALLMARKS OF LUTHERAN IDENTITY

The General Absolution came to be a part of the church's liturgy "from the ninth to the fourteenth centuries."[20] The Authoritative Absolution appeared between "the tenth and eleventh centuries."[21]

And in regard to Confession and Absolution in the liturgy, Peter Brunner (1900–81), Lutheran professor at Heidelberg University in Germany, advised Lutherans that "under no circumstances should the confession of sins by the entire congregation and the resultant comforting promise of forgiveness be omitted."[22]

The Authoritative Absolution is found in Luther's revised order of confession in the 1531 edition of his Small Catechism. It reads, "I, by the command of Jesus Christ our Lord, forgive thee all thy sin in the name of the Father and of the Son and of the Holy Ghost. Amen. Go in peace."[23] And in Germany in 1570, a Lutheran church order, the *Kurländische Kirchenordnung*, also has the pastor pronounce the Authoritative Absolution. "Upon your belief and confession, in accordance with the command of our Lord Jesus Christ, I forgive and absolve you of all your sins, in the name of the Father, the Son, and the Holy Spirit. Amen."[24]

As noted above, the first Lutheran liturgy in the United States appeared in German in 1748 in the Pennsylvania Ministerium's *Kirchenagende (Church Agenda)*. It used only the General Absolution. But not long after this liturgy's appearance, members of the Pennsylvania Ministerium, desiring to accommodate themselves to the American culture of non-Lutheran Protestants, made significant revisions in their hymnal's liturgy, both in 1786 and in 1818. Both were "revisions downward."[25] The 1818 revision contained a Confession of Sins, but it had no Absolution, neither general nor authoritative.[26]

In 1917, three American Lutheran synods (General Synod, General Council, and Synod of the South) published *The Common Service Book of the Lutheran Church*. Similar to the General Council's hymnal of 1877, this hymnal's liturgy contained a Confession of Sins and a General Absolution.

In 1941, the Synodical Conference of North American Lutherans (formed in 1872) published *The Lutheran Hymnal*. It had two settings. The non-Communion setting had a confession of sins with the General Absolution. The second setting, a Communion service, had the Confession of Sins followed by the Authoritative Absolution. This was the first Lutheran liturgy in English to use the Authoritative Absolution in North America. It was similar to the *Kirchenagende* of the Lutheran Church in Saxony, the liturgy the Missouri Synod used in some of its German services as early as 1856.[27]

In 1993, the Wisconsin Evangelical Lutheran Synod (WELS) published its *Christian Worship: A Lutheran Hymnal.* Two of its three settings have only the Authoritative Absolution, and the other has the General Absolution.

In 2006, the Lutheran Church—Missouri Synod published its most recent hymnal, *Lutheran Service Book.* Each of its five liturgical settings has the Authoritative and also the General Absolution. The pastor has the option of choosing either one. Also in 2006, the Evangelical Lutheran Church in America (ELCA) produced its latest hymnal, *Evangelical Lutheran Worship.* It has ten settings. Setting One and Setting Two have only the General Absolution. The remaining eight settings have no Absolution.

Regarding the Authoritative Absolution, many people wonder, "How can a pastor forgive sins? Is God not the only one who forgives sins?" Luther said it well: "The people [congregation] as a whole cannot do these things, but must entrust or have them entrusted to one person."[28] Lutheran theology teaches the act of forgiveness is vested in every Christian, not only in the pastor. Thus, when the pastor forgives repentant Christians their sins, he is not pronouncing the forgiveness as his but is speaking on behalf of the congregation that called him to forgive sins in its place.

As Lutherans, we want to remember the authority for a Christian (pastor or layperson) to forgive the sins of fellow Christians comes from what Christ told His disciples: "If you forgive the sins of anyone, they are forgiven, if you withhold forgiveness from anyone, they are withheld" (John 20:23). Briefly stated, the pastor's forgiveness is based on Christ's command, not on some man-made notion. So when Lutherans hear their pastors say, "I forgive you all your sins," they should be comforted as though Christ Himself had pronounced the forgiveness.

INTROIT (ENTRANCE)

Historically, the Introit ("entrance" in Latin) was sung as the clergy entered the church and processed to the altar located in the sanctuary (chancel). The Introit is an appointed Psalm sung for the day. It is usually preceded and followed by an antiphon, sung by the congregation in response to each verse of the Psalm or to a group of verses; the antiphon summarizes the theme of the particular Sunday.[29]

At this juncture in the discussion of the liturgy, it is fitting to note today's frequent use of the word *sanctuary*, now commonly also used by many Lutherans to refer to the entire interior of a church building. Liturgically, architecturally, and theologically, this is an incorrect use of the word *sanctuary*, whose meaning is derived from the Latin *sanctuarium*, a holy place for holy acts. It is the designated location in front of the church's interior, elevated and furnished with an altar, a pulpit, and sometimes a lectern. It is from this site where the holy acts of God are administered; namely, His Word is read, preached, sins absolved, and the Lord's Supper is received. The sanctuary does not include the nave and its pews, for it is not in the nave or the pews from where God's sacred acts are offered. Today's use of the word *sanctuary* by English-speaking Christians, now including many Lutherans, is largely an unconscious adoption of Reformed Evangelical theology that also uses the word *worship* with its nonsacramental meaning, as opposed to the sacramental meaning of "Divine Service." Fifty years ago, Lutherans did not talk that way.

In recent years, liturgically minded Lutheran pastors, instead of using the term "worship service," have been making concerted efforts to speak of "Divine Service," thus reclaiming the German word *Gottesdienst*, meaning "God's service." Perhaps, before long, a similar change will occur in regard to Lutherans reclaiming the proper theological understanding of the term *sanctuary*.

GLORIA PATRI (GLORY TO THE FATHER)

Following the Introit, the congregation sings the Gloria Patri, giving glory to the Father, to the Son, and to the Holy Spirit. It is derived from Romans 16:27; Ephesians 3:21; and Philippians 4:20. In the old Roman liturgy, the Gloria was the opening hymn.[30] In effect, the Gloria Patri is a doxology sung in response to the Introit's reading of a given Psalm, often referred to as the lesser doxology. It should be noted that when Christians sing this part of the liturgy, they are also affirming their belief in the Holy Trinity. The Gloria Patri became part of the Church's liturgy in the fourth century, both in the East and the West.[31]

THE KYRIE (LORD, HAVE MERCY)

The Kyrie, short for *Kyrie eleison* ("Lord, have mercy" in Greek), usually follows the Gloria Patri. It is not a confession of sins, although it may appear as such. It is a brief prayer sung by the congregation. It is the congregation's first prayer in the Divine Service in which God's mercy is sought by its members, who in this vale of tears will face trials and tribulations in their service to Him and their neighbor.

According to some historians, the Kyrie appeared in the latter part of the first century in the East.[32] Egeria, a Spanish nun in the latter part of the fourth century, traveled to the Holy Land and visited numerous sites in and around Jerusalem. In her diary, she wrote that she had heard the Kyrie Eleison sung in Jerusalem by a boys' choir.[33]

It is not known for certain which biblical reference(s) first prompted Christians to use the Kyrie liturgically, for there are a number of passages in the Bible that suggest its biblical origins. Psalm 51:1, for instance, reads: "Have mercy on me, O God." Another reference is from the ten lepers who cried, "Jesus, Master, have mercy on us" (Luke 17:13).

GLORIA IN EXCELSIS (GLORY TO GOD IN THE HIGHEST)

This part of the liturgy is in response to the Kyrie, as the parishioners voice their joy in the mercy of God's goodness for sending His Son to save them from their wretched sinfulness. Given that the Gloria in Excelsis is based on Luke 2:14, where the angels are recorded singing, "Glory to God in the highest" to the shepherds on the Judean plains of Bethlehem at the birth of Jesus Christ, Luther called it the "angelic hymn." He said this portion of the liturgy "did not grow, nor was it made on earth, but it came down from heaven."[34] It is thus the oldest hymn of the Christian Church.

It is thus the oldest hymn of the Christian Church.

Since the Gloria in Excelsis was first sung by the angels to the shepherds on the fields of Bethlehem, Lutherans recall that glorious event when they sing this portion of the liturgy on Sunday mornings.

Liturgical historians contend when some churches substitute a "Hymn of Praise" for the Gloria in Excelsis, the selected hymn does not equal the majesty of the Gloria in Excelsis that contains some of the very words the angels sang.

SALUTATION

In this portion of the liturgy, the pastor says to the congregation, "The Lord be with you." These biblical words, and others quite similar, are found in a number of places in Scripture. For instance, St. Paul's words to Philemon: "The grace of the Lord Jesus Christ be with your spirit" (Philemon 25). The Salutation also reminds us of the archangel Gabriel's greeting to the Virgin Mary: "The Lord is with you!" (Luke 1:28).

Liturgically, the Salutation, according to Luther D. Reed, is "a reciprocal prayer of the minister for his people and of the congregation for its pastor before they unitedly offer their petitions to God."[35] Thus, the pastor's words, "the Lord be with you," are not a friendly greeting extended to the congregation, as is the new response, "And also with you," in the new Salutation of some recent Lutheran hymnals. Rather, as Australian Lutheran Hermann Sasse says, the phrase "the Lord be with you" expresses the pastor's desire that the prayer of this Salutation that he is about to offer will really be Christ's prayer. The congregation's response, "and with thy spirit," expresses this desire to the pastor—namely, that his prayer on behalf of the congregation will indeed be received by God, in the prayer's words, "through Jesus Christ, our Lord."[36]

However, since 1978, many Lutheran congregations have been using a new Salutation. It has the pastor saying to the congregation, "The Lord be with you," to which the congregation responds, "And also with you." This new response replaces the traditional, biblically based response, "And with thy spirit." This change has its origin in the liturgical innovations of the Catholic Church's Vatican II of the 1960s. The new Salutation, vis-à-vis pastor and congregation, as above, is now equivalent to a friendly greeting, something it historically and liturgically never was intended to be. Liturgical critics say the new response, "And also with you," violates what the original Latin "*et cum spiritu tuo*" (and with thy spirit) means. One critic has stated, "*Et cum spiritu tuo* is not part and parcel of everyday language. It is a biblical expression and part and parcel of all liturgical forms of worship from the time of

Hippolytus, who is the first known witness for this dialogue between celebrant and people."[37] Thus the new respond is an anomaly.

Regarding the modern response, "And also with you," Gerald L. Bray, a liturgical expert in the Church of England, asks, "What kind of response is 'and also with you'? Why has the pseudo-colloquial form replaced 'and with thy spirit'? Is it that we no longer believe that man has a spirit, and that the level of our discourse is primarily spiritual?" He continues, "We do not go to church just to chat or to wish each other well."[38]

It is important to remember the words "And with thy spirit" are derived from 2 Timothy 4:22, where St. Paul says, "The Lord be with your spirit." Thus, the traditional Salutation is biblically based, whereas the response in the new Salutation is not. It is merely a colloquial expression.

Interestingly, soon after Vatican II had issued its new Salutation, the Lutheran Church in America, together with the American Lutheran Church, adopted it for their new hymnal, *Lutheran Book of Worship* (1978). Four years later (1982), the Missouri Synod published its hymnal, *Lutheran Worship*. It, too, adopted this Salutation. And in 1993, the Wisconsin Synod's hymnal, *Christian Worship: A Lutheran Hymnal*, did the same. They all replaced the biblical response of "And with thy spirit" with "And also with you," thus making it a cordial greeting instead of a prayer.

Here Lutherans will be interested in knowing that on June 16, 2006, *The New York Times* reported that the Conference of Catholic Bishops in the United States voted 173 to 29 to return the traditional liturgical response, "And with thy spirit." The three largest American Lutheran bodies, however, continue to use the unbiblical response "And also with you." The Missouri Synod's current hymnal, *Lutheran Service Book* (2006), has five settings. Settings one, two, four, and five have only the modern response of "And also with you." Only setting three has the biblical response of "And with thy spirit."

THE COLLECT OR PRAYER OF THE DAY

The traditional Collect follows the Salutation. It is a brief summary that "collects" the congregation's petitions it wants to address to God. Before the Collect is prayed, the pastor says, "Let us pray." This is "an invitation and admonition and should not be inappropriately replaced by 'We pray' or 'God's people pray.'"[39] The Collect commonly concludes with the words "through Jesus Christ, Thy Son, our Lord, who lives and reigns with You and the Holy Spirit, world without end." This trinitarian conclusion goes back to the fourth century, at that time intended to counter the Arian heresy that denied the deity of Christ.[40]

Old Testament Reading

Since the late 1970s, some Lutheran hymnals, apparently influenced by one of the liturgical changes made by Vatican II in the 1960s, now appoint a reading from the Old Testament. The Old Testament is often coordinated with the appointed Holy Gospel to present a prophecy-fulfillment dynamic. This reading is commonly the first of three readings in the Divine Service.

The Epistle Reading

This part of the liturgy consists of reading a selection from one of the New Testament's epistles, designated by the liturgy's proper for a given Sunday in the Church Year. According to Reed, "The Epistle is the word of Christian law, but law in the spirit of Christ."[41] Each reading urges Christians to live sanctified lives, similar to what the early Christians were urged to do.

The Gradual

This portion of the liturgy received its name from the Latin *gradus*, meaning "step." Historically, the church's choir chanted a Psalm from a step, one level up in the chancel area. In the Middle Ages, the Gradual then, as now, was sung between the reading of the Epistle and Gospel, and it always included the joyful proclamation of Alleluia (meaning "praise God") in anticipation of soon hearing the Gospel.

The Holy Gospel

The reading of the Holy Gospel is taken from one of the New Testament's four Gospels. The reading is chosen to fit the theme for a given Sunday in the Church Year. Hearing the pastor's announcement of the Gospel selection, the congregation responds, "Glory be to You, O Lord." And when the reading of the Gospel is completed, the congregation responds again, this time with "Praise be to You, O Christ." The first response is one of admiration; the second is a response of gratitude.

It is a tradition in liturgical churches, including the Lutheran Church, to have the congregation stand for the reading of the Holy Gospel to honor the words and work of Christ that it proclaims. It is an old custom that goes back at least to the Apostolic Constitutions (ca. AD 375) where it is first mentioned.

THE CREED

When spoken after the Holy Gospel, the Creed is a corporate confession and an expression of thanks for the message of salvation that the congregation just heard.

Whether it is the Apostles' or Nicene Creed, Lutherans confess the creed to others and to themselves in a Divine Service. When spoken after the Holy Gospel, the Creed is a corporate confession and an expression of thanks for the message of salvation that the congregation just heard in the readings from God's Word.[42]

The Apostles' Creed has pristine origins. Some of its statements go back at least to the early third century. For instance, the Apostolic Tradition of Hippolytus (ca. AD 217) asked baptismal candidates questions that had words remarkably similar to the Apostles' Creed.

The Nicene Creed is the product of both the Council of Nicaea (AD 325) and the Council of Constantinople I (AD 381). These Church councils met in response to the heretical teachings of Arius (AD 256–336), who denied the deity of Jesus. The Nicene Creed is more polemical than the Apostles' Creed.

THE SERMON

It is through the sermon that God serves His people by bringing them His message of Law and Gospel.

The distinctive nature and purpose of preaching are lost on many today who think of and see the sermon as just another part of a disjointed liturgy, such as that seen in churches where the historic liturgy is no longer used and where the sermon is little more than a presentation of moral teachings. But it is well to remember that the sermon is an important liturgical component. It is through the sermon that God serves His people by bringing them His message of Law and Gospel.

HALLMARKS OF LUTHERAN IDENTITY

According to St. Paul, the sermon is a divine institution. He told Timothy to "preach the word" (2 Timothy 4:2). Similarly, Luther said, "Know first of all that a Christian congregation should never gather together without the preaching of God's Word."[43] And the Apology of the Augsburg Confession assures us, "There is nothing that keeps people at church more than good preaching" (Ap XXIV [XII] 50).

Roland H. Bainton notes, "The Reformation gave centrality to the sermon. The pulpit was higher than the altar, for Luther held that salvation is through the Word and without the Word the elements are devoid of sacramental quality, but the Word is sterile unless it is spoken."[44] And Luther scholar Ernest G. Schwiebert (1895–2000) says Luther's "sermons presented a wholly new interpretation of Christian ethics, which normally flowed from his doctrine of justification by faith."[45] In short, Luther's emphasizing the importance of the sermon in the Church's divine liturgy is a historic hallmark of Lutheran theology and identity.

THE OFFERTORY

Commonly, the Offertory comes right after the sermon. It consists of singing an appropriate Psalm selection. The Offertory is not just a prayer but a sacrificial response to God for the blessings He has given us. That is why the Offering (collection) is usually taken right after the singing of "Create in Me a Clean Heart, O God" or some other appropriate liturgical response.

GENERAL PRAYER

The General Prayer is a prayer for the church and the world and often consists of three parts: thanksgiving, commemoration, and intercession. The thanksgiving portion thanks God for all of His gifts and blessings. The General Prayer also implores God's mercy for peace, for healing the sick, for sustaining those suffering persecution in their Christian witness, for faithful pastors and teachers, for success in spreading the Gospel to the unbelieving world, for guidance in not falling prey to false doctrine, for God-fearing leaders in government, for good weather, and for keeping us faithful to the end.

THE PREFACE

The name for this portion of the historic liturgy comes from *praefari* in Latin. It means "to pray aloud"; it is not as we think of a preface today, as a preview of something still to come. The Preface is a dialogue (one of the oldest in the liturgy) between the pastor and the congregation. It begins when the pastor says to the congregation, "The Lord be with you." The congregation responds, "And with thy spirit." The dialogue continues as the pastor says to the congregation, "Lift up your hearts," to which the congregation replies, "We lift them up unto the Lord." Finally, the pastor says, "Let us give thanks unto the Lord, our God." Many Lutheran congregations respond, "It is meet [an old term that means proper or good] and right so to do."[46] The themes of the Church Year influence the Preface, and certain ones are appointed to the various seasons. The Preface for Christmas, for instance, focuses on the Word made flesh in the person of Jesus Christ, and for Easter, it accents Christ's bodily resurrection.

THE SANCTUS

Before Lutheran communicants hear the Words of Institution and receive the body and blood of Christ in the Lord's Supper, they sing the Sanctus. It is the concluding climax to the Preface that reminds us that Christ, the Lord of the universe, is present in His body and blood. As noted earlier, the Sanctus was already in existence in about AD 96. In large measure, it is based on Isaiah 6:3, which reads, "Holy, holy, holy is the LORD of hosts; the whole earth is full of His glory!" The words "Hosanna, hosanna, hosanna in the highest" and "Blessed is He, blessed is He, blessed is He who comes in the name of the Lord!" echo Psalm 118:26.

THE LORD'S PRAYER

The Lord's Prayer is the chief prayer of the Christian Church.

The Lord's Prayer is the chief prayer of the Christian Church. Prayed here as we prepare to meet Jesus in His Supper, we acknowledge that it is in the Supper we receive that for which we pray. We pray, "Thy kingdom come"; then receive the kingdom of God in the coming of Christ in His body and His blood. We pray, "Thy will be done"; then we become part of His distribution of grace in the Sacrament. We pray for the forgiveness of sins; then we hear that forgiveness is accomplished for us in Christ's sacrificial death. We pray for daily bread; then by the Sacrament, our faith is strengthened and we are prepared to be the answer to that prayer to others through our vocation, just as we receive our daily bread through their vocation. Historically, as Reed has noted, while its location may vary, the Lord's Prayer is found in every liturgy connected to the Lord's Supper.[47]

WORDS OF INSTITUTION (CONSECRATION OF THE ELEMENTS)

This portion of the liturgy repeats the words Christ spoke just before He gave the disciples the bread (body) and wine (blood) in the Upper Room, shortly before He and the disciples went to the Garden of Gethsemane. The words Christ spoke at the Supper not only instituted the Lord's Supper but also taught the disciples and us that His body and blood are present and received in the bread and wine of the Supper. This is evident from His words, "This is My body, which is given for you. Do this in remembrance of Me. . . . This cup that is poured out for you is the new covenant in My blood" (Luke 22:19–20).

The Words of Institution are not spoken as a mere historical reminder of what occurred in the Upper Room. Rather, they are words spoken by Christ that validate and authenticate the essence of the Lord's Supper; namely, that His body and blood are truly, supernaturally present, and that through faith the repentant communicants receive the forgiveness of sins by receiving the consecrated bread and wine. Without the words of consecration, there is no body and blood of Christ present in His Supper, for they are the command and promise of Christ that define what the Lord's Supper is and does for the recipients.

PAX DOMINI (PEACE OF THE LORD)

Following the Words of Institution, the liturgy has the pastor proclaim the Pax Domini to the communicants. This is another dialogue between the pastor and the people, similar to the Salutation. The Pax is the voice of the Gospel announcing the remission of sins through the pastor. Being at peace with God, the faithful are invited to the Supper.

AGNUS DEI (LAMB OF GOD)

The Agnus Dei, introduced by Pope Sergius I in the late 600s, is another beautiful part of the liturgy. It is really a Communion hymn derived from John 1:29: "Behold, the Lamb of God, who takes away the sin of the world!" It is sung just before communicants receive the Lord's Supper. In many Lutheran congregations, following Luther's recommendation, the pastor communes himself while this hymn is sung.[48] In singing the Agnus Dei, the parishioners are asking for God's mercy and peace, the anticipated result of receiving the Lord's Supper.

THE DISTRIBUTION

Lutherans commonly receive the Lord's Supper at the altar rail. During the distribution, one or more hymns may be sung. Since the bodily presence of Christ in the Lord's Supper is denied by Reformed Protestants, some Lutheran pastors, in order to underscore Christ's bodily presence, add the word *true* to the words *body* and *blood*, as they distribute the bread and wine. Adding the word *true* was first approved by the Lutheran faculty at Wittenberg University in 1579.[49]

Upon receiving the elements, it is common for the pastor to dismiss the communicants with words of comfort and assurance. For instance, "The body and blood of our Lord Jesus Christ strengthen and preserve you in body and soul to life everlasting. Depart in peace."[50] At this point in the Communion service, many Lutheran communicants make the sign of the cross.

NUNC DIMITTIS (DEPART NOW)

This biblically derived hymn, commonly sung right after the reception of the Lord's Supper, is based on Simeon's response to his having seen God's incarnation of the Christ Child (Luke 2:28–32). Upon seeing the baby Jesus (the promised Messiah) in the temple, Simeon was now ready to depart his life on earth in peace.

The Christian Church sang the Nunc Dimittis already as early as the fourth century.[51] It is thus appropriate for Christians to sing this ancient hymn after they have received Christ's body and blood for the forgiveness of their sins and for the strengthening of their faith. They can now truly "depart in peace."

Singing the Nunc Dimittis at the end of the Lord's Supper is reminiscent of what Christ's disciples did after they had received the first Holy Meal. They sang a hymn as they departed and proceeded to the Garden of Gethsemane (Matthew 26:30).

THE THANKSGIVING

Here, the pastor says, "O give thanks unto the Lord, for He is good," and the congregation responds, "And His mercy endures forever." These words are another dialogue between the pastor and congregation. Both pastor and congregation are filled with gratitude for what they have received in this Sacrament.

THE BENEDICTION

The Benediction may be given in the words of Aaron or those of St. Paul. The former declares, "The LORD bless you and keep you; the LORD make His face shine upon you and be gracious unto you; the LORD lift up His countenance upon you and give you peace" (Numbers 6:24–26). Paul's Benediction declares, "The grace of the Lord Jesus Christ and the love of God and the fellowship of the Holy Spirit be with you all" (2 Corinthians 13:14). Both Benedictions are spoken by God's appointed agent, the pastor, who announces the Lord's blessings to the people.

Benedictions are spoken by God's appointed agent, the pastor, who announces the Lord's blessings to the people.

MATINS AND VESPERS

Thus far, we have refreshed our memory regarding the liturgical parts that are commonly included in a Lutheran Divine Service. While the Divine Service is the chief service used by congregations for the celebration of the Sacrament of the Altar, the Church also has liturgies for other times when Christians gather to hear God's Word. Two common and ancient services are Matins and Vespers. According to Reed, "Matins represents the most ancient public service of the church apart from the Eucharist itself."[52] In its earliest form, it goes back to the fourth century, when Christians used it in Jerusalem.[53]

At the time of the Reformation, Martin Luther brought Matins and Vespers out of the monastery and formulated these two prayer services for congregational use. While both services focus on praise and reflection on Scripture, Luther's modifications made Matins and Vespers "preaching services." Matins and Vespers as preaching services tend to offer a strong emphasis on the progress of the Church Year.[54]

Matins (*matutinas*, "morning prayers"), as we have it in our hymnbooks today, is the combination of the ancient prayer offices for the morning. One of its outstanding features is the hymn "Te Deum Laudamus" (Lord, we praise You).

As the Order of Matins seeks to impart God's grace and mercy to His people, it is commonly used as a service in the morning. Similarly, the Order of Vespers (*vespera*, "evening") does this at the end of the day. As with Matins, it begins by pastor and people asking God to open their lips so that they might praise Him. The great hymn "Magnificat," the Song of Mary, is featured in Vespers.

THE SPIRITUAL VALUE OF THE HISTORIC LITURGY

When Lutherans speak and sing the historic liturgy, they reflect a spiritual bond with fellow liturgically minded Christians. Regardless where they might be geographically, a spiritual bond is formed with those Christians who also are participating in the liturgy. Thus, when a congregation eliminates the historic liturgy, it breaks that bond and becomes an island unto itself, ignoring the importance of the *Una Sancta* (the one Holy Church). Today, however, the concept of the church for many tends to be only the local congregation.

But there is more. Given that the historic liturgy is almost entirely based on texts of Holy Scripture, abandoning the liturgy not only eliminates significant portions of Holy Scripture, but it also deprives parishioners of an important instrument (God's inspired Word) through which the Holy Spirit can strengthen their faith. Abandoning the historic

> When Lutherans speak and sing the historic liturgy, they reflect a spiritual bond with fellow Christians.

liturgy also prevents parishioners from becoming familiar with what endures and has endured biblically.

Writing new "liturgies" for church services has in recent years become quite common in many Lutheran parishes. This practice increases the possibility of subjecting people to un-Christian worship content. Below is an example from an LCMS congregation. In its printed Sunday morning bulletin, the Invocation read as follows:

> Pastor: God of burning bushes and burning hearts.
>
> **People: Hear our longings.**
>
> Pastor: God of verdant valleys and scorching deserts.
>
> **People: Hear our prayer.**
>
> Pastor: God bless those who dance and those who weep.
>
> **People: Bless our lives.**
>
> Pastor: God of streaming storms and deep silences.
>
> **People: Receive our worship.**

This Invocation is not only Christless, but it also ascribes to God some questionable attributes. Thus, innovative contemporary services may sometimes unwittingly teach questionable ways of worshiping, along with possibly presenting other dubious content that misleads God's people.

When biblical content is not present in many contemporary services, as in the above example, the counsel of Peter Brunner is pertinent. He has wisely stated, "Everything that is inconsistent with the Gospel of Jesus Christ and of the Holy Spirit effective in it must be excluded from the form of worship."[55]

Congregations engaged in forsaking the historic liturgy may find it helpful to remember that Luther desired no liturgical innovations. In 1526, he undertook the task of producing the *Deutsche Messe* (German Mass) from the Latin Mass in order to stop individual pastors, who thought they were free to do as they wished, from designing their own orders of service. Thus, in translating and revising the Latin Mass, Luther said he had made no innovations.

> For I have been hesitant and fearful, partly because of the weak in faith, who cannot suddenly exchange an old and

accustomed order of worship for a new and unusual one, and more so because of the fickle and fastidious spirits who rush in like unclean swine without faith or reason, and who delight in novelty and tire of it as quickly, when it is worn off.[56]

Similarly, the Apology of the Augsburg Confession states, "We cheerfully maintain the old traditions made in the Church for the sake of usefulness and peace" (XV [VIII] 38).

Making changes in the liturgy, unfortunately, is not totally new to Lutheran churches in America. As noted above, in the 1800s some Lutheran clergy tried to "Americanize" the liturgy by making deletions and revising down certain liturgical components. In response to those changes, Charles Porterfield Krauth lamented, "Must Lutheranism be shorn of its glory to adapt it to the times or our land?"[57]

Today, some Lutherans believe the traditional liturgy can be replaced by what they call "evangelical style" without harming the theology so long as the "Lutheran substance" [Lutheran doctrine] is retained.[58] This argument overlooks that style or form tends to become the new substance, reminiscent of the renowned Canadian media analyst Marshall McLuhan, who in the 1960s and '70s in his book, *The Medium Is the Message*, showed that the medium (or the style) that is used to convey an intended message, ironically, becomes the message itself. Thus, by eliminating the biblically based traditional liturgy, the substance of Lutheran theology will not long endure.

By eliminating the biblically based traditional liturgy, the substance of Lutheran theology will not long endure.

The spiritual vitality of the Lutheran Church is not enhanced when some pastors, having accepted the criticisms of contemporary service advocates, see the historic liturgy as irrelevant.[59] The desire for variety in church services was not one of Luther's values, and for nearly five centuries it was also not a value of Lutheran churches that desired to follow his biblically based teachings and advice. Producing liturgical innovations is not a hallmark of Lutheran theology and identity.

CONCLUSION

It would be edifying if today's Lutheran pastors taught parishioners in sermons and Bible classes what the historic liturgy is and does for them spiritually, and why it has been used by Christians for centuries. Pastors want to remember the liturgy, as noted earlier by Hermann Sasse, is essentially the product of the Lord's Supper. It is a vital instrument that conveys the Gospel of Jesus Christ. "The liturgy does not exist to provide edifying entertainment, motivation for sanctified living, or therapy for psychological distresses, but the forgiveness of sins."[60]

Congregations would also benefit if pastors preached on the different parts of the liturgy so that parishioners would gain a better understanding and appreciation of why the Lutheran Church values the biblically based divine liturgy. Such preaching would help Lutherans to be more conscious that their church not only is a liturgical church but that its liturgy is also a hallmark of Lutheran theology and identity that contemporary services tend to minimize or undermine.

1. What is the significance of knowing that the word *liturgy* is derived from the Greek word *leitourgia*?

2. What is the difference between the concepts "worship service" and "Divine Service"?

3. What is the purpose of the Kyrie in the liturgy?

4. Why did Lutherans in 1579 introduce the word *true* in regard to the body and blood of Christ during the distribution of the Lord's Supper?

5. Since so much of the liturgy is derived from Scripture, what arguments might pastors use to persuade those desiring to adopt contemporary worship styles not to depart from the traditional liturgy?

6. How does the liturgy connect Christians today to Christians of the past?

7. In Lutheran theology, what is another term for the "Words of Institution"?

8. Why does Lutheran theology teach that the Words of Institution are not just a historical description of the Lord's Supper, as many non-Lutheran Protestant churches teach?

9. What do you think Luther would say about pastors today ignoring the historic liturgy and writing their own orders of service? Explain.

10. How are "contemporary services" incompatible with the historic liturgy? Explain.

11. How does the liturgical phrase "and with thy spirit" differ theologically from the recent, modern expression "and also with you"?

12. What key word is missing in the preceding Salutation?

13. From whom did Lutherans "borrow" the preceding Salutation?

14. When in history did the preceding Salutation appear?

15. What does the Latin word *vespera* mean?

CHAPTER 15

THEOLOGY OF THE CROSS

Luther's Unique Insight

"Far be it from me to boast except in the cross of our Lord Jesus Christ, by which the world has been crucified to me, and I to the world." —St. Paul; Galatians 6:14

Among Luther's many spiritual insights and contributions is his concept of the "theology of the cross" (*theologia crucis* in Latin), another prominent Lutheran hallmark.

In explaining what the theology of the cross means, Luther largely derived his insights from the inspired words of St. Paul, who on more than one occasion spoke on the theology of the cross, even though he did not use that term. To the Corinthian Christians, he said, "The word of the cross is folly to those who are perishing, but to us who are being saved it is the power of God" (1 Corinthians 1:18). He further stated that though the message of Christ crucified is seen as foolishness by the world, this "foolishness of God is wiser than men, and the weakness of God is stronger than men" (v. 25).

Luther's theology of the cross focuses on three things: (1) how God can only be found in Jesus' state of humiliation as the incarnate Son of God, especially in His suffering on the cross; (2) how Jesus' sufferings are relevant and applicable to the lives of Christians as they experience various sufferings and afflictions in this world's vale of tears; and (3) how the cross dethrones our good works as a means of salvation.

THEOLOGY OF THE CROSS
VS. THEOLOGY OF GLORY

Luther laid some of the groundwork for the theology of the cross in his Heidelberg Disputation in the spring of 1518, six months after he had posted his Ninety-Five Theses on the door of All Saints' Church in Wittenberg. In his Heidelberg presentation, he contrasted "theology of the cross" with what he called "theology of glory." These two concepts differ dramatically; they are explored below.

FINDING GOD

The theology of the cross, as Luther stated, tells us that God can only be found in the incarnate, humiliated, and crucified Jesus Christ.[1] Apart from the cross, said Luther, one only finds a false god. On the other hand, the theology of glory looks for God outside the cross by trying to find Him in His power and glory. The latter is illustrated by Christ's disciple Philip, who once asked Jesus to show him the Father. Philip wanted to see God in His power and majesty, but Jesus told him, "Whoever has seen Me has seen the Father. How can you say, 'Show us the Father?'" (John 14:9).

Philip, as we also sometimes do, thought in terms of the theology of glory. He failed to see that God had revealed Himself in the human flesh of Jesus, a true man, not some suprahuman being. Jesus did not look like God to him. But that is precisely where God was present and visible, right before Philip's eyes.

Finding and seeing God in Jesus Christ, in His humiliation and suffering, is what the theology of the cross underscores. This, however, is *not* how or where the world thinks God can be found. St. Paul understood this when he wrote, "For Jews demand signs and Greeks seek wisdom, but we preach Christ crucified . . . the power of God and the wisdom of God. For the foolishness of God is wiser than men,

Finding and seeing God in Jesus Christ, in His humiliation and suffering, is what the theology of the cross underscores.

and the weakness of God is stronger than men" (1 Corinthians 1:22–25). Another time, Paul said God "emptied Himself, by taking the form of a servant, being born in the likeness of men. And being found in human form, He humbled Himself by becoming obedient to the point of death, even death on a cross" (Philippians 2:7–8). Similarly, eight hundred years before the birth of Christ, the prophet Isaiah spoke of Jesus' suffering as a human being "despised and rejected by men, a man of sorrows and acquainted with grief . . . stricken, smitten by God, and afflicted. But He was pierced for our transgressions . . . and with His wounds we are healed" (Isaiah 53:3–5).

The theology of glory looks for God in power and glory. But Luther said if this is where He is to be found, then there would have been no need for Him to come down to earth in the incarnation of His Son. To people seeking God in power and glory, it sounds ridiculous that He can only be found in the cross, a symbol of ignominy and utter defeat. Indeed, hanging and dying on the cross did not make Jesus look like God. It prompted the mockers at the foot of His cross to say, "Save Yourself and come down from the cross!" (Mark 15:30). The mockers reflected a theology of glory, for they wanted to see Jesus in power and majesty. They failed to see God present in Christ's suffering and dying for the sins of the world, including their sins. God was hidden to them in the cross. But it is also important to note that God was not hidden to the centurion who, standing at the foot of the cross, through the eyes of faith, declared, "Truly this man was the Son of God!" (Mark 15:39). As Luther stated, "He who does not know Christ does not know God hidden in suffering."[2]

The theology of glory tends to look for God in His power and law rather than looking for Him in His grace revealed in the message of the cross. Hence, the theology of glory unwittingly looks to see a fearful or awesome picture of God; ironically, one whom individuals could never face or physically endure, for as Luther said, if God were to reveal Himself outside of Christ, He would be a "consuming fire."[3] Theology of glory seekers forget what God told Moses: "You cannot see My face, for man shall not see Me and live" (Exodus 33:20). Similarly, the prophet Isaiah said, "Truly, You are a God who hides Himself" (Isaiah 45:15). In short, the theology of the cross says God only shows His back to us. The theology of glory, however, wants more. God's back is not enough.

THE NATURE OF GOD

The theology of the cross correctly understands the true nature of God. It sees His nature in His grace, love, and mercy. St. Paul declared, "God, being rich in mercy, because of the great love with which He loved us, even when we were dead in our trespasses, made us alive together with Christ" (Ephesians 2:4–5). Paul Gerhardt, the seventeenth-century Lutheran pastor and hymnwriter, understood this in His hymn, "O Sacred Head, Now Wounded."

> My burden in Thy Passion, Lord,
>   Thou hast borne for me,
> For it was my transgression
>   Which bro't this woe on Thee.
> I cast me down before Thee;
>   Wrath were my rightful lot.
> Have mercy, I implore Thee;
>   Redeemer, spurn me not! (*TLH* 172:4)

The theology of the cross does not deny God's greatness and power, but it sees them both revealed in the Gospel, in the crucified Son of God. It reflects the words of St. Paul, "For the word of the cross is folly to those who are perishing, but to us who are being saved it is the power of God" (1 Corinthians 1:18).

The theology of the cross sees the glory of God in Christ's suffering and agony on the cross.

In the words of Herbert B. Workman, Methodist scholar and Early Church historian, the theology of the cross states that "a cross-less Savior would be a crown-less king; for Christ the 'hour' of His crucifixion was the 'hour' of His glory."[4] Therefore, in contrast to the theology of glory, which sees the glory of God in His majesty and power, the theology of the cross sees the glory of God in Christ's suffering and agony on the cross.

THEOLOGY OF THE CROSS AND HUMAN SUFFERING

The theology of the cross not only says God revealed Himself in Christ's suffering on the cross but that He also reveals Himself in the suffering of Christians. It says Christians should not be surprised when things in life go wrong, often drastically wrong, bringing tremendous pain and suffering. Here it is well to recall what happened to the young lad Joseph in the Old Testament. He was scorned and hated by his brothers. When he was about seventeen, his brothers sold him to Egyptian caravan merchants; this resulted in slavery for him. In time, Potiphar, his slave master, made Joseph overseer of all that he possessed. Although enslaved, God blessed Joseph. But his good fortune was not to last, for one day Potiphar's wife tried to seduce him sexually. Joseph replied, "How then can I do this great wickedness and sin against God?" (Genesis 39:9). The spurned woman then falsely accused him of trying to rape her, and he was thrown into prison. This was the second time that things went terribly wrong for him, and once again as a child of God he endured a lot of suffering. We can well imagine what went through his mind while in prison. Undoubtedly, he wondered and likely questioned why God let two major misfortunes happen to him. Yet, God had not forgotten him, even if it looked that way humanly speaking, for Genesis 39:21–23 says that even in his imprisonment God extended kindness to him.

Joseph had the gift of interpreting dreams. In time, this gift resulted in correctly interpreting one of Pharaoh's perplexing dreams. This led Pharaoh to appoint Joseph to be in charge of storing grain during Egypt's seven years of abundance, which Joseph had predicted according to Pharaoh's dreams, and then distributing the stored grain during the seven years of famine that would follow. During the pervasive famine that also affected adjoining regions, Joseph's brothers came from Canaan to Egypt to buy grain. The famine was so severe that they came to Egypt a second time, and on the second visit, Joseph identified himself to his brothers (ch. 45). Then, complying with Pharaoh's request, Joseph had his father, Jacob, his eleven brothers, and their families migrate to Egypt. But soon after their father, Jacob, died, the brothers feared Joseph would punish them for the evil they had previously done to him. But Joseph assured them, "As for you, you meant evil against me, but God meant it for good" (50:20). Joseph, as a child of God, understood the theology of the cross.

Another biblical example of someone who understood the theology of the cross is Job in the Old Testament. He lost his sons and daughters and all his material possessions. In response, he said, "The LORD gave, and the LORD has taken away; blessed be the name of the LORD" (Job 1:21). The writer of the Book of Job states, "In all this Job did not sin or charge God with wrong" (1:22). In short, Job saw God hidden in his suffering. Similar to Joseph, he, too, understood the theology of the cross.

UNDERSTANDING SUFFERING

Indeed, physical and emotional suffering occur frequently in the life of Christians, and when pain and sorrow strike, we often think God is angry with us or that He has forgotten us. But it is precisely at such times, says Luther, that He has not forgotten us. To our sinful nature, this sounds strange, even unacceptable. When we react this way, it is an indication that we have much to learn about the theology of the cross. It is at such times we need to remember that "the LORD reproves him whom He loves, as a father the son in whom he delights" (Proverbs 3:12).

The theology of the cross means no matter how terrible life may be at times for us Christians, whether it is war, famine, disease, natural disaster, persecution, or personal calamities, God is still with us, His redeemed children. He is not mindless or asleep at the proverbial switch.

The theology of the cross assures us Christians that no matter what evil or suffering may come our way, God never intends to harm us; it is always for our spiritual well-being. That is what St. Paul meant when he wrote, "And we know that for those who love God all things work together for good, for those who are called according to His purpose" (Romans 8:28). Similarly, St. Peter assured the Christians of his day: "Beloved, do not be surprised at the fiery trial when it comes upon you to test you, as though something strange were happening to you. But rejoice insofar as you share Christ's sufferings, that you may also rejoice and be glad when His glory is revealed" (1 Peter 4:12–13).

When afflictions and sufferings in life are difficult to understand, and they often are, God wants His stricken children to remember the words of Isaiah: "For My thoughts are not your thoughts, neither are your ways My ways. . . . For as the heavens are higher than the earth, so are My ways higher than your ways and My thoughts than your thoughts" (Isaiah 55:8–9). In short, it is only through the theology of the cross that the human suffering of Joseph and Job, as well as the suffering of Christians at any time, can be understood by faith in God's promise: "Just as I was with Moses, so I will be with you. I will not leave you or forsake you" (Joshua 1:5).

Although the theology of the cross helps Christians understand their afflictions, it does not mean they can ever understand them fully. Our sinful nature makes that impossible. St. Paul summed it up well: "For now we see in a mirror dimly" (1 Corinthians 13:12). And when our faith is weak in regard to believing God is present in our sufferings, we need to remember and pray the words of the father whose son Jesus had just healed: "I believe; help my unbelief!" (Mark 9:24).

INEVITABILITY OF SUFFERING

Although Christians inevitably experience suffering in the form of physical or psychological pain—sometimes both—the theology of the cross provides them with God's divine consolation. It tells every Christian that Christ, who Himself suffered unfathomable pain, anguish, and sorrow, fully understands any and all afflictions when they become a Christian's lot. The faithful Christian also knows that his or her suffering, however immense it might be, is never equal to what Christ endured on the cross when He suffered for the sins of the entire world.

Luther said there were several reasons why it is inevitable that Christians experience the cross of suffering, pain, and agony. One, though Christians are God's redeemed children, they are still sinful creatures who at times need to be humbled. As noted earlier, God chastens (humbles) those whom He loves. Suffering has a way of humbling God's loved ones, as it did in the case of Joseph and Job.

Two, God seeks to teach His followers, including us, patience through suffering. In the words of the psalmist, "Be still, and know that I am God" (Psalm 46:10). When tragedies, pain, and sorrow enter our lives, Luther counseled, "Therefore be patient in your suffering. This is true Christian consolation."[5]

Three, as Christians we need to be reminded of the presence and gravity of original sin that remains and affects us until we enter eternal life. Some of the consequences of the tragedy of original sin are sickness, pain, grief, and affliction.

Four, when things go well for us Christians, Luther said, we often and easily forget God. Therefore, God, who does not want anyone to perish, but that all should come to the knowledge of truth, will some-times let the cross of physical or psychological suffering enter our lives so that we might remember His love and mercy, which He showed by Christ's death on the cross. While this seems contradictory to the world's way of thinking, God in His wisdom wants to keep His children from falling away spiritually by letting them endure the cross of suffering.

SUFFERING FOR THE SAKE OF THE GOSPEL

The insights of Luther's theology of the cross are also relevant in the life of Christians when they experience suffering apart from sicknesses or life's tragedies; namely, suffering for the sake of the Gospel. When Christians let their light shine, for instance, by proclaiming Christ as the only way of salvation in a multicultural world that sees all religions as having equal value, or when Christians refuse to deny Christ, they will often experience the cross of suffering for His name's sake. Today, the latter is especially true where Christianity is openly despised; for example, in Communist countries (China and North Korea) and in predominantly Islamic countries (Saudi Arabia, Iran, Iraq, Syria, and Egypt).

The severe, widespread persecutions of Christians today are, to some degree, documented on television and even more informatively in *The Voice of the Martyrs*, a monthly newsletter published in Bartles-ville, Oklahoma. The suffering of today's Christians in Communist and Islamic countries reminds us of Christ's words: "You will be hated by all for My name's sake" (Luke 21:17). These persecutions also demonstrate that the sufferers have taken up their cross to follow their Lord (Matthew 16:24), and their suffering also underscores the truth of these words as well: "Indeed, the hour is coming when whoever kills you will think he is offering service to God" (John 16:2). With regard to these words, Luther said, "That is what Christ Himself experienced on the cross." And he added, "That is where the sublime and profound wisdom of God lies hidden; that is where He deals wonderfully with His saints."[6]

To a lesser degree, Christians, even in free societies, at times have to suffer and bear the cross of ridicule or rejection when they, for example, publicly oppose immoral behavior (abortion, unmarried cohabitation, homosexuality, transsexuality, etc.) that today's secular culture condones and often promotes. When such crosses enter the life of Christians, they need to take comfort in Christ's words, "Whoever does not take his cross and follow Me is not worthy of Me. Whoever finds his life will lose it, and whoever loses his life for My sake will find it" (Matthew 10:38–39). Thus, suffering will often occur in the life of the faithful as they seek to let their Christian light shine.

Luther once remarked, "He who is no *crucianus* is also no *christianus*,"[7] meaning he who does not bear the cross is not a Christian. This remark has wide application. It tells us if we, who live in a free society, for example, experience no ridicule or rejection for the sake of Christ, we need to take another look at our life as professing Christians. For if we truly live as Christ wants us to live, crosses will invariably be part of our lot. Luther did not mean that Christians were to impose crosses on themselves, for he once said, "You need not run after it yourself. If it is to be, that is, if God disposes that you must suffer, accept it, and console yourself with bliss that is eternal, not temporal."[8]

> If we truly live as Christ wants us to live, crosses will invariably be part of our lot.

THE CROSS AND CRUCIFIX AS CHRISTIAN SYMBOLS

When Luther spoke of the theology of the cross, he primarily underscored God's hiddenness in Christ's cross of suffering, ridicule, and death He experienced for the sins of world, as well as the suffering and misfortunes Christians experience living under the cross. This focus differs from another aspect of Luther's theology of the cross; namely, the spiritual meaning the symbol of the cross has for Christians when, for example, they make the sign of the cross to bless themselves. It was the latter why Luther in the Small Catechism instructed Christians to sign themselves, as discussed in chapter 10. To make the sign of the cross was to remind Christians of what Christ had accomplished for them on the cross for their salvation. It was another way Luther emphasized the meaning of the cross, theologically.

To expand a little in regard to what was discussed earlier in chapter 10, making the sign of the cross, it is interesting to know that Luther valued this custom because it symbolized "to the whole world [Christ's] destruction of sin."[9] In his Large Catechism, he said, "Children should continue to cross themselves when anything monstrous or terrible is seen or heard. They can shout, 'Lord God, protect us'" (I 74). He saw this as a wholesome response to their fear. And he once gave this advice for when Christians are tempted by the devil to think of themselves as unworthy of God's grace: "In that event cross yourself and do not let the question of your worthiness or unworthiness assail you."[10]

In a sermon on the Gospel of John, Luther also placed high value on the crucifix as a spiritual aid for Christians. Said he, "The custom of holding a crucifix before a dying person has kept many in the Christian faith and has enabled them to die with a confident faith in the crucified Christ."[11] In another sermon, he told his hearers it is "a good practice to hold a wooden crucifix before the eyes of the dying person or to press it in their hands."[12]

Given that in Luther's day, Lutherans blessed themselves with the sign of the cross, plus on Ash Wednesday pastors traced a cross from the ashes of burned palm fronds on their foreheads, it would be interesting to know why and when both of these centuries-old customs were widely discontinued after Luther's day. Regarding the question why Lutherans in the post-Reformation period practically stopped both practices, it is commonly assumed they were discontinued because they were seen as "Catholic." However, there appears to be no documented information in articles or books as to why Lutherans abandoned both customs, and there is also no published information on when the majority of Lutherans stopped signing themselves. Interestingly, upon abandoning making the sign of the cross, Lutherans for several centuries were virtually indistinguishable from non-Lutheran Protestants who had little or no regard for the cross as an important and meaningful spiritual symbol for Christians.

The post-Reformation absence of Lutherans blessing themselves with the sign of the cross in Divine Services or in their private devotions, in a related manner, was also evident in the absence of any cross in Lutheran hymnals. For the longest time, Lutheran hymnals, published by different Lutheran bodies, had no cross visible on their hymnals' pages. The first Lutheran hymnal in America to appear with a small cross printed by the hymnal's Invocation in the liturgy (indicating parishioners could make the sign of the cross at that point) was the *Lutheran Book of Worship* (1978), a hymnal of the American Lutheran Church (ALC) and the Lutheran Church in America (LCA). Four years later, in 1982, the Missouri Synod's hymnal *Lutheran Worship* also had a small cross printed by the Invocation. And in 2006, Missouri Synod's newest hymnal, *Lutheran Service Book,* again has a small cross printed by the Invocation for each of this hymnals' five liturgical settings. To date, however, not all Lutheran bodies have taken this step.

These relatively recent changes in some Lutheran hymnals indicate there is a growing acceptance today among many Lutheran laypeople with respect to making the sign of the cross. This acceptance is now also evident in many Lutheran congregations on Ash Wednesday. As part of the Ash Wednesday service, many congregations now have parishioners come voluntarily to the altar where the pastor uses ashes of burned palm fronds to trace a cross on their foreheads, a rite conducted to remind the participants of their mortality and repentance.

The rite of imposing ashes is an adiaphoron in Lutheran theology, and some Lutheran bodies in that sense have seen no problem in adopting it (more on adiaphora in chapter 18). For instance, the LCMS *Lutheran Service Book: Altar Book* (2006) has such a rite for an Ash Wednesday service. In this rite, as the pastor traces the cross on each person's forehead, he reminds them, "Remember that you are dust, and to dust you shall return," a paraphrase of Genesis 3:19. The 2006 hymnal of the Evangelical Lutheran Church in America (ELCA) also has a similar rite. And in February 2012, the editors of *Forward in Christ*, the Wisconsin Evangelical Lutheran Synod's official publication, wrote positively about the imposition of ashes on Ash Wednesday.

These recent changes indicate Lutheran pastors and laity are showing renewed interest in the sign of the cross as a spiritual symbol, and they also indicate that both are realizing that making the sign of the cross is a salutary Christian custom. These belated changes, of course, support Luther who, in spite of his having eliminated some of Rome's ecclesiastical practices, wanted Christians to retain this ancient Christian custom and not neglect it in their day-to-day living.

Although Lutherans for the longest time had stopped making the sign of the cross in their prayers and private devotions, many pastors, it needs to be noted, had not totally abandoned the custom. For some pastors still made the sign of the cross in some church-related functions. Some, for instance, traced the cross on the forehead and on the breast of persons they baptized. In addition, many pastors with the right hand extended made the sign of the cross when they pronounced the Benediction at the end of Divine Services. And countless Lutheran churches, though not all, in the New World were built with a cross on their steeples, reflecting a Lutheran hallmark dating back to the days of the Reformation.

THE CROSS IN CHURCH ARCHITECTURE

Ordinarily, there is a conspicuous difference in the architecture of most Lutheran churches versus many other Protestant churches. For the most part, the interior and exterior of Lutheran churches commonly reflect the cruciform architectural design, similar to that of the Gothic cathedrals. Before the Reformation, countless Catholic churches were built with this design, and when some Catholic churches during the Reformation era left Rome for Lutheran theology, they became Lutheran churches, bringing the cruciform church design to Lutherans.

The cruciform architecture, so prominent in the Gothic cathedrals, has been described as the architecture that best exemplifies Christianity. One historian has said Gothic cathedrals made Christians "aware of the invisible and infinite, and that the divine became immanent."[13] The peaked arches of the cathedrals and churches pointed to the heavens, and their cross-capped steeples were visible from miles away. The center aisle in the church's nave symbolized the vertical arm of the Latin cross; the transept symbolized its horizontal arms, and the chancel and altar symbolized its vertical top. Many of these churches also had a cross or crucifix on the altar, along with crosses often visible in stained-glass windows.

They wanted their churches to be visible reminders to themselves and to others of the apostle Paul's words, as noted in the epigram at the beginning of

> The cruciform architecture, so prominent in the Gothic cathedrals, has been described as the architecture that best exemplifies Christianity.

this chapter: "Far be it from me to boast except in the cross of our Lord Jesus Christ, by which the world has been crucified to me, and I to the world" (Galatians 6:14).

Lutheran theology, however, has never insisted that Law-and-Gospel sermons cannot be preached or taught, or the Sacraments administered, in buildings that do not have such architectural symbolism. For instance, in foreign mission fields, it is not uncommon that many church buildings are simple structures, frequently with little or no cruciform symbolism. Still, even though architectural church design is a matter of adiaphoron, it is not uncommon in foreign mission fields for Lutheran missionaries, conducting Divine Services in very immodest church buildings, to add or display a Christian cross or crosses to help reinforce their preaching of Christ crucified. Doing so, they indicate the presence and visibility of the cross is to them an important hallmark of Lutheran theology and identity.

CONCLUSION

The theology of the cross accents Luther's strong conviction that God can only be found in the cross of His Son, Jesus Christ. To agree with Luther, as Alister E. McGrath (renowned Britisth theologian) has shown, we must remember there is an immense "gulf between the preconceived God and the revealed God." Accepting the latter, McGrath says, "forces [us] to abandon [our] preconceptions."[14] It is only then that we can understand the theology of the cross. And as Robin Leaver says, "At the centre of the Christian faith there is Jesus Christ, and at the centre of His life is the cross."[15]

Paradoxically, the theology of the cross teaches us that God reveals Himself in the hiddenness of the cross of His Son and also in the hiddenness of Christians suffering illnesses, tragedies, and other misfortunes. It teaches, as Luther so strongly emphasized, "that punishments, crosses, and death are the most precious treasury of all and the most sacred relics which the Lord of this theology himself has consecrated and blessed."[16] It also teaches that "through the cross works are dethroned and the old Adam, who is especially edified by works, is crucified." And Luther continued, "It is impossible for a person not to be puffed up by his good works unless he has first been deflated and destroyed by suffering and evil until he knows that he is worthless and his works are not his but God's."[17] In short, the cross dethrones human works, even good works, by elevating God's grace in His Son, Jesus Christ.

In addition, the cross has a long history as an important visual symbol in Christian devotional life and church architecture. It has always reminded Christians of what their Lord Jesus Christ suffered and endured for their sins and what He accomplished for them as a result of His suffering; namely, eternal life. Hence, through the ages, countless Christians have been moved to say with the British hymnwriter George W. Kitchin, "Lift high the cross."

Although influenced to some degree by the culture of non-Lutheran Protestantism with its low value of the cross as a meaningful symbol, Lutherans (as noted above) never totally abandoned all uses of the cross as an important Christian symbol. This has made it easier for making the sign of the cross to return among Lutherans as a spiritually edifying experience.

1. When tragedy happens in a Christian's life, he or she might ask, "I went to church every Sunday and what good did it do for me?" Does this question reflect the theology of the cross or the theology of glory? Why?

2. Can one accept the theology of the cross without faith in Jesus Christ? Why or why not?

3. Why do Christians find it difficult to see God hidden in the cross?

4. Why do Christians often think God has neglected them in their suffering?

5. Why does God let suffering and tragedies enter the lives of Christians?

6. Why is it paradoxical to say God reveals Himself hidden in the cross?

7. Why does our sinful nature favor the theology of glory?

8. Why does our sinful nature not take kindly to the theology of the cross?

9. Why have so many Lutherans over the years failed to make the sign of the cross?

10. Why have so many churches in America ignored the cross in art and architecture?

11. Do you think most Lutherans know that most Lutheran churches are architecturally built on the pattern of the Latin cross? Explain.

12. Why do some Lutherans erroneously think it is a Roman Catholic practice for Lutheran churches to have a crucifix on the altar?

13. When we go to church to please God, are we practicing the theology of glory or the theology of the cross? Explain.

14. When we complain about misfortunes in our life, are we practicing the theology of glory or the theology of the cross? Explain.

CHAPTER 16

THE AUGSBURG CONFESSION

Birth of the Lutheran Church

"[The Augsburg Confession] is the most churchly, the most catholic, the most conservative creed of Protestantism."
—Philip Schaff (1819–93)

I n April 1521, Luther appeared before Emperor Charles V and the territorial princes at the Diet of Worms in Germany. There he was asked to renounce all his writings, to which he responded, "Unless I am convinced by the testimony of the Scriptures or by clear reason . . . I cannot and I will not retract anything, since it is neither safe nor right to go against conscience. . . . God help me, Amen."[1] Nine years later, another imperial diet took place, this one in Augsburg, Germany. At this diet, Luther was not permitted to attend because Elector John Frederick feared for Luther's safety.

The closest Luther could come to Augsburg was Coburg, about 280 kilometers (175 miles) north. Here he was regularly consulted on a document the Lutheran reformers were creating to present to the emperor. When the document was completed, the Lutheran reformers presented it and read it aloud before Charles V and the princes on June 25, 1530, without Luther's presence. It became known as the Augsburg Confession, a key hallmark of Lutheran theology and identity.

In 1540, and also in 1542, Philip Melanchthon tried to make this historic document more doctrinally compatible with Reformed theology. He altered parts of it without authorization. The altered versions were never accepted by Luther or by the ten signatories who signed the original Confession in 1530. Thus, the original document became known as the "Unaltered Augsburg Confession" (U.A.C). These three letters can be seen imprinted on cornerstones of many Lutheran churches. They indicate that these congregations adhere to the original, unaltered Augsburg Confession of 1530, which soon became a hallmark of Lutheran theology and identity.

The Augsburg Confession consists of twenty-eight articles that show Lutherans were not teaching anything new or contrary to what Christ's apostles had taught in the New Testament, and that they were only desirous of restoring the apostolic doctrines that had become greatly abused and corrupted under Rome's many popes. Before the diet adjourned, ten governmental officials (eight princes and two city officials) "professed adherence to it."[2] No theologians signed it, for it was believed the document would have greater impact with signatures of only lay dignitaries. The signing of this bold profession of faith had great historical and theological significance. It marked the formal break between Catholics and Lutherans, and thus June 25, 1530, the day it was signed, became the birthday of the Lutheran Church. Roland H. Bainton, a Yale University professor, says the signing of the Augsburg Confession marked "the death day of the Holy Roman Empire."[3]

Since the Augsburg Confession was signed by ten governmental officials, did they violate or mix Luther's doctrine of the two kingdoms, as will be discussed in chapter 17? The answer is no. Their mere signing was simply a confession or profession of what they as Christians believed, quite aside from their position as governmental officials. They did not on this day use any governmental means to force their subjects (the citizens) to accept the Augsburg Confession. What soon followed in terms of their assuming the position of "emergency bishops" is briefly discussed in the next chapter.

The Augsburg Confession: A True Exposition of God's Word

Ever since the signing of the Augsburg Confession, Lutherans have contended this document is a true and faithful exposition of Holy Scripture. After the document had been publicly read, Duke William of Bavaria stated, "Never before has this matter and doctrine been presented to me in this manner."[4] Hearing this remark, John Eck, the renowned Catholic theologian and adamant opponent of Luther, told the duke he would refute the Augsburg Confession with citations from

HALLMARKS OF LUTHERAN IDENTITY

the Church Fathers but admitted he could not refute it with the Scriptures. The Bavarian duke then replied, "Then the Lutherans, I understand, sit in the Scriptures and we of the Pope's church beside the Scriptures!" Another Catholic, Bishop Stadion of Augsburg, stated, "What has been read to us is the truth, the pure truth, and we cannot deny it."[5]

Authorship of the Augsburg Confession

As already noted, Luther was not permitted to be present at the Diet of Augsburg in 1530 because it was outside Elector Prince John Frederick's Saxony territorial jurisdiction, thus he had no authority to protect Luther from being captured and killed as a condemned heretic. Luther was still under the emperor's ban for refusing to recant at the Diet of Worms nearly a decade earlier in 1521. Therefore, Luther stayed in Coburg (175 miles north of Augsburg) while Elector John Frederick, Philip Melanchthon, Justus Jonas, Johann Bugenhagen, and others of the Lutheran party went to Augsburg, arriving May 2, 1530.

Melanchthon, a talented, unordained lay theologian, had already begun drafting the Augsburg Confession while in Coburg, en route to Augsburg, but upon arriving in Augsburg, he devoted himself totally to the task. In formulating it, he remained in close contact with Luther in the Coburg Castle in regard to his revisions, informing and checking with him via daily messengers.

To assist him in writing the Augsburg Confession, Melanchthon leaned on three documents that Luther and his colleagues had recently formulated. These were the Marburg Articles and the Schwabach Articles (both October 1529), and the Torgau Articles (March 1530). On June 25, 1530, nine days after the diet had opened, the completed Augsburg Confession was read in German to Emperor Charles V,

Lutherans have contended this document is a true and faithful exposition of Holy Scripture.

though the emperor also had a Latin copy in hand. The reading in German took about two hours, and the emperor reportedly fell asleep. After it was read, as indicated above, eight brave princes and two city officials signed the document in defiance of the emperor.

When Melanchthon warned Elector John Frederick of possible dire consequences if he as elector signed the Augsburg Confession, Frederick answered that "he would do what was right, without concerning himself about his electoral dignity; he would confess his Lord, whose cross he prized higher than all the power of the world."[6] He was only twenty-seven years old and remained a stalwart defender of the Augsburg Confession to the end of his earthly sojourn; he died in 1554 at the age of sixty-two. He is often referred to as John the Steadfast.

The Document's Twenty-Eight Articles

This historic document consists of twenty-eight articles of varying lengths. In part, each article's length was the result of the degree of disagreement that existed between the papal side of the church versus the Lutheran side. Each article is written in a thesis-antithesis format, stating what the Lutherans believed and what they rejected. A brief summary of each article follows.

Article I: God

As might be expected, the first article of the Augsburg Confession begins with what Lutherans believe about God. In rather brief form, this article affirms the doctrine of the Trinity: Father, Son, and Holy Spirit. It further states that these three persons have only one divine essence. And it briefly notes anti-Trinitarian heretics that once plagued the Early Church, along with the Church's condemning them. Among the heretics this article includes are Muslims (*Mahometisten* in the original German edition).

Article II: Original Sin

This article states that all persons "who are naturally born" are born in sin and hence without fear and trust in God. The phrase "who are naturally born," exempts Jesus from original sin because He was conceived by the Holy Spirit and born of the Virgin Mary. The article calls original sin a disease that brings about eternal death to every person unless he or she is born again through Baptism and the Holy Spirit. All heresies pertaining to original sin are condemned. The primary heresy cited is Pelagianism, taught by a fifth-century monk, Pelagius, who denied that human beings were totally depraved at birth.

ARTICLE III: THE SON OF GOD

This article states that Jesus Christ, Son of God, was born of the Virgin Mary. It further notes that He possesses two natures, human and divine, and hence He is true man and true God. As God's only-begotten Son, He was crucified, died, buried, descended into hell, rose from the dead, and, after these experiences, He ascended to heaven. The article also asserts that all who believe in the Son, as a result of being sanctified by the Holy Spirit, are comforted and defended against the devil and the power of sin. In conclusion, the article declares that the Son of God will come again to judge the living and the dead.

> He possesses two natures, human and divine, and hence He is true man and true God.

ARTICLE IV: JUSTIFICATION

Lutherans call this article on justification the foundation on which the Christian Church stands or falls. It succinctly asserts that individuals are justified only by faith in Christ without any works or efforts on their part. The faith a person has in Christ is imputed to him or her as righteousness in God's sight. Compared to the other articles of the Augsburg Confession, this one is only four sentences long, which is rather surprising given that justification was a major point of conflict between supporters of the pope and Lutherans. The entire article reads as follows:

> Lutherans call this article on justification the foundation on which the Christian Church stands or falls.

> Our churches teach that people cannot be justified before God by their own strength, merits, or works. People are freely justified for Christ's sake, through faith, when they believe that they are received into favor and that their sins are forgiven for Christ's sake. By His death, Christ made satisfaction for our sins. God counts this faith for righteousness in His sight (Romans 3 and 4 [3:21–26; 4:5]).

ARTICLE V: THE MINISTRY

God instituted the ministry, says this article, so that the Holy Spirit, through Word and Sacrament, might instill faith in people, where and when it pleases Him. The article condemns the Anabaptists in particular for teaching that the Holy Spirit comes to individuals directly, apart from God's external Word.

ARTICLE VI: NEW OBEDIENCE

A Christian's faith that is not dead produces good works in Christ. Such works, though they do not contribute to anyone's salvation, are necessary because God commands them. For instance, "Let your light shine before others, so that they may see your good works and give glory to your Father who is in heaven" (Matthew 5:16).

ARTICLE VII: THE CHURCH

This article asserts that the Christian Church is the congregation of saints in which the Gospel is rightly taught and the Sacraments rightly administered. The article also states it is not necessary for the unity of the church that human traditions—that is, ceremonies and rites—be alike in all places.

ARTICLE VIII: WHAT THE CHURCH IS

As in Article VII, the church is called the congregation of saints, but it recognizes that in its midst there also are hypocrites and evil persons. The article continues to say though the latter are present among God's faithful, they do not negate or nullify the validity of God's Word and Sacraments. This part of the article is in response to the heresy of the Donatists, a highly divisive fifth-century group within the church. They taught that evil men or hypocrites made the Word and Sacraments ineffective if they administered them. Donatists also taught that the effectiveness of God's Word depends on the faith of the transmitter. This article condemns this false teaching, for the power and effectiveness of God's Word does not depend on the faith of any person conveying it. It is effective and efficacious apart from anyone who administers it.

ARTICLE IX: BAPTISM

This article declares that Baptism is necessary for salvation and that it bestows God's grace (the forgiveness of sins) on its recipients, including infants. Given that the Anabaptists, who appeared in the 1520s, rejected infant Baptism, the article condemns their teaching that taught children were saved without Baptism. Although no religious denomination is formally known as Anabaptist today, Baptist, Mennonite, and Pentecostal churches similarly reject infant Baptism and the forgiveness of sin it bestows.

ARTICLE X: THE LORD'S SUPPER

This brief article states that Christ's body and blood are truly present in the Lord's Supper, and it rejects all contrary teachings. But it does not mention any contrary teachings.

ARTICLE XI: CONFESSION

This article says that private confession and the absolution of sins ought to be retained in churches, but it also notes that it is not necessary for Christians to enumerate sins in order to confess them. The article cites Psalm 19:12 in support of its latter point: "Who can discern his errors?"

ARTICLE XII: REPENTANCE

All Christians after their Baptism, this article states, commit sins and therefore need to repent. The article also says it is the church's function to impart absolution to all penitent Christians. Upon being absolved, Christians are expected to do good works as fruits of repentance. The article condemns the teaching that Christians cannot lose their faith, along with rejecting the teaching that asserts Christians can attain spiritual perfection and hence no longer need to repent. Also rejected is the teaching that says remission of sins can be achieved by making restitution for one's sins, apart from faith in Christ.

ARTICLE XIII: THE USE OF THE SACRAMENTS

This article teaches the Sacraments were instituted by God as signs and testimonies of God's gracious will toward us in order "to awaken and confirm faith in those who use them." The article rejects the teaching that states mere outward participation in the Sacraments is spiritually beneficial without faith that one's sins are forgiven.

ARTICLE XIV: ORDER IN THE CHURCH

In only a few words, this article declares that no one should publicly teach, preach, or administer the Sacraments without a regular call to do so. In other words, self-appointed preachers or teachers are not a part of the church's formal ministry.

ARTICLE XV: CHURCH CEREMONIES

Rites and ceremonies in the church, according to this article, should be conducted without sin and contribute to peace and good order in the church. This advice should especially be heeded in regard to holy days and festivals. The article further notes that Christian consciences are not to be burdened in regard to observing given rites. They are, after all, not necessary to salvation. And finally, the article states it must be remembered that if vows and traditions pertaining to foods and special days are observed to merit grace, they are contrary to the Gospel.

Christian consciences are not to be burdened in regard to observing given rites.

ARTICLE XVI: CIVIL GOVERNMENT

In the early 1520s, the Anabaptists taught that Christians were not to serve in civic affairs. In response, this article asserts that Christians may indeed hold various offices or positions in the civic or worldly realm. As servants in government, Christians may make legal contracts, own property, take oaths, marry, and be given in marriage. In conclusion, the article states that the Gospel of Christ does not destroy or remove the civic realm. Christians are obligated to obey the ordinances and laws of the state. Only when the state's laws violate God's Word are Christians to obey God rather than men.

ARTICLE XVII: CHRIST'S RETURN FOR JUDGMENT

In keeping with Scripture and the Apostles' Creed, this article professes that at the end of time Christ will return to resurrect and judge all the dead. The godly and elect will receive eternal life, whereas the ungodly will receive everlasting punishment. In stating this confession, the article also condemns the Anabaptist position that taught at the end of time punishments of condemned unbelievers and devils would cease. In addition, the article rejects opinions that maintain before the resurrection of the dead the godly will rule this world, everywhere suppressing the ungodly.

ARTICLE XVIII: FREE WILL

Regarding free will, this article argues that man has some liberty to choose in matters pertaining to civil righteousness—that is, whether to labor, to marry, to raise produce for food, to construct buildings, to appreciate the arts, and so on. But relative to choosing the righteousness of God he has absolutely no power without the prompting of the Holy Spirit. The article cites 1 Corinthians 2:14: "The natural person does not accept the things of the Spirit of God, for they are a folly to him." In conclusion, the article condemns the Pelagians and others who taught that individuals are able to love God above all things and keep God's commandments without the Holy Spirit.

ARTICLE XIX: THE CAUSE OF SIN

This article teaches that though God creates and preserves the natural world, the cause of sin is the will of the wicked; namely, the devil and ungodly individuals. This brief article also points out that unless prevented by God, the evil and wicked turn away from God.

ARTICLE XX: GOOD WORKS

In comparison to some of the other articles, this one is quite lengthy. But given that Lutherans taught Christians were saved by faith alone, without good works, it required a longer response. Rome accused Lutherans of teaching that Christians did not need to do good works. This article rejects this accusation. It also rejects Rome's teaching that Christians are saved by faith *and* works, and it faults Rome for not having even taught Christians about faith for the longest periods of time. Rome is also criticized for having a faulty concept of faith, one that consists only of historical or intellectual knowledge, whereas biblically speaking, faith does not merely pertain to the historical knowledge of Christ but also includes believing in the benefits and effects of His work of salvation. Finally, the article states that while good works are necessary in the life of a Christian, they are not necessary for salvation, and they are only pleasing to God if they are done in faith as a response to what God has done in Christ.

ARTICLE XXI: WORSHIP OF THE SAINTS

Although this article declares that departed saints are to be honored and from whose lives Christians may learn about Christian piety, they are not, however, ones to whom we pray or worship. The article argues the primary reason departed saints are not to be

worshiped is based on the fact that there is only
one mediator between God and man, the God-
man Jesus Christ, as indicated by the apostle Paul in
1 Timothy 2:5. The article further notes that Lutherans have been falsely accused by Rome of having
abolished all ceremonies honoring saints.

ARTICLE XXII: BOTH KINDS IN THE SACRAMENT

Giving communicants both bread and wine in
the Lord's Supper is strongly defended in this article.
At the time of the Augsburg Confession, the Roman
Church only gave lay members the host (bread); only
the clergy received the wine. The article cites Matthew 26:27 in support of distributing both elements.
When Christ instituted the Lord's Supper, He told
the disciples to eat and drink. In addition, the article
points out both were given to communicants in the
Early Church.

ARTICLE XXIII: THE MARRIAGE OF PRIESTS

Rome attacked Lutherans for permitting priests
to marry. This article defends marriage of priests by
noting that the apostle Paul wrote in 1 Timothy 3:2
that an "overseer [bishop] must be above reproach,
the husband of one wife." The article also notes that
not only does Rome's compulsory celibacy of priests
have no biblical command, but it has also caused
many scandals and other sinful acts.

ARTICLE XXIV: THE MASS

This article rejects the false accusation that Lutherans had abolished the Mass. It notes that the
Sacrament was distributed in Lutheran churches on
every holy day, as well as on other days when people asked for it. The article also mentions abuses of
private Masses in that they were often given for the
sake of money. It states that now among Lutherans
the people are advised and taught the dignity of
the Lord's Supper. In conclusion, the article indi-

cates that the Lord's Supper only benefits Christians if they partake of this Holy Meal through faith in Christ for the remission of their sins. Receiving the Lord's Supper perfunctorily, without faith in the forgiveness of sins, bestows no spiritual benefit.

ARTICLE XXV: CONFESSION

In this article, the Lutherans at Augsburg told their papal adversaries that confession in Lutheran churches, contrary to false accusations, had not been abolished but was actively practiced along with absolution. They also said that confession of sins and absolution commonly occurred before parishioners received the Lord's Supper. While the article notes confession in Lutheran churches had not been eliminated, it states that private confession is not biblically mandated. The Lutherans corrected the false teachings surrounding confession, such as that confession made "satisfaction" for sin or that there were certain activities that could "make up" for sins.

ARTICLE XXVI: THE DISTINCTION OF MEATS

Abstaining from certain foods or fasting, this article argues, is abused when people practice either one to merit God's grace. In addition, many consciences were burdened by feeling guilty when, for various reasons, they were not able to observe given food rules. The article admits abstaining from certain foods was acceptable if it enhanced outward bodily discipline, but it was sinfully wrong to make it a mandatory practice. In support of this position, the article cites two Church Fathers, Irenaeus (d. ca. 202) and St. Augustine (d. 430).

ARTICLE XXVII: MONASTIC VOWS

This article gives a brief history of monasteries and how they once were important centers of learning and spiritual discipline, taught theology, and even provided the Church with pastors and bishops. However, in time, their original purposes were greatly changed and even abused. At the time of the Diet of Augsburg, monastic vows had taken on values equal to Baptism, seen as meriting forgiveness of sins and justification in the sight of God. Other egregious abuses were common too. For instance, many monasteries taught that monks could reach the state of spiritual perfection. Hence, this article condemned most of the prevailing values and practices of monasteries, arguing that they contradicted the Gospel of Jesus Christ.

ARTICLE XXVIII: CHURCH AUTHORITY

Luther made much of the doctrine of two kingdoms—the spiritual and the secular. This article is largely an exposition of what the two kingdoms (governments) or realms mean in the lives of Christians, both in church and in society. The spiritual realm—the Church—rules only with the Gospel of Jesus Christ, without force or coercion of any kind. The secular or worldly realm is where law, coercion, and punishment are exercised to keep peace and quiet in society. In this sphere, the sword rules. This article shows that the Church of Rome had commingled the two realms. Many popes, for example, had preempted the role of the secular realm and made the Gospel of Jesus Christ into a new law, thereby engendering fear in the hearts of people rather than having them see the Gospel as God's unconditional love for repentant sinners.

CONCLUSION

The Augsburg Confession has been cited as the Magna Carta of the Christian Church in that it restored the apostolic teachings of the New Testament to their original truth and purity. This renowned document, as already noted, gave birth to the Lutheran Church and serves as an abiding hallmark of Lutheran identity.

Over the years, Lutherans have honored this hallmark by celebrating its importance. In 1580, the fiftieth anniversary of the Augsburg Confession was celebrated by Lutherans as they published the Book of Concord. In 1930, Missouri Synod Lutherans in various parts of the United States celebrated the four hundredth anniversary of the Augsburg Confession by having special church services. In Fairmont, Minnesota, three thousand Lutherans came together to honor the Augsburg Confession in a special church service. In Albany, New York, more than two thousand Lutherans gathered to pay tribute to this historic document, and in the small town of Chappell, Nebraska, twelve hundred Lutherans did the same. Lutherans today would also do well to celebrate this historic document's existence every year, especially on the Sunday closest to June 25, the day that ten laymen (eight princes and two city officials) signed this historic Christian treatise to preserve biblical teaching in an era when false teachings were permeating the Church.

Finally, the Augsburg Confession has not been honored and extolled only by Lutherans. Reformed theologian and church historian Philip Schaff, in the early part of the twentieth century, paid the highest compliment to this Lutheran masterpiece: "The Augsburg Confession breathes throughout an earnest and devout evangelical Christian spirit, and is expressed in clear, mild, dignified language."[7]

Chapter 16 Discussion Questions

1. What did the Lutherans at the Diet of Augsburg say about the nature of the Augsburg Confession?

2. Why did Martin Luther not attend the Diet of Augsburg?

3. Who was the author of the Augsburg Confession?

4. How did the Augsburg Confession distinguish Lutherans from some of the other Protestant groups that arose during the time of the Reformation?

5. How does Article IX on Baptism differ from what many non-Lutheran Protestants believe and teach?

6. How does Article X on the Lord's Supper differ from what other non-Lutheran Protestants believe and teach?

7. Why was the Augsburg Confession only signed by laymen, not by any theologians?

8. How had the monasteries in time become corrupted?

9. On what basis does the Augsburg Confession reject the celibacy of priests in Article XXIII?

10. What are the two kingdoms mentioned in Article XXVIII?

11. What effect did the signing of the Augsburg Confession have on the Holy Roman Empire?

12. In what year, month, and day was the Augsburg Confession formally signed?

13. Who tried to modify the Augsburg Confession in 1540 and in 1542?

14. What do the three letters U.A.C. stand for?

CHAPTER 17

TWO DIFFERENT GOVERNMENTS

Spiritual and Secular

"Therefore render to Caesar the things that are Caesar's,
and to God the things that are God's."
—Jesus Christ; Matthew 22:21

Luther's contributions to Christian theology were numerous and significant. One of these contributions, a unique hallmark of Lutheran theology and identity, states that God has established two governments: the spiritual and the secular. Sometimes these two governments are referred to as the two kingdoms, realms, or spheres. Although Luther in part borrowed the concept of two governments from St. Augustine (354–430), many of the insights were uniquely his own, insights that he extracted from Scripture and statements made by Jesus Christ.

In Lutheran theology, the spiritual government is known as the realm of grace, and the worldly government is the secular realm. Sometimes Lutherans refer to the spiritual realm as the operation of God's right hand and to the worldly realm as the operation of God's left hand.

It is important to remember Luther taught that God instituted both governments in order to govern His world. But He governs each very differently. In the spiritual sphere, He governs with Christians through the Gospel; in the secular sphere, He governs through individuals irrespective of their religious or nonreligious affiliations.

These two governments, however, are not in conflict with one another because each exists for distinctively different reasons and purposes. Christians, unlike non-Christians and atheists, live in both realms; or, as international journalist and Lutheran lay theologian Uwe Siemon-Netto has stated, Christians really possess two passports.[1]

According to Luther, God established the worldly, or secular, government because without it human life would not endure. He adds that we were in this realm before we became Christians, and we will remain in it as long as we live on earth, for "our outward life and our physical existence"[2] depend on it. Hence, the secular sphere "includes everything that contributes to the preservation of this earthly life, especially marriage and family, the entire household, as well as property, business, and all the stations and vocations which God has instituted."[3] Luther referred to the worldly sphere as the "external matter"[4] that serves people's external or nonspiritual needs. The sphere of grace, on the other hand, serves the spiritual (nonexternal) needs of Christians, who are members of this realm by faith in Christ. In addition, as citizens of this world, they are also members of the worldly realm.

CHARACTERISTICS OF THE TWO GOVERNMENTS

As already noted, the two governments have totally different characteristics and serve distinctly different purposes. Varying interpretations and applications have been published on this important subject, and the brief discussion below notes some of the more common characteristics of each realm.

PERSUASION VS. COERCION

Coercion has no place in the spiritual realm.

God governs the spiritual sphere, His Church, by the persuasive, noncoercive power of the Gospel of Jesus Christ. Coercion has no place in the spiritual realm. Jesus said, "My kingdom is not of this world. If My kingdom were of this world, My servants would have been fighting" (John 18:36). Christ's kingdom is, said Luther, "a kingdom of grace and mercy, not of wrath and punishment. In it there is only forgiveness, consideration for one another, love, service, the doing of good, peace, joy, etc."[5]

The worldly or temporal realm is governed and ruled by means of the law and the sword. Retribution, coercion, and punishment are preeminent. In the words of St. Paul, "For he [the government] is the servant of God, an avenger who carries out God's wrath on the wrong-doer" (Romans 13:4).

SPIRITUAL VS. NONSPIRITUAL

In the spiritual government, or the sphere of grace, the focus is on things spiritual; namely, preaching and teaching the Gospel of Jesus Christ, baptizing would-be members, administering the Lord's Supper, admonishing and reproving erring Christians, and offering repentant individuals forgiveness. As noted in chapter 7, the spiritually uncomfortable are made comfortable, and the spiritually comfortable are made uncomfortable. In this government, God reveals Himself in His Word and Sacraments.

The worldly government focuses on people's nonspiritual (external) needs by providing them with protection from various exigencies and from harm and evil by keeping in check would-be violators of the law and by punishing them in accordance with the law when it is broken. Forgiveness is not a norm in this realm, nor are Jesus' words "love your enemy" a part of this realm. These activities apply only to Christians in the spiritual realm of grace.

MEMBERSHIP IN THE TWO GOVERNMENTS

Only baptized believers in Jesus Christ are members in the realm of spiritual government, the Christian Church. They become members by virtue of their Baptism and faith in Jesus Christ, not by means of natural birth. Nominal or pseudo-Christians in this spiritual realm (the Church) function as hypocrites.

In the worldly realm, everyone is a member merely by living in it. Christians, agnostics, atheists, pagans, and other non-Christians are all members of the worldly realm, and God provides for them all. As Christ said, "For [God] makes His sun rise on the evil and on the good, and sends rain on the just and on the unjust" (Matthew 5:45).

Revealed Law vs. Positive Law

The spiritual government operates with the revealed Law of God in the Bible. In Lutheran theology, as taught in Luther's Small Catechism, for instance, this Law (the Ten Commandments) functions as a curb, a mirror, and a guide. As a curb, it deters us Christians from breaking the Law; as a mirror, it reveals to us the laws we broke; and as a guide, it teaches us what God wants us to do in living a God-pleasing life. Obeying or honoring God's Law is prompted and motivated by the Holy Spirit.

In the worldly or secular government, positive (legislated) law rules and governs outward human behavior in the civil realm of society. Obeying or honoring the law is commonly the result of people having internalized the values reflected in the law, as well as desiring to live quiet, peaceful lives. Those who do not respect the law are kept in check through formal instruments or forces of coercion. Thus, when they break the law, judgment and punishment are administered by proper governmental authorities on the basis of enacted laws.

Spiritual Peace vs. Earthly Peace

The spiritual government exists to give its members inner, or spiritual, peace and comfort. It does so by offering penitent Christians in this realm God's forgiveness in Jesus Christ.

The worldly government, on the other hand, exists to give people outward, or social, peace and quiet. Its authorities are charged with protecting all citizens, Christians and non-Christians alike. Those who break the law or disturb the public peace are arrested, prosecuted, and punished when found guilty.

> The spiritual government exists to give its members inner, or spiritual, peace and comfort.

Private Values vs. Public Duty

In the spiritual realm, for example, Christian judges, in their private lives, may grieve regarding the decisions they must make to pronounce the death sentence for individuals found guilty of murder. Privately, as Christians, they may pray for such individuals. But in the worldly or secular sphere, Christian judges must set aside their feelings of pity and emotions. In regard to the persons being sentenced, they say to themselves, "As a Christian I feel sorry for you, but as a judge I must sentence you according to the law."

Luther states the judge in no way sins in handing out his or her judgment, and hence there is no need for him or her to ask for forgiveness, as once was erroneously required of executioners in the Middle Ages. The judge's official action in the worldly realm is done on behalf of God, as though God did it Himself. Moreover, Luther says, the judge is not acting as a Christian but as a government official.[6]

The situation is very similar with Christian soldiers on the battlefield, where they are obligated to protect their country. Here it is their God-given duty to fight and even kill, if necessary. When Jesus said to turn the other cheek (Matthew 5:39), His words were meant for individuals in their interpersonal relationships as Christians with other people, not what they were to do as soldiers serving their country on the battlefield. Turning the other cheek is behavior expected in the spiritual realm. Fighting and protecting one's country is behavior that belongs in the secular realm.

SUFFERING FOR THE GOSPEL VS. OTHER SUFFERING

According to Luther, Christians, members of the spiritual realm, must not defend themselves *personally* by means of force when suffering for the sake of the Gospel. He stated, "Especially should you be willing to do so for the sake of the Lord Christ, if you are threatened on account of the Gospel."[7] Similarly, Christians must never defend the Gospel by means of force or violence. Even collectively, the Church may not use force to defend itself. Here the words of Christ in John 18:36, cited earlier in this chapter, are relevant. Only the secular government, the worldly realm, has the right to enact and enforce laws, preserve and maintain peace, protect human lives (prenatal and postnatal), maintain armies, outlaw racism, protect free speech, build prisons, and so on. Christians are obligated to obey secular government's laws but not if such obedience requires disobeying God. For Scripture states, "We must obey God rather than men" (Acts 5:29).

Even when Christendom in the West was gravely threatened by the Muslim Turks, who in 1529 besieged Vienna, Austria, Luther argued it was only the secular rulers' role, not the Church's, to declare war against them. Speaking specifically about that Islamic invasion, he said, "They [princes and the emperor] have God's command to protect their subjects and are duty bound to do so."[8] Luther was firmly opposed to ecclesiastical authorities waging physical war(s). He once remarked, "If I were a soldier and saw a priest's banner in the field, or a banner of the cross, even though it was a crucifix, I should run as though the devil were chasing me."[9]

Suffering in matters not related to the Gospel, the Christian, who is also a member of the secular realm, may certainly call upon civic authorities for protection. Luther said, "In the realm of the emperor, there should be no tolerance shown toward any injustice, but rather a defense against wrong and a punishment of it, and an effort to defend and maintain the right, according to what each one's office or station may require."[10]

THE CHRISTIAN'S ROLE IN SECULAR GOVERNMENT

The doctrine of the two governments maintains when Christians hold office in some form of secular government, their obligation is not to evangelize or Christianize the worldly kingdom but to humanize it. This principle must be upheld even when Christians are motivated by the Gospel to enter public service. Evangelization may only be done on the private level and even then quite apart from the Christian's position as a public servant. To not evangelize in the position of a public servant engaged in his or her work is not denying the Christian's biblical obligation to witness to the Gospel. Luther's statement on two governments only says that in the worldly or secular realm, which exists to uphold peace, law, order, and justice, the Christian as a public servant in government is to serve the public in a civic capacity. That is how God wants the secular government to function. However, Christians in the secular sphere can still let their Christian light shine (Matthew 5:16) by being morally upright, courteous, patient, and considerate.

Some Lutherans often ask whether they may address moral issues in the secular or public square. The answer is yes. But they must address moral issues on the basis of natural/moral law, rather than by quoting biblical passages. If Christians oppose, say, abortion by citing only Scripture, the pro-abortionists will call that opposition a religious matter and thus will more likely receive the support of nonreligious individuals. Abortion, contrary to what many secularists think, is not a religious issue. Rather, it is a moral issue and a crime against humanity. To be sure, abortion is also a biblical sin, but in the public square Christians as citizens oppose abortion as a moral evil.

As Christians, we need to keep in mind we are members of both realms, or governments, and God wants us to be actively engaged in both. Here Luther serves as a good example to emulate. He spoke out against evil in the spiritual realm (the Church) and also against evil behavior in the secular realm (the world). As Christians, we must not be guilty of an old accusation that says many Christians are so heavenly minded that they are of no earthly good.

Hence, we as Christians should be involved in aiding and assisting in the area of charitable and humanitarian service, regardless of whether they are provided by the spiritual or secular realm. When it comes to charitable humanitarian services, the early Christians in the Greco-Roman world serve as an exemplary model. In the fourth century, they introduced the world's first hospices and hospitals.[11] They understood and took seriously what Christ said, "I was sick and you visited Me" (Matthew 25:36), and "As you did not do it to one of the least of these, you did not do it to Me" (25:45). Their humanitarian actions were also prompted by another of Jesus' sayings: "Let your light shine before others, so that they may see your good works and give glory to your Father who is in heaven" (5:16). Indeed, the early Christians set noble precedents in the area of charity and humanitarian services. Interestingly, many modern hospitals still remind us of their Christian origin in that they still bear Christian names, such as St. John's, St. Luke's, St. Mary's, or St. Stephen's Hospital, and some bear the name of a particular denomination; for instance, Lutheran Hospital, Methodist Hospital, or Presbyterian Hospital.[12]

> As Christians, we need to keep in mind we are members of both realms, or governments, and God wants us to be actively engaged in both.

Two Governments and Separation of Church and State

Although there are differences between the concepts of two governments and the separation of church and state, there are also certain similarities. Both concepts assert that the church should not rule the worldly government, and the worldly government should not dictate to the church. This principle really stems from what Jesus said to the Pharisees when they tried to ensnare Him regarding a person's obligation to God vis-à-vis Caesar (government). In response to them, He said, "Render to Caesar the things that are Caesar's, and to God the things that are God's" (Matthew 22:21). In light of these words, Luther says Christ's answer laid the foundation for distinguishing between the two realms or, in today's language, the separation of church and state.[13]

The separation of church and state principle was first formally invoked by Hosius, bishop in Cordoba, Spain (353–56). He reprimanded Constantius II (337–61), the Roman emperor, on account of his meddling in ecclesiastical matters. Constantius II tried to get the Western bishops to condemn Athanasius for opposing Arius, who had denied the deity of Jesus Christ. Hosius said, "Intrude not yourself into ecclesiastical affairs. . . . God has put into your hands the [secular] kingdom; to us [bishops] he has entrusted the affairs of the church."[14]

Intermingling the Two Governments

When Emperor Constantius II tried to get Bishop Hosius to condemn the supporters of Athanasius, it was a definite act of intermingling the two governments—the spiritual and the secular. Similarly, when the pope crowned Charlemagne the Great on Christmas Day in 800, he, too, intermingled the two governments. This act by the pope essentially abolished the distinction between the two governments. Later, when Pope Urban II in November 1095 preached a sermon in Clermont, France, in which he called for the Crusades to begin, it, too, was an intermingling of the two governments. This intermingling was true even though the Crusades began as a defensive war,[15] as well as a war to recover lost territory in ancient Palestine that nominally still belonged to Christians.[16] (The latter is a fact of history not commonly known.) It was not the pope's or the church's role to launch the Crusades. In so doing, Pope Urban II clearly violated the principle of two governments.[17] Given that the empire in 1095/1096 was divided geographically, the emperor in the West and the emperor in the East together should have launched the Crusades, not Pope Urban II.

In 1529, when the Islamic Turks were besieging Vienna, Luther wrote, "It is not right for the pope . . . to lead a church army, or army of Christians, for the church ought not to strive or fight with the sword."[18] And he added, war against the Turks "should be fought at the emperor's command, under his banner, and in his name."[19]

When Thomas Münzer (1489–1525), the main agitator in the Peasants' War in 1525, argued that he was fighting for the Gospel, he, too, intermingled the two governments. The rebellious peasants, said Luther, "put wrath into God's kingdom and mercy into the world's kingdom; and that is the same as putting the devil in heaven and God in hell."[20] Briefly put, the two realms must never be confused or intermingled.

Whenever social or political demands are made in the name of the Christian Gospel, the two governments are commingled.[21] For instance, many American churches in the early 1900s joined hands with Walter Rauschenbush (1861–1918) in his Social Gospel movement. Although this particular movement no longer exists in America, some clergy in some denominations still preach social gospel sermons or sociopolitical sermons from their pulpits, thus obfuscating the distinction between the two spheres or governments.

Confusing the two realms is not a mere academic concern but an error that has serious implications for preserving and spreading the Gospel. The Gospel is God's love and grace in Jesus Christ. It is a message of forgiveness to repentant sinners. It is not a prescription for changing society. Rather, the Gospel motivates Christians to do good works in society. The Gospel also does not provide an agenda to address or solve social and political problems. When the two governments are intermingled, the Gospel becomes law, and the secular realm preempts the spiritual realm. That is why Luther saw the commingling of the two governments as the work of the devil. "The

> The two realms must never be confused or intermingled.

devil," he said, "never stops cooking and brewing these two kingdoms into each other."[22]

Conclusion

The doctrine of the two governments or realms helps us understand and appreciate how God governs the world apart from the Church. It also helps us understand the important words Jesus spoke but which are often ignored or misunderstood. For instance, when He said, "Love your enemies, do good to those who hate you" (Luke 6:27), He was not speaking to the secular government but to individuals in the spiritual realm. If the secular government were to love its enemies, it not only would deny the reason for its existence but it would also court disaster. According to Romans 13:1–7, God commands the worldly government to keep its enemies in check, even prosecute and punish them when they break the law or threaten the security and safety of the general public. At no time did Jesus tell the secular government to love its enemies. However, when individuals do not know or understand how the two governments differ, they have sometimes expected the secular government to love its enemies. For instance, it is not the function of secular government to love today's Islamic terrorists and hope they will cease being terrorists. Rather, it is the role and duty of the secular government to apprehend them and bring them to justice.

The role of the secular government is not to love or forgive but to bring the murderer to justice.

Similarly, some well-meaning Christians, in opposition to capital punishment, say the government should love and forgive the murderer, not execute him or her. Here, too, the role of the secular government is not to love or forgive but to bring the murderer to justice. To forgive belongs to the spiritual sphere. Others argue that capital punishment violates the Fifth Commandment ("You shall not murder"), because by exercising capital punishment the government is murdering the criminal. This argument is even more erroneous, for it ignores the commandment's context. Moses gave this commandment to individuals, not to governmental authorities. When an earthly, secular government executes a criminal, it is not engaged in murder. It is simply using the sword, as the apostle Paul wrote, to avenge its wrath on the evildoer (Romans 13:4).

Although the doctrine of the two governments has been an important plank in Lutheran theology for nearly five centuries, it has not always been adhered to consistently. For instance, in the early years of the Reformation, it was a crime to promote the Reformation's theology under existing canon law and German law; the territorial princes, as supreme adjudicators, had the power to punish or tolerate violators of either law. This sometimes included princes who promoted the Lutheran Reformation.

As the Reformation unfolded, some of the German princes (those who favored the Augsburg Confession in 1530) gave direct support to the Reformation's theology. They did so by assuming the role of "emergency bishops" when Luther asked them to implement reforms he advocated, given that Lutherans had no bishops. Luther knew that without the princes functioning as emergency bishops (a position he intended to be only temporary) the Reformation would fail. Each prince, as the foremost member of the church (*praecipuum membrum ecclesiae*), exercised the authority that traditionally belonged to a bishop. The princes, in turn, appointed "visitators" to visit and implement Reformation reforms within their territorial jurisdiction.[23]

In light of the above, Luther's doctrine of the two realms of government was not strictly followed in the early years of the Reformation. For interestingly, the Apology to the Augsburg Confession, addressing Emperor Charles V, stated it was his "duty to preserve sound teaching and hand it down to future generations, to those who teach what is right" (Ap XXI [XI] 44). Similarly, the Treatise on the Power and Primacy of the Pope, one of the Lutheran Confessions, asserted, "the kings and princes should especially guard the interests of the Church. They should see to it that errors are removed and consciences are healed" (54).

Finally, notwithstanding the exceptions that occurred regarding Luther's doctrine of the two governments in the sixteenth century, this doctrine has not only remained an important doctrine in Lutheran theology but also has influenced many modern states. Thus, Dominique

Colas, the French scholar, argues that Luther's formulation of the two spheres of government "was essential to the genesis of the modern state."[24] If this is a valid assessment, then the separation of the two governments or realms is not only a Lutheran hallmark among Lutherans but also a doctrine that has made significant contributions in the West that extend far beyond the boundaries of the Lutheran Church.

1. Although Luther's concept of the two governments (realms or kingdoms) in part came from St. Augustine, he drew most of his insights regarding this doctrine from what source?

2. What are some synonyms for the spiritual realm and the worldly realm?

3. Biblically speaking, why is it not the function of government to forgive violators of the law, even when they confess and are sorry for what they did?

4. Why should Christians be active participants in the secular or worldly government?

5. Why must Christians in the worldly realm not try to Christianize or convert it?

6. Why may the Church never defend itself or the Gospel by means of force?

7. What scriptural evidence is there that the worldly government is instituted by God?

8. How does preaching a social gospel confuse the distinction between the two governments?

9. What are some current examples of churches or clergy commingling the two governments?

10. How does the devil operate in both the spiritual and secular realms?

11. How does pacifism relate to the two governments?

12. In light of the two governments, does a Christian soldier in war function as a Christian or as a citizen? How so?

CHAPTER 18

ADIAPHORA

A Look at Christian Liberty

"Nothing is an adiaphoron when confession and offense
are involved."—Matthias Flacius (1520–75)

A *diaphora* is a plural Greek word referring to things that are indifferent. The concept's origin harks back to the Greek Stoic philosophers (fourth century BC). Acts that were neither a virtue nor a vice, which the Stoics considered to be indifferent, they called adiaphora. Later, some Christian theologians used the concept of adiaphora when they referred to biblical teachings they saw as indifferent; that is, as neither commanded nor forbidden. Thus, adiaphora are teachings or practices that Christians in their God-given liberty are free to accept or reject with impunity.

Most Lutheran laypeople are not familiar with the concept of adiaphora. Many may never have heard of it. But Lutheran pastors and theologians often use this concept in theological discussions. The Lutheran Church's Epitome to the Formula of Concord even has a section titled "Church Practices Which Are Called Adiaphora or Matters of Indifference" (Article X). It appears safe to say that no other Christians are so conscious of this concept as are pastors and theologians in the Lutheran Church.

Brief Background of Adiaphora
in Lutheran Theology

The concept of adiaphora took on major significance in German Lutheran circles during the Adiaphora Controversy. This controversy plagued Lutherans from 1548 to 1574, and especially during the Leipzig Interim. Luther died in February 1546, and the Smalcald War broke out in July of the same year. In this war, the pope's armed forces of Emperor Charles V and Duke Maurice (a turncoat who had once defended Lutherans) defeated the Lutheran princes in May 1547. This defeat brought ultimatums for Lutherans to conform to given theological dictates issued by the pope, who ordered Emperor Charles V to implement them. Lutherans were to accept Catholic ceremonies and practices that they had previously reformed or removed in their churches. They were ordered to accept Rome's seven sacraments, pray to departed saints, have confirmation rites performed by bishops, and no longer teach the doctrines of *sola Scriptura* and *sola fide*. Rome's demands were first issued at the beginning of the Augsburg Interim in May 1548. Some of these demands were modified during the Leipzig Interim, which began seven months later in December.

During the Leipzig Interim, which lasted until the Peace of Augsburg in 1555, many Lutherans, especially Philip Melanchthon (formerly Luther's co-worker), acquiesced to Rome's demands. To justify his compliance, Melanchthon and his supporters (known as Philippists) invoked the concept of adiaphora, claiming the Catholic ceremonies and practices Rome was forcing on Lutherans were a matter of theological indifference; namely, adiaphora. Many unwavering Lutherans, however, refused to capitulate, including Duke John Frederick of Saxony. Melanchthon had become a theological deviant.

Without noting the many details in the controversy, Lutherans today will find it helpful to know that the adiaphora concept was grossly misused by Melanchthon and his associates during the Leipzig Interim. Its misuse did considerable damage to numerous Lutherans and their theology for nearly a decade. Some twenty years later (1577), in response to this tragic misuse, the Formula of Concord in Article X spelled out the proper use of adiaphora. It stated even when an act is theoretically an adiaphoron, it loses that status when it causes spiritual offense among Christians.

The Importance of Adiaphora

In light of Lutheran theology's insistence that Law and Gospel must be clearly distinguished from each other and not confused, Lutherans are extra cautious in labeling certain beliefs or practices as biblically wrong when in fact they may be biblically acceptable. There are specific biblical references that Lutheran theology cites in support of certain teachings and practices it calls adiaphora. One biblical verse is Colossians 2:16–17, "Let no one pass judgment on you in questions of food and drink, or with regard to a festival or a new moon or a Sabbath. These are a shadow of the things to come, but the substance belongs to Christ." These words to the Colossian Christians, according to Lutheran seminary professor Lorenz Wunderlich, indicate "there were no restrictions on their selection of their diet, their drink, or their day or days of worship. The Old Testament's ceremonial prescriptions no longer applied to them. And these Apostolic words mean nothing less to us."[1] Another relevant passage regarding adiaphora is Galatians 5:1, "Stand firm therefore, and do not submit to a yoke of slavery."

> Lutherans are extra cautious in labeling certain beliefs or practices as biblically wrong when in fact they may be biblically acceptable.

There are a host of activities or practices that can be subsumed under the aegis of adiaphora. The following are some examples that Lutherans say Christians are free to do or not to do.

1. Although Baptism is commanded by God, its method is not. Hence, it may be done by immersing, pouring, or sprinkling.

2. The circumcision of boys is also no longer commanded; it is an adiaphoron.

3. Although God wants Christians to instruct people in His Word, the Church's formal Rite of Confirmation is not found or commanded in Scripture.

4. The wearing of vestments by pastors is neither commanded nor forbidden in the Bible, thus an adiaphoron.

5. Whether Christians assemble for Divine Services on Sundays or some other day in the week is a matter of Christian liberty.

6. A Christian's moderate use of alcohol is also an adiaphoron.

7. The use of leavened or unleavened bread in the Lord's Supper is an adiaphoron. The Church in the West uses unleavened bread, but the Church in the East uses leavened bread.

8. Although highly recommended by Luther, signing oneself with the cross is a matter of Christian liberty.

9. In the Lord's Supper, Christians are free to use either the common cup (chalice) or individual cups.

10. Although a salutary custom, having sponsors at the Baptism of an infant is not a biblical requirement; again, it is an adiaphoron.

These and other adiaphora show that God has not locked Lutheran Christians in a legalistic iron cage but has given them freedom to use or not to use certain activities to glorify and honor His holy name. As the apostle Paul reminds us, "So, whether you eat or drink, or whatever you do, do all to the glory of God" (1 Corinthians 10:31).

God has not locked Lutheran Christians in a legalistic iron cage.

ADIAPHORA AND CONTEMPORARY CHURCH SERVICES

In the last several decades, many churches in North America have experienced an influx of new and differing orders or forms of church services, commonly known as "contemporary services." These church services, as noted in chapter 14, have since the 1980s also made their way into many Lutheran congregations and thus largely replaced the traditional, historic liturgy. To some degree, this phenomenon is found in virtually all American Lutheran bodies or synods today. To justify and defend the use of newly devised contemporary services, Lutheran pastors who use them argue that such practices are simply a matter of adiaphora.

Those who make this argument sometimes cite Article VII of the Apology of the Augsburg Confession to justify their composing new orders of services, even though this article does not use the concept of adiaphora. Rather, it merely states, "the true unity of the Church is not injured by dissimilar ceremonies instituted by humans" (VII and VIII 33). A closer look, however, indicates it is questionable to apply these words from the Apology to defend producing new and different church services, as is done today. For they speak only about ceremonies already in existence at that time, rather than the writing of new ones. Moreover, the lack of modern printing facilities in the 1500s would have made it extremely difficult to produce many new orders of service, as is done now in contemporary services. Thus, the Apology of the Augsburg Confession does not support devising new rites and ceremonies, as found in today's contemporary services.

It is also important to note when the Augsburg Confession and the Apology speak about "our churches," they have in mind territorial churches, not a local congregation. Thus, a local congregation could not necessarily do as it pleased. Moreover, the Augsburg Confession had no interest in encouraging innovative church services, for in Article XXI it states, "It can easily be judged that if the churches observed ceremonies correctly, their dignity would be maintained and reverence and piety would increase among the people" (par. 6).

To contend that Article VII does not support writing new and different orders of service is consistent with Luther's views. While translating and revising the Latin Mass into German, he was concerned about innovations. "We cannot," he said, "have one do it one way today, and another way tomorrow, and let everybody parade his talents and confuse the people so that they can neither learn nor retain anything."[2] As already noted, neither does the discussion of adiaphora in Article X of the Formula of Concord support frequent changes in church services, particularly if they spiritually offend some Christians. For as Charles

P. Arand (scholar of the Lutheran confessions) has shown, the Lutheran Confessions do not say adiaphora make every kind of church service permissible, even if it is not contrary to Scripture. Arand says if an adiaphoron is seen in that permissive light, it "creates not only chaos, but disunity."[3]

It was a faulty, superficial understanding of adiaphora, held by Melanchthon and his supporters, that prompted the writers of the Formula of Concord in Article X to address this erroneous understanding. They rejected the concessions Melanchthon had made in the name of adiaphora, most of which pertained to ceremonial or liturgical practices, but were nevertheless theologically wrong. And it is interesting to know what *Gnesio* (loyal) Lutherans, who opposed Melanchthon and the Philippists, said regarding liturgical practices, thirty years before Article X was written. They maintained, "there was no such thing as mere liturgy. Liturgy was intimately connected with theology and practice."[4]

Prompted largely by a faulty understanding of adiaphora, similar to Melanchthon's behavior, numerous Lutheran pastors since the 1980s have replaced the historic Lutheran liturgy with contemporary services. It has been a decision that in recent years has frequently resulted in disunity, division, and in offending many faithful Lutherans.

ADIAPHORA AND CONGREGATIONS DOING THEIR OWN THING

To see Article VII of the Augsburg Confession in the light of adiaphora in order to justify the perpetual changing of contemporary church services permits every congregation to do its own thing. Such was not the intent of Article VII, and this is further evident from what it says regarding the use of different traditions, rites, and ceremonies. It states, "It is pleasing to us that, for the sake of peace, universal ceremonies are kept" (par. 33).

Congregations doing their own thing results not only from their faulty understanding of adiaphora but also from overlooking an important element of the historic liturgy; namely, its uniformity. As Theodore Graebner has stated, "Uniformity in externals, while an adiaphoron, is nevertheless not a matter of slight importance. The Lutheran Church is a liturgical church, and the essence of liturgy is uniformity."[5]

ADIAPHORA AND THE CHURCH CATHOLIC

It needs to be pointed out that congregations doing their own thing in the name of adiaphora are in danger of forgetting they are part of the Church catholic. When members of the Lutheran Church confess the Apostles' Creed, they publicly say they believe "in the one holy Christian [catholic] Church." Making this confession, a congregation states its spiritual ties and bonds go beyond the borders of its local members, even back to the early, pristine Church. Hence, every congregation that has contemporary services should examine its many newly printed orders of service to see whether they are compatible with the congregation being a part of the Church catholic. And it is important to know that the new and various kinds of church services often reflect certain aspects of the culture at large. This enhances the danger of a congregation losing its catholicity, for the culture at large and the catholicity of the church are rarely compatible. As the apostle Paul told the Christians in Rome, "Do not be conformed to this world, but be transformed by the renewal of your mind, that by testing you may discern what is the will of God, what is good and acceptable and perfect" (Romans 12:2).

To be sure, though some pastors and congregations think it is merely a matter of adiaphora for them to use new and different orders of service every Sunday, there is much more at stake theologically. These congregations, in their divorce from the Church's historic liturgy and their false understanding of adiaphora, are unknowingly contributing to severing their ties to the one Holy catholic Church, the *Una Sancta*.

ADIAPHORA AND SPIRITUAL OFFENSE

As already noted, when the Epitome of the Formula of Concord (Article X) addressed the misuse of adiaphora that occurred during the Leipzig Interim, it specifically focused on the matter of spiritual offense to show that adiaphora were not absolutes, and thus they sometimes needed to be qualified or even abandoned. Article X therefore declared,

> We believe, teach, and confess that the community of God
> ‹the churches of God› (in every place ‹in every land› and at
> every time according to its circumstances) has the power
> to change such worship ceremonies in a way that may be
> most useful and edifying to the community of God, as it

may be most profitable and edifying to the community of God ‹the churches of God›.

Nevertheless, all frivolity and offense should be avoided in this matter. Special care should be taken to exercise patience toward the weak in faith (1 Corinthians 8:9–13; Romans 14:13). (FC Ep X 4–5)

The two biblical references at the end of this citation take us to what St. Paul told the early Christians. To those in Corinth, he said, "Therefore, if food makes my brother stumble, I will never eat meat, lest I make my brother stumble" (1 Corinthians 8:13). In short, he told Christians it was fine if they had no trouble eating meat previously dedicated to pagan idols. But if their eating such meat offended some of their fellow Christians, then they were not to eat that meat so their fellow believers would not stumble spiritually. Romans 14 similarly accents the importance of Christians not putting a spiritual stumbling block in their fellow Christians' way.

Although there is no specific biblical reference that forbids a pastor, for example, during a church service from preaching outside of the pulpit in blue jeans, walking around in the church's chancel, and wearing a flashy Hawaiian shirt, such behavior in a Lutheran church service would be spiritually offensive to many Lutherans who expect to see the pastor preach from the pulpit and clad in liturgical vestments. Just because something is not specifically prohibited in the Bible does not mean it is spiritually edifying to members in the household of faith.[6] In short, this unusual demeanor in a church service, offensive to many Lutherans, is not an adiaphoron.

The Lutheran formulators of Article X stated when certain ceremonies or practices (theoretically adiaphora) spiritually offend Christians, they in effect are no longer adiaphora. Matthias Flacius, a

> Romans 14 similarly accents the importance of Christians not putting a spiritual stumbling block in their fellow Christians' way.

defender of Lutheran orthodoxy at that time, underscored this point, as noted in the epigraph at the beginning of this chapter. "Nothing is an adiaphoron when *confession and offense* are involved"[7] (emphasis added). The matter of giving spiritual offense is often overlooked by many pastors when they, for instance, introduce contemporary church services.

As noted above in chapter 14, in the mid-1800s some American Lutherans adapted their Lutheran hymnal and liturgy to the prevailing non-Lutheran Protestant culture, and these changes offended fellow Christians. Lutheran pastor Theodor Kliefoth lamented these changes, saying that for many Lutherans the lack of liturgical "conformity [was] a stumbling block to them."[8]

It is well-known that contemporary church services often spiritually offend many devout Lutherans, resulting in many offended members transferring their membership to another congregation. And when pastors who introduce contemporary services are not bothered by the spiritual offense that these services often create among many members, they fail to heed what St. Paul taught the Christians in Corinth; namely, that they were not to offend their fellow believers by their behavior, even though their behavior was not biblically forbidden.

ADIAPHORA AND CHRISTIAN COLLEGIALITY

Adiaphora in Lutheran theology gives Lutherans a great deal of Christian liberty and freedom. This freedom, however, has at times been misused, especially when some pastors adopt a new practice without having devoted any serious theological thought or study regarding it and also failed to consult with their peers before making a final decision. Here, one wonders if, in the 1980s, Lutheran pastors had given serious theological thought and study to the matter of contemporary church services, which then were so quickly accepted as adiaphora, whether they might not have been averted, at least for many Lutheran congregations.

With the background of Article X, such studies might have revealed to many pastors that though a certain practice is theoretically an adiaphoron, its potential to give spiritual offense cancels its status as an adiaphoron. Here it is helpful to recall the error Philip Melanchthon made during the Leipzig Interim. In his acquiescing to Rome, he argued his concessions were adiaphora in that the externals in worship were separate from doctrine; but later, upon more theological reflection, he admitted his adiaphora arguments were wrong and that his concessions were not adiaphora after all.[9]

Charles P. Arand gives Lutheran pastors helpful advice when he urges all pastors who plan to adopt some new practice(s) to consult their colleagues in ministry so they might know how their contemplated "practice will affect them."[10] Arand cites historical precedent for such collegial interaction, even when the change(s) planned may be adiaphora. He recalls Lutherans in the 1520s, who were falsely accused of having abandoned ecclesiastical rites and ceremonies in order to introduce innovations, "expressed a strong desire to work with their opponents on matters of adiaphora where it did not involve a compromise of the Gospel."[11]

This past Lutheran posture not only revealed a spirit of collegiality but also an awareness of wanting to be true to the Church catholic. The Lutheran Reformers were concerned about how their actions, even though they were matters of adiaphora, might affect others in the church. If pastors in the future were collegially to discuss new practices with one another before actually implementing them, it would greatly minimize the influence of our American culture's exaggerated individualism that encourages everyone, including congregations, to do their own thing.

> The Lutheran Reformers were concerned about how their actions, even though they were matters of adiaphora, might affect others in the church.

❧❧ CONCLUSION

Although certain rites and ceremonies not commanded or forbidden in Holy Scripture may theoretically be practiced in congregations, they must not be used simply because there is no specific biblical passage prohibiting them. Before new rites and ceremonies are to be used by a pastor or congregation, the law of Christian love must be operative so that giving spiritual offense does not occur. As we have seen, St. Paul told the Christians in Corinth he would no longer eat meat once dedicated to idols if it caused weaker brothers and sisters to stumble spiritually (1 Corinthians 8:9–13). Hence, if contemporary church services spiritually offend some fellow Lutherans, then the concept of adiaphora at that juncture, in the spirit of Christian love, should be abandoned.

There is a certain irony often not recognized by many Lutheran pastors and congregations when they invoke the concept of adiaphora to justify abandoning the traditional liturgy. For in defending their use of contemporary church services, they do not seem to realize that Article X in the Formula of Concord (which they have vowed to uphold) was formulated in response to the "liturgical changes which Melanchthon and other Wittenberg theologians [during the Leipzig Interim] had made under pressure from the Roman Catholic emperor."[12]

Finally, the concept of adiaphoron is important in Lutheran theology, one that has great value regarding the freedom Christians have in the Gospel of Jesus Christ. But in regard to Christian freedom, adiaphora must be seen in the light of St. Paul's spiritual counsel that urges Christians not to give spiritual offense by their behavior, even though a specific behavior or activity is not forbidden in Scripture. Hence, the words of Matthias Flacius, cited in the chapter's epigraph, offer sage spiritual counsel, "Nothing is an adiaphoron when confession and offense are involved."[13] Thus, when we Lutherans engage in behavior that is biblically permitted and does not offend fellow believers, the concept of adiaphora is a treasured hallmark of Lutheran theology.

1. What are some synonymous terms for adiaphora?

2. Why is the moderate use of alcohol, for example, an adiaphoron?

3. Why do Christians see circumcision as an adiaphoron?

4. What role does Christian love for weaker Christians play in the use of adiaphora?

5. Why do you think pastors sometimes say a given church practice is an adiaphoron without having really studied the practice in question?

6. Do you think we Lutherans need to give more attention to the matter of giving spiritual offense to fellow believers? Why or why not?

7. What is meant by the Church catholic, the *Una Sancta*?

8. In what document or doctrinal confession do we Lutherans profess to be part of the Church catholic?

9. When a congregation ignores the Church catholic, what does it risk becoming?

10. When, according to Article X of the Epitome of the Formula of Concord, does an adiaphoron practice become a nonadiaphoron?

11. What relationship can a practice called adiaphoron sometimes have to false doctrine?

12. Do you think Lutheran laypeople need to know more about adiaphora? Why or why not?

CHAPTER 19

THE BOOK OF CONCORD

Lutheran Handbook

"The Book of Concord deals either explicitly or implicitly with every doctrinal aberration of the contemporary period and, for that matter, of every period in the church's history."
—F. E. Mayer (1892–1954)

To honor and celebrate the fiftieth anniversary of the signing of the Augsburg Confession (June 25, 1530), Lutherans published the Book of Concord on June 25, 1580. This book includes all the chief doctrinal documents of the Lutheran Church. They appear in the following order: the Three Universal or Ecumenical Creeds; the Augsburg Confession (1530); the Apology of the Augsburg Confession (1531), the Smalcald Articles (1537); the Treatise on the Power and Primacy of the Pope (1537); the Small Catechism (1529); the Large Catechism (1529); and the Formula of Concord (1580).

THE THREE CREEDS

The Ecumenical Creeds are listed as the first confessional documents in the Book of Concord. By placing these historic creeds first, Lutheran theology asserts that it is not a new or different faith but a continuation of the historic Christian teachings confessed by Christians of all times and all places. These ancient statements of faith are the Apostles', the Nicene, and the Athanasian Creeds.

THE APOSTLES' CREED

This creed consists of three articles. The First one states that Christians believe in God the Father. The Second Article spells out what we believe regarding Jesus Christ and His redemptive work. The Third Article states our belief in the Holy Spirit, the Christian Church, the communion of saints, the forgiveness of sins, the resurrection of the body, and everlasting life, which we await.

Although the specific date of this creed is not known, certain portions of it are similar to the Roman Creed of the second century. Luther saw it underscoring the doctrine of the Trinity, given that the First Article speaks about God the Father, the Second Article about God the Son, and the Third Article about God the Holy Spirit. He also said that the Christian's faith could not be expressed any shorter or more clearly. It has sometimes been called the litmus test of Christianity.

He also said that the Christian's faith could not be expressed any shorter or more clearly.

THE NICENE CREED

This creed was formulated largely by the Christian Church's first ecumenical council at Nicaea (modern Turkey) in AD 325, at which approximately three hundred bishops[1] attended from the Eastern and Western parts of the Church. This council dealt with heretical teachings of Arius (256–336), a presbyter from Alexandria, Egypt. Arius taught there was a time that Jesus, the Son of God, did not exist; Arius also denied that Christ was God. The council condemned his teachings. The second ecumenical council met in 381 in Constantinople. It expanded some parts of Nicaea's formulations, particularly regarding the Holy Spirit, as in the present-day's Nicene Creed. Although this creed would be more accurately called the Nicene-Constantinopolitan Creed, it is commonly known as the Nicene Creed, largely because of the latter title's brevity.

This creed contains most doctrinal points found in the Apostles' Creed, but there are some differences. In response to the false teachings of Arius, it provides a more detailed description of who Jesus Christ is. Unlike the Apostles' Creed, the Nicene Creed confesses "one Baptism for the remission of sins," and it does not state that Christ descended into hell. The reason for this is because the Nicene Council was asked to address the Arian heresy, and thus this creed is more polemical than the Apostles' Creed.

THE ATHANASIAN CREED

It was once thought that Athanasius (d. 379), the ardent opponent of Arius at the Council of Nicaea, wrote this creed. Research, however, has shown it to be a fifth-century document and written by an unknown author. In considerable detail, it spells out the doctrine of the Trinity and the Incarnation. And similar to the Apostles' and Nicene Creed, it asserts that Christ will come again to judge the living and the dead and that someday all people will rise from the dead and be required to give "an account concerning their own deeds." It concludes, "This is the catholic faith; whoever does not believe it faithfully and firmly cannot be saved."

Although the Book of Concord refers to the three creeds as "ecumenical," the Roman Catholic Church and the Eastern Orthodox Church do not see the Athanasian Creed as an ecumenical creed. Eastern Orthodox churches have never recognized it as such, though it is found in some of their publications. But to Roman Catholics, it is largely unknown today. Rome sees the Nicene Creed as more important, largely because it is the product of two ecumenical councils. Non-Lutheran Protestant churches often do not include the Apostles' or Nicene Creed in their hymnals, and Baptists and Pentecostals, who say they are noncreedal, do not formally confess them either.

It is important to note when Lutherans placed the three ancient creeds in the forefront of the Book of Concord, they signaled to Rome and the Reformed churches that their theological documents that followed conformed to the doctrines of these creeds. It was the Lutheran way of showing the Book of Concord did not contain any new doctrines after the Augsburg Confession had been publicly confessed and signed in 1530.

Unlike Lutherans, many Christian denominations do not use or emphasize the creeds. It is common in most Lutheran churches to confess either the Apostles' or the Nicene Creed in their Divine Services on Sundays. And many Lutheran congregations confess the Athanasian Creed one week after Pentecost Sunday, on Trinity Sunday. Thus, by regularly confessing one of the three creeds in their Sunday services, Lutheran churches indicate the custom is a hallmark of their Lutheran identity.

The Augsburg Confession

Immediately following the three creeds, the first document in the Book of Concord is the Augsburg Confession. But given that chapter 16 is entirely devoted to the Augsburg Confession, the present chapter focuses on the Book of Concord's next document, the Apology of the Augsburg Confession.

The Apology of the Augsburg Confession

Although the Augsburg Confession was read aloud in an irenic tone before Charles V at the Diet of Augsburg on June 25, 1530, it did not mitigate the tension and conflict between Lutherans and Catholics. Almost immediately after its presentation, the Catholics tried to discredit it by issuing their *Roman Imperial Confutation*. In response to the Confutation, Philip Melanchthon (Luther's co-worker) took it upon himself to write an apology (a defense) of the Augsburg Confession. He completed the Apology by September 20, 1530, while the Diet was still in session. Two days later, it was presented to Emperor Charles V, but he rejected it. This enabled Melanchthon to revise and more sharply hone its arguments as a rebuttal to the Confutation. His revision was completed in 1531, but it did not receive formal approval until it was signed by an assembly of Lutheran clergy and princes in the town of Smalcald in 1537. With its formal approval, the Apology took its place alongside the Augsburg Confession as an official theological document of the Lutheran churches. Now there were two

With its formal approval, the Apology took its place alongside the Augsburg Confession as an official theological document of the Lutheran churches.

major Lutheran documents that exposed the numerous departures in the theology and practice of the Catholic Church.

The Apology comments on each article of the Augsburg Confession. Many of the Augsburg Confession's articles are very brief, but because the Confutation had rejected some articles and disputed many others, Melanchthon had to engage in a relatively long defense of the disputed articles. For instance, Article II (Original Sin) of the Augsburg Confession in the original German and Latin version contained only two sentences, but given that the Catholics had a substantially different doctrine regarding original sin, they largely rejected the Lutheran position. Therefore, the Apology in its final form has seven pages defending the Lutheran position on original sin.

The situation is similar with the article on justification, Article IV. The Augsburg Confession has only two sentences explaining how Christians are justified in God's sight through faith in Jesus Christ, but the Apology has sixty-two pages defending the Augsburg Confession's statement on justification. The long defense resulted because the Confutation had rejected the Lutheran position that stated a person is saved and justified through faith in Christ alone, as taught in Romans 3:28 and Ephesians 2:8–9. The Catholic Church, as noted earlier in chapter 3, taught (and still teaches) that Christians are saved by faith *and* works, not by faith in Christ alone.

In many of its lengthy defenses, the Apology cites numerous biblical passages in support of what the Augsburg Confession proclaims. These passages indicate Lutherans "were thoroughly acquainted with the Word of God."[2] These passages also demonstrate that their theology was firmly grounded in *sola Scriptura.*

THE SMALCALD ARTICLES

Anticipating that the pope would call a general council, Elector John Frederick of Saxony asked Luther in December 1536 to prepare a document of doctrinal articles that could be presented at such a council, assuming Lutherans would be permitted to attend and set forth their case. Before the month was over, Luther had fulfilled the elector's request and he presented the document "for review by a small group of theologians assembled in Wittenberg."[3] This group proposed that the document, along with other concerns, add an article on the invocation of saints.[4]

After the Wittenberg group had reviewed the document's articles, Elector John Frederick took it to the town of Smalcald, where the representatives of the Smalcaldic League were to assemble on February 8, 1537, to discuss and approve the articles. When that day arrived, Luther's illness prevented him from attending. A number of clergymen, however, without Luther's presence, signed the document, even though it had not been officially approved.[5] Many of these forty-four signers were men in responsible positions in their regions and had "a decisive voice in directing doctrine taught there."[6] Later, when "the Formula of Concord was completed and adopted in 1577, Luther's articles were highly regarded and adopted as part of the Lutheran Church's formal confession of faith."[7] They became known as The Smalcald Articles.

CHRIST AND FAITH

This, the first article, underscores what the Augsburg Confession proclaimed a few years earlier; namely, that Jesus Christ suffered, died, and rose for our justification. Citing Romans 3:28, it further states Christians are saved by faith alone in Christ, apart from any good works. It also cites Acts 4:12, asserting that there is no salvation outside of Jesus Christ.

THE MASS

The first sentence of Article II regarding the Mass (Rome's name for celebrating the Lord's Supper) calls it "the greatest and most horrible abomination" (SA II II 1). The article goes on to say the celebration of the Mass is riddled with "popish idolatries," and hence it should be rejected and abandoned. The article further asserts that the Mass falsely teaches Christ is sacrificed each time it is performed. Additionally, it asserts the Mass also supports the doctrine of purgatory; it has clergy communing themselves in private; it contributes to the selling of indulgences; it encourages people to venerate relics, and it gives them a false hope of the forgiveness of sins for worshiping relics.

In this article, Luther and his associates used the term *Mass* not because they saw it as an acceptable theological term but because they were writing to their adversaries relative to what was wrong with the Mass. The ungodly abuses of the Mass apparently prompted Luther already in 1529 not to use the term when he wrote his Small and Large Catechisms. In both, he speaks of "the Sacrament of the Altar," and in his Large Catechism, he also uses the term *Lord's Supper*. And it is noteworthy that only a few articles after the present one on the Mass,

HALLMARKS OF LUTHERAN IDENTITY

there is an article on "The Sacrament of the Altar," indicating that the term *Mass* found no favor among confessional Lutherans. Similarly, the writers of the Formula of Concord, when speaking about the Lord's Supper, used the terms *Lord's Supper, Holy Supper, Sacrament of the Altar,* and *Supper,* but not *Mass.* The Formula of Concord uses the word *Mass* only twice, and then only to find fault with its theological aberrations. To this day, confessional Lutherans do not use the term *Mass* when they speak about the Lord's Supper. Hence, abandoning the word *Mass* is a hallmark of Lutheran theology and identity.

THE INVOCATION OF SAINTS

This section, contained in Article II, contends that the invocation of saints is an Antichrist's abuse, and "it is neither commanded nor counseled, nor has it any warrant in Scripture" (SA II II 25). This practice is also called "idolatrous" (28). It further argues that while saints in heaven may pray for Christians (26), there is no biblical command or apostolic precedence telling Christians to pray to them.

CHAPTERS AND CLOISTERS

This article says that at one time chapters and cloisters (monasteries) were useful instruments of education, but they had lost their original purpose in that they were now given to many abuses, one being that monasteries were seen as means of salvation. It concludes by saying all monasteries should be abandoned and discontinued.

THE PAPACY

The office of the pope, as head of the Church, according to this article, has no biblical basis and is also unnecessary. There is only one head of the Church; namely, Jesus Christ. So strong is the criticism of the papal office and its numerous corruptions that the article says the pope "is the true . . . Antichrist." He has "exalted himself above and opposed himself

There is only one head of the Church; namely, Jesus Christ.

against Christ. For he will not permit Christians to be saved without his power, which, nevertheless is nothing, and is neither ordained nor commanded by God" (II IV 10).

SIN

Concerning sin, this article asserts all men are born as sinfully corrupt beings; so corrupt, in fact, that "no reason can understand it. Rather, it must be believed from the revelation of Scripture" (III I 3). The article is highly critical of what the Scholastic theologians taught concerning sin. They taught (1) man could by his natural powers keep God's Law; (2) if he did the best he could, God would grant him grace; (3) mere participation in the Lord's Supper—that is, even without repentance and without faith—bestowed God's forgiveness. The article rejects these false Scholastic teachings.

THE LAW

Immediately following the article on sin is a brief treatise on the purpose of the Law. It states the primary function of the Law is to show people the depths and gravity of their sin. Another of its functions is to restrain human beings from engaging in sinful behavior. It also contends that people by nature despise the Law because it forbids behavior that they by nature desire to do.

REPENTANCE

Having shown the Lutheran position on sin and the Law, the next article at some length focuses on repentance. It argues that the Law produces repentance and the Gospel offers forgiveness. The article cites Mark 1:15, "Repent and believe in the Gospel." An additional argument is put forth, saying the Law must never be preached alone, apart from the Gospel, because without the Gospel individuals despair. King Saul and Judas are two biblical examples of men who despaired; both committed suicide.

THE GOSPEL

This article reminds Catholic opponents of Lutheran theology that the Gospel of God's forgiveness in Christ comes to Christians in five ways: through the spoken Word, through Baptism, through the Lord's Supper, through the power of the keys, and finally, "through the mutual conversations and consolation of brethren" (III IV 1). Regarding the latter, the article quotes Matthew 18:20: "Where two or three are gathered in my name, there am I among them."

BAPTISM

Following the article on the Gospel is a short treatise on Baptism. It reminds Christians, "Baptism is nothing other than God's Word in the water, commanded by His institution" (III V 1). Briefly put, it is the "washing . . . with the Word" (Ephesians 5:26). The article concludes by defending infant Baptism, saying that children, too, are included in the promise of Christ's redemption, and therefore the Church must continue baptizing them.

THE SACRAMENT OF THE ALTAR

Similar to in the Augsburg Confession, this article teaches that the consecrated bread and wine in the Lord's Supper are "Christ's true body and blood." The Supper should not be administered in one form only, as was the practice of the Catholic Church since the late Middle Ages. Withholding the wine from the laity was formally reaffirmed at the Council of Constance in 1414–18. In 1415, this council declared those desiring wine along with the bread were heretics.[8]

This article also rejects the Catholic doctrine of transubstantiation; namely, that the bread and wine are changed into the body and blood of Christ by the presiding priest, and that they are then no longer bread and wine.

THE KEYS

Christ told His apostles that in their forthcoming ministry they would be given the power to retain the sins of the impenitent and forgive the sins of those who repented. "I will give you the keys of the kingdom of heaven, and whatever you bind on earth shall be bound in heaven, and whatever you loose on earth shall be loosed in heaven" (Matthew 16:19). Article VII

> Children, too, are included in the promise of Christ's redemption, and therefore the Church must continue baptizing them.

of the Smalcald Articles calls this authorization of Christ "the Keys." Consistent with Jesus' words, this article explains, "The Keys are an office and power given by Christ to the Church for binding and loosing sin. This applies not only to gross and well-known sins, but also the subtle, hidden sins that are known only to God" (III VII 1). This function assures Christians that when their pastor on behalf of the congregation absolves them upon confessing their sins as penitent sinners, their sins are forgiven in the eyes of God.

Readers may be interested in knowing that "the Keys" (also known as the Office of the Keys and Confession) now found in Luther's Small Catechism initially was not part of his Small Catechism in 1529. Andreas Osiander, a Lutheran pastor in Nuremberg, as noted in chapter 10, added this part in 1531.[9]

CONFESSION

Closely related to the matter of repentance, this article discusses the practice of Christians confessing their sins. It notes that, while confession of sins is a necessary practice in the Church, it does not mean Christians must be able to recall or enumerate all their sins. The article says it is not possible to enumerate all of one's sins because human memory is too fallible. The discussion also notes that the absolution a remorseful sinner receives in the confession is part of the Keys.

The confession of sins includes private confession, a practice Lutherans did not discontinue at the time of the Reformation. In fact, the article says, "it should not be despised, but greatly and highly esteemed, along with all other offices of the Christian Church" (III VII 2). Although private or individual confession is not common in many Lutheran parishes today, it is still practiced by some. In fact, some present-day Lutheran hymnals still contain an order of private confession.

EXCOMMUNICATION

At the time of the Reformation, the Catholic Church practiced what it called the "greater excommunication"; namely, punishing individuals who committed civil wrongs outside the context of the church. This practice, says the article, does not belong to the church but rather to authorities outside the church. The church may only discipline or excommunicate Christians who are manifest and impenitent sinners in the spiritual realm. The article concludes by saying that clergy should not mingle or confuse the civil realm with the spiritual sphere,

HALLMARKS OF LUTHERAN IDENTITY

commonly called the two governments (kingdoms or realms) in Lutheran theology.

ORDINATION AND THE CALL

Here the extant ordination and vocation of clergy are criticized. The article contends ordaining ministers to serve in Christ's Church need not be done only by bishops. It also says the pope has no right to issue unbiblical laws that permit only bishops to ordain pastors and priests. Ordination is not a biblically mandated rite, nor has the Church always had bishops. In support of this argument, reference is made to the Early Church in Alexandria that had only priests and preachers, not bishops, governing its affairs.

THE MARRIAGE OF PRIESTS

At the time of the Reformation, the Catholic Church had for a number of centuries barred priests from marrying. The Smalcald Articles strongly opposed this practice on the grounds that it had no biblical basis. It argues priests should be free to marry, and that compulsory celibacy is wrong and unbiblical. The article calls preventing the marriage of priests a teaching "of demons" (III XI 3)

THE CHURCH

This article insists that the papacy is not the Church; rather, the Church consists of those who see Jesus Christ as their spiritual shepherd. Nor does the holiness of the Church consist of "albs, tonsures, long gowns, and other ceremonies they made up without Holy Scripture, but from God's Word and true faith" (III XII 3).

HOW ONE IS JUSTIFIED BEFORE GOD AND DOES GOOD WORKS

Here Rome's doctrine that man is justified by faith and good works is refuted. The article unequivocally states that man is justified by faith in Christ. Good works are the fruits of faith. They do not contribute

> Good works are merely the fruits of faith. They do not contribute to man's justification.

to man's justification. The article also states if good works are not present in the life of a Christian, then his or her "faith is false and not true" (III XIII 4).

Monastic Vows

In a few words, this article rejects not only monastic vows but also the biblical legitimacy of monks. It contends if anyone in the monastic way of life thinks he is living a more God-pleasing life and thus more likely to enter heaven than the ordinary Christian, he denies Christ's atonement.

Human Traditions

This article states the Catholic teaching that says human traditions provide "the forgiveness of sins or merit salvation is unchristian and condemned." The article also condemns "the pope's bag of tricks about foolish and childish articles, such as the dedication of churches, the baptism of bells, the baptism of the altar stone. . . . Such baptizing is a mockery and scorning of Holy Baptism, and so should not tolerated." The article's last sentence proclaims, "We will have nothing to do with them" (III XV 1–5).

The Treatise on the Power and Primacy of the Pope

This document rejects the legitimacy of the papal office on the basis of Scripture, the Early Church's history, and the Early Church Fathers, none of which provide any support for such an office in the Church. The document also notes and condemns the various abuses the papacy over the years imposed on the Church. It concludes that the office of the pope reveals marks of the Antichrist.

Philip Melanchthon wrote this treatise in 1537 at the request of the representatives of the Smalcaldic League that met the same year. The representatives of the League, who anticipated the convening of the general council in Mantua, felt circumstances made it necessary to address the un-Christian nature of the papal office. The treatise was officially adopted as a confession of faith by the representatives at Smalcald. And as noted earlier, Luther's illness prevented him from being present to sign it.

THE FORMULA OF CONCORD

Soon after Luther died in 1546, serious theological disagreements arose among Lutherans, resulting in the formation of two groups, the Gnesio-Lutherans and the Philippists. The former said they adhered to Luther's teachings, whereas the latter, followers of Philip Melanchthon, tried to compromise with the Calvinists and the Catholics. These two groups were unable to resolve the theological issues that divided them, but by the late 1560s and early 1570s, a third group, totally loyal to Martin Luther, entered the scene. This group consisted of men such as Martin Chemnitz, Jacob Andreae, Johannes Brenz, David Chytraeus, Christopher Koerner, Joachim Moerlin, and Nicholas Selnecker, along with a number of loyal laymen, some of whom were reigning dukes.[10] This latter group, after thirty years of theological debates and conflicts, was most instrumental in bringing about the Lutheran unity that produced the Formula of Concord, agreed upon and signed in 1577 and published on June 25, 1580, exactly fifty years to the date when the Augsburg Confession was signed in 1530.

Several items are noteworthy regarding the Formula of Concord. First, it is important to know it was signed by dukes, counts, barons, mayors, pastors, and theologians—8,188 signatories in all, whose acceptance brought about Lutheran unity after several decades of dissensions. They represented about two-thirds of the Lutheran territories in Germany.[11] Second, had it not been for Martin Chemnitz and Jacob Andreae, this historic document would likely not have seen the light of day. These two theologians were the prime movers in formulating the Formula's theology. With regard to Martin Chemnitz, the Catholics (as noted earlier in chapter 4) said, "If the second Martin had not come, the first would not have prevailed."[12] What would have become of the Lutheran Church without it no one knows. Third, it is important to note that in numerous instances the Formula of Concord uses the assertive phrase "We believe, teach, and confess" as its doctrinal positions are enunciated. These words reveal the writers' staunch theological and confessional convictions. Thus, their assertion, "we believe, teach, and confess" is an important hallmark of Lutheran theology and identity, with the Formula of Concord being the more prominent hallmark.

The Formula of Concord consists of two parts. The first part is the Epitome; the second part is the Solid Declaration. The Epitome has twelve articles: Original Sin; Free Will; the Righteousness of Faith before God; Good Works; the Law and the Gospel; the Third Use of

God's Law; the Holy Supper of Christ; the Person of Christ; the Descent of Christ to Hell; Church Practices, Which Are Called Adiaphora or Matters of Indifference; God's Eternal Foreknowledge and Election; and Other Factions and Sects. These articles were in controversy among Lutheran theologians after Luther's death but were resolved in the Epitome.

The Solid Declaration spells out in greater detail each of the twelve articles in the Epitome. Given that some of the articles, such as the doctrine of Original Sin, the Lord's Supper, Law and Gospel, and Good Works, are discussed in other parts of the present book, either as separate chapters or as parts in other chapters, not all are summarized in the present chapter, even though they are a part of the Formula of Concord.

FREE WILL

On the basis of 1 Corinthians 2:14, this article declares that natural man does not have the will to become a child of God; that is, to become a Christian. It further asserts that only God can turn the will of man to convert him, and that God does this through the means of His Word and Sacraments. Here the reader may refer above to chapter 8, "Word and Sacrament: Two Means of Grace."

> On the basis of 1 Corinthians 2:14, this article declares that natural man does not have the will to become a child of God; that is, to become a Christian.

This article on free will in part reflects Luther's book-length treatise known as *The Bondage of the Will* (1525), published in response to the learned scholar Erasmus of Rotterdam. The article refers to Luther's saying that before conversion, no human being can cooperate with the Holy Spirit, but after conversion, "a person's regenerate will is not idle, but also cooperates in all the Holy Spirit's works that He does through us" (SD II 88).

HALLMARKS OF LUTHERAN IDENTITY

The Righteousness of Faith before God

This topic pertains to the Lutheran teaching that a person is saved by grace through faith alone in Jesus Christ, as discussed above in chapter 3. The present article reaffirms that position. It states a person is righteous before God not because of any good works but solely on the basis of the person's faith in Christ and His atoning work of salvation. Faith in Christ makes a person righteous in God's sight. In the antitheses section, a number of false teachings regarding this article are stated and rejected.

The Third Use of God's Law

Here the Formula of Concord states that the Law, in addition to functioning as a curb and a mirror, also functions as a rule or a guide for human behavior, directing Christians to God-pleasing behavior. The article was largely written to refute those who argued that Christians no longer needed the Law. Those who taught and preached the latter at various times in the Christian Church were known as Antinomians, from the Greek *anti* (against) *nomos* (law).

The Person of Christ

This article reaffirms the two natures of Jesus Christ, which some false teachers, as early as in the fifth century, confused or denied. The article asserts that Christ's divine and human nature are united in such a way so that there are not two Christs—namely, one the Son of God and the other the Son of man. The article reinforces this position by stating,

> We believe, teach, and confess that now, in this one undivided person of Christ, there are two distinct natures: the divine, which is from eternity, and the human, which in time was received into the unity of the person of God's Son. These two natures in the person of Christ are never either separated from or mingled with each other. (SD VIII 7).

With this statement, Lutherans reiterated in the Formula of Concord what the Church confessed and declared at the Council of Ephesus in AD 451 when it said that Mary gave birth not only to Jesus but also to God. As noted in chapter 4, the council used the Greek term *theotokos* (God-bearer) to describe the Virgin Mary as having given birth to Jesus Christ, the God-man.

CHRIST'S DESCENT INTO HELL

As stated in the Apostles' Creed, this portion of the Formula of Concord underscores the truth that Christ did, in fact, descend into hell. It teaches that we should not speculate whether the descent took place before or after Christ's death, whether He descended spiritually or corporeally, or whether the descent was part of his suffering or glorious triumph. But rather, "We simply believe that the entire person (God and man) descended into hell after the burial, conquered the devil, destroyed hell's power, and took from the devil all his might" (SD IX 2–3).

CHURCH PRACTICES

This article in the Solid Declaration states that certain customs, practices, or rites in the church that are not biblically mandated must not be treated as though they are required. They are a matter of Christian liberty, provided their behavior does not give spiritual offense to fellow Christians. (For more on things not commanded or forbidden in Scripture, see chapter 18, which provides a detailed discussion on the topic of adiaphora.)

GOD'S ETERNAL FOREKNOWLEDGE AND ELECTION

Briefly put, this article makes several observations. One, God through Christ has elected all those who will enter eternal life, even before the world was created (Ephesians 1:4). Two, God alone does the electing; man has absolutely no role in electing himself to eternal life (1 Peter 1:2). Three, God does not want anyone to perish, for His Word says God "desires all people to be saved and to come to the knowledge of the truth" (1 Timothy 2:4); yet not all will be saved or elected. Four, if God wants all to be saved and He alone does the saving (electing), then why are not all saved? The article says this question must not be answered on the basis of reason but must be left to the inscrutable wisdom and mystery of God. Scripture only permits us to conclude that those who die outside of Christ are lost and have no one to blame but themselves. Finally, though God's foreknowledge knows all of the elect, it is not His foreknowledge that determines who is elected or not elected.

OTHER FACTIONS AND SECTS (THAT NEVER CONFESSED THE AUGSBURG CONFESSION)

This article rejects the teachings of the Anabaptists, Schwenk-felders, the New Arians, and the New Anti-Trinitarians. The Anabaptists are criticized for rejecting infant Baptism, refusing to serve in civil government, declining to take oaths, opposing the death penalty, faulting Christians for possessing private property, and so on. The Schwenkfelders are faulted for denying Baptism and the Lord's Supper as means of divine grace and for their faulty doctrine regarding the two natures of Christ. The New Arians and New Anti-Trinitarians are rejected for denying the deity of Christ.

CONCLUSION

The Book of Concord, which contains all Lutheran Confessional documents, has appropriately attained the reputation as the authoritative source of orthodox Lutheran theology in regard to what confessional Lutherans believe, teach, and confess to be the true and correct teachings revealed in the Old and New Testaments of the Bible. Given the Book of Concord's longstanding, authoritative position among Lutherans and Lutheran theology, it is indisputably and widely known as a major hallmark of Lutheran theology and identity.

1. What anniversary does the publication of the Formula of Concord in 1580 commemorate?

2. How many confessional documents does the Book of Concord contain?

3. Why was the Apology of the Augsburg Confession written?

4. Who was the primary author of the Apology of the Augsburg Confession?

5. Why is the Apology of the Augsburg Confession so much longer than the Augsburg Confession?

6. Why and by whom were the Smalcald Articles written?

7. What articles are found in the Smalcald Articles that are not in the Augsburg Confession?

8. When and by whom was the Office of the Keys added to Luther's Small Catechism?

9. The Lutheran Church did not abolish private confession during the Reformation or after. But today, private confession seems to have fallen by the wayside. Why do you think this has happened?

10. How many Lutherans signed the Formula of Concord?

11. What are Lutherans conveying to non-Lutherans by including the three Ecumenical Creeds in the forepart of the Book of Concord?

12. Who in the Lutheran Church is often called "the second Martin"? Why?

CHAPTER 20

WORK AND VOCATION

God's Mask

"All our work to God . . . are the masks of God, behind
which He wants to remain concealed and do all things."
—Martin Luther

Among the gems in Lutheran theology is Luther's perspective on work and vocation, especially as it relates to the work and vocation of Christians. This perspective is another important hallmark of Lutheran theology and identity. Unlike secular society, which tends to see work and vocation as synonymous terms, Luther saw them as similar or related but not as synonymous. He considered work as a more limited phenomenon compared to vocation, a concept derived from the Latin *vocatio*, a calling. It was a calling in which God wanted Christians to carry out their vocation that encompassed all a person does in his or her given station(s). Stations include being a husband, wife, parent, son, daughter, employee, employer, citizen, pastor, lawyer, or civic official. And a person may belong to several stations simultaneously; for example, a husband, a father, and school teacher.[1] In short, to Luther, vocation no longer referred only to religious orders and their related activities, as it was understood in Catholic thought before he theologically reconceptualized this important concept.

WORK AS A DIVINE CALLING

Luther saw both work and stations in the context of a Christian's vocation as a calling from God. Therefore, he said, "Let everyone . . .

rejoice that he is in a divine calling when he assumes and performs . . . ordinary duties of this life." He underscored this point by saying, "When a maid milks the cows or a hired man hoes the field—provided that they are believers; namely, that they conclude that this kind of life is pleasing to God."[2]

This view was radically different from what the Catholic Church had been teaching since at least the Middle Ages. Rome said only the clergy and those in religious orders had a vocation, a divine calling. Nonreligious work or domestic occupations did not qualify as vocations. Luther notes how this faulty teaching affected some people by citing what two jurists in Erfurt requested: "When the time came for them to die, they said to each other, sighing deeply: 'Oh, if we had not been doctors of law but monks, how much more blessedly we would now die!'"[3] Hoping to compensate for not having chosen a religious occupation, these two men had themselves clothed in the garb of monks in their coffins, an act for which they paid a lot of money to the church.[4]

For nearly five centuries, Lutheran theology has taught that every Christian's work and station are a divine calling, but this understanding does not appear to have been grasped very well by many Lutherans, and perhaps even less so by non-Lutheran Protestants. This is evident when one hears many, both Christians and non-Christians, giving the distinct impression that the occupation of a pastor or priest is a higher calling than a janitor, factory worker, mechanic, sales clerk, police officer, firefighter, teacher, mayor, executive, and so on. In the minds of many people, nonreligious occupations are divorced from the concept of a divine calling. Thus, the teaching of medieval Catholicism is still with us.

Most people commonly see certain occupations as having higher social statuses than others. To do so seems to be quite natural. But Luther argued that work, as a divine calling, means that in God's eyes all work has the same status and value. God is neither a respecter of persons (Acts 10:34) nor a respecter of status that humans attach to given occupations. In God's perspective, work performed by a clergyman has no higher status than any kind of work done by laypeople. This concept did not demean or lower the value of the office of the Christian ministry but rather elevated all occupations outside the Christian ministry. To God, all work is equally valuable and pleasing because it serves our neighbors and society, and hence His purpose. Luther taught that God does not need our good works but our neighbors do.

He further argued that what Christians do for God are not good works. Good works are what Christians do for their neighbors. This is an important distinction not well-known by many Christians, including many Lutherans.

Luther's understanding of work as vocation, says Emil Brunner, had revolutionary consequences. For if God does not assign social status to work, it makes no difference what kind of work Christians do so long as they perform it in faith to the glory of God and for their fellow human beings. Brunner says this Lutheran perspective shifted the meaning of work from *what* and *how* to *why*.[5]

Some forty years ago, Aaron Levenstein published a book called *Why People Work: Changing Incentives in a Troubled World* (1962). His research revealed while the incentives for work were changing, most Americans did not see work as having lost its purpose and meaning. However, his study makes no reference to work having purpose and meaning because it serves one's neighbors or that it is an important way to glorify God. Apparently, most Americans do not have the sense that their work is a vocation, a divine calling to serve their neighbors and thereby also glorify God.

WORK AS ONE OF GOD'S MASKS (*LARVAE DEI*)

In chapter 15, "Theology of the Cross," it was noted that Luther taught that God is hidden in the cross—not just in the cross on Calvary but also in our crosses of suffering and sorrow. Similarly, Luther saw God hidden in people's daily work and in their vocations. It was one of God's masks (*larvae Dei*), as noted in the present chapter's epigraph. "What else is all our work to God—whether in the fields, in the garden, in the city, in the house, in war, or in government. . . . These are the masks of God, behind which He wants to remain concealed and do all things."[6]

Luther saw God hidden in people's daily work and in their vocations.

As I have noted in *How Christianity Changed the World,* "So hidden is God in one's work that unless the Christian consciously thinks about it (and only the Christian with the Spirit of God in him or her can do so), he will have no awareness of God's presence in his work."[7] In a similar vein, popular Evangelical writer Philip Yancey has rightly stated, "It requires a trained set of eyes to see God in the details [of our work]."[8]

God is also hidden in the work of the non-Christians, but they do not know it. It is through their work, as well as through the work of Christians, that society's citizens are served and by which God maintains His created world. But this is not common knowledge—often not to most Christians either. Moreover, even when we Christians are told that God is hidden in our work or vocation, we have difficulty remembering this mysterious fact. Influenced by the world, it is hard for Christians to see work in that light.

Seeing God hidden in people's work and vocations is a highly beneficial insight for Christians. It reveals that there is a spiritual dimension to their work's activities, many of which often seem routine, monotonous, and at times even boring. Hence, though we Christians may often feel this way too, it is good to remind ourselves that God, in spite of our lack of awareness, is nevertheless hidden in our work. Keeping this truth firmly and daily in mind, by God's grace, gives added meaning and purpose to our work and vocations.

WORK AS HOLY AND UNHOLY

Not only is God hidden in our work, but He also sees work as either holy or unholy, depending on whether it is done by Christians or non-Christians. Hence, Luther says,

> Heathens and non-Christians do their work without God's Word, in sin and unbelief. But Christians do their work according to God's Word by faith in Christ and in obedience to God's Word. That is why the work of Christians is holy in God's sight, whereas the work of non-Christians is unholy.[9]

According to Luther, two things make work holy; namely, (1) God's Word, which commands man to work, and (2) faith in Jesus Christ. Luther said, "God's Word and faith make work pleasing to God and the angels." He goes on to say that without God's Word, work, as done by heathens, is vulgar in His sight, but the same work done mindful of God's Word and faith makes it "holy and God-pleasing."[10]

To say that work is holy only when performed by Christians and unholy when done by non-Christians may lead many in today's pluralistic society to conclude that such a statement is unkind, narrow-minded, and bigoted. Not to be taken aback by such criticism, we Christians need to remember St. Paul's words, "For whatever does not proceed from faith is sin" (Romans 14:23). On the other hand, it needs to be noted that though work done by non-Christians is not holy in God's sight, it is, however, still desired by God, for it is through the work of all people that He keeps His created world in operation.

DIGNITY AND HONOR OF WORK

Logically speaking, if God is hidden in one's work, it must then have dignity and honor. However, in the non-Christian world, work has not only become divorced from God's design but it also lacks dignity and honor. For instance, the latter belief harks back to the ancient Greeks and Romans, who had an extremely low opinion of manual work and labor. Their philosophers and freemen saw work, especially physical work, as demeaning and undignified. Manual labor was suitable only for slaves and the lower classes. It is rather well-known that renowned Greek philosopher Aristotle (384–322 BC) said no man could practice virtue if his livelihood was that of a mechanic or laborer. Plutarch (AD 46–ca. 120), another Greek thinker, reported that Plato (427–347 BC), renowned Greek philosopher, was incensed at two men for having constructed an apparatus to solve geometry problems. Manually constructed devices were to be crafted by artisans, who were usually slaves, not philosophers or freemen. Plato said mechanical devices corrupted "the pure excellence of geometry."[11] Cicero (d. 43 BC), Roman philosopher and rhetorician, said working daily for one's livelihood was "unbecoming to a gentleman" (a freeborn man), and "vulgar are the means of livelihood of all hired workmen whom

Logically speaking, if God is hidden in one's work, it must then have dignity and honor.

we pay for mere manual labor. . . . And all mechanics are engaged in vulgar trades."[12]

With the advent of Christianity, work began to receive dignity and honor, as Christians were influenced by their knowing that Jesus was once a carpenter and Paul a tentmaker. Neither Jesus nor Paul despised work. Moreover, Paul told the Thessalonians, "If anyone is not willing to work, let him not eat" (2 Thessalonians 3:10). The Apostolic Constitutions (ca. AD 375), a collection of apostolic precepts, reinforced Christianity's concept of work as honorable and God-pleasing by saying, "For the Lord hates the slothful."[13]

Luther's concept that all work is a calling in which God is hidden apparently stems in part from his familiarity by knowing that the early Christians saw all work in the light of dignity and honor. He was also keenly aware that God, through Moses, taught His people not to "muzzle an ox when it is treading out the grain" (Deuteronomy 25:4) and "the laborer deserves his wages" (Luke 10:7). Luther cites these passages many times in his writings, urging Christians to remember that their work has dignity and honor in the eyes of God.

Finally, our work has dignity and honor because it is commanded by God and because work is part of His created order. Even before sin entered the world, God told Adam to work: "The LORD God took the man and put him in the garden of Eden to work it and keep it" (Genesis 2:15). Luther cites this passage to show that even in paradise God gave Adam work to do. Work is not a consequence of man's fall into sin, as is sometimes erroneously assumed.

> Our work has dignity and honor because it is commanded by God and because work is part of His created order.

THE SIGNIFICANCE OF VOCATION (A CALLING)

As already noted, Luther saw vocation in a broader context than merely one's work or occupation. It included what he often called "stations" in life, such as being a father, mother, son, daughter, citizen, employee, or employer. Regarding these, Luther said, "This is my office; this is my vocation [a calling]. Such a person is pleasing to God. It is God's will that I be a father or mother, a husband or wife."[14]

According to Luther, the Christian's vocation is grounded in his or her Baptism. In one context, where he mentions Baptism and absolution, Luther urged all Christians, "Be anxiously concerned about the things that pertain to your faith and calling."[15] Hence, what a Christian does in his or her vocation is the fruit of faith and justification. He further adds that the Christian in his or her vocation "pleases God even in the lower stations in the kind of life . . . whether he is a servant, a maid, a magistrate, or a subject."[16] In these stations, Christians in their vocations serve their neighbors and society, and thereby glorify God.

Humanly speaking, being a parent, a maid, a laborer, a butcher, a baker, or a candlestick maker may seem quite mundane and even insignificant. But, according to Luther, we as Christians must not forget that we have been called by God to fill these and other stations in life. That is how God maintains His world on a daily basis, and He wants us to know and believe that our work or vocation is part of His divine will.

To Christians, work is part of their vocation, their calling from God. They are not just called to their work to provide for their own needs but also to serve their neighbors and society. It is one thing for Christians to receive therapeutic benefits from their work by its occupying their time, engaging their talents, providing a feeling of accomplishment, and overcoming the boredom of idleness, but for them to know that their work pleases God gives it the ultimate therapeutic value.

WORK AND ALIENATION

For some time, sociological studies have reported that modern workers (particularly in the West) are alienated from their work—that is, they do not identify with what they help produce and hence find no real satisfaction or meaning in it. This alienation has often been explained as being largely the consequence of modern society's high degree of specialization that prevents workers from seeing how their individual efforts have contributed to the final product that comes off the factory assembly lines. In the past, a worker who made a chair, a table, a garment, a buggy whip, or prepared food from the garden at home was able to see the product of his or her hand's labor and hence derived a feeling of satisfaction, as well as personally identifying with it. But now, as workers make mass-production items on factory assembly lines, the feelings of satisfaction, meaning, and identification with the products are essentially gone. It is virtually impossible for, say, factory workers to identify with a product they helped produce, such as an automobile, a television, a computer, or even factory canned foods, for they cannot see the part they, as individuals, contributed. Thus, modern workers are alienated from the products of their labor—so goes the argument.

If, however, in today's complex society, Christian workers were more cognizant of their work as a calling or vocation, and that God is hidden in it, alienation from work, it might be argued, would probably be greatly mitigated. Deriving satisfaction and meaning from work is important, but according to Luther's concept of vocation, meaning and fulfillment must not become ends unto themselves, divorced from why God really wants His people to work.

REMAINING TRUE TO ONE'S VOCATION

According to Luther, when Christians see their vocation as God-given and God-pleasing, the devil is highly displeased. The devil tries to get Christians to see their work as having nothing to do with God or with serving their neighbors. The devil wants Christians to see work only as that which provides for their own needs. He never wants to see God factored into any equation, and the concept of vocation is no exception. Thus, Swedish theologian Gustaf Wingren, in his book *Luther on Vocation*, says the devil is always at work tempting "to get man out of his vocation."[17] If he succeeds, then the Christian's work will take on a totally secular, worldly meaning. This may lead, as Lutheran educator and author Gene E. Veith Jr. points out, to various temptations, such as "to get a divorce, to leave one's children, to quit the job, to give up writing or making music, or whatever talents one has."[18]

The devil wants Christians to see work only as that which provides for their own needs.

How, then, do we Lutherans resist and overcome the devil's temptations regarding our vocation? We must daily remind ourselves that God has placed us in our various stations that make up our work. We also need to make use of God's Means of Grace, Word and Sacrament, and remember His promise of grace and faith embedded in our Baptism. And in the words of Jesus, we must say, "Get behind me Satan" when we are tempted to leave our vocation or to see our work divorced from God hidden in it. When we remember that God, though hidden, is truly in our work and vocation, not only are we conforming to His will but that truth also gives sacred meaning to what we do, contrary to what the world would have us believe.

CONCLUSION

Although God could indeed maintain His world without peoples' work or vocation, He nevertheless chose to use the various human activities to accomplish this end. As Luther phrased it, "God could easily give you grain and fruit without your plowing and planting. But he does not want to do so."[19] In other words, God uses people to produce goods and services needed to maintain the world He created, and it is well to remember, as Luther phrased it so well: "Our work, in and of itself, does not produce the goods that are necessary for life. God Himself must add His blessing to our work."[20] These words reflect still another hallmark of Lutheran theology and identity.

1. According to Luther, what is the difference between work and vocation?

2. What did Luther mean by "the mask of God" in work?

3. How did the ancient Greeks and Romans view manual labor?

4. How and why is a Christian's work or occupation a calling?

5. Why is it often difficult for Christians to see their work as a calling?

6. Why is work not the result of man's fall into sin?

7. What helped the early Christians see work as having dignity and honor?

8. How can Christians glorify God in their work as a calling?

9. How is being a parent, husband, wife, citizen, or an employee a vocation?

10. What makes a Christian's work or vocation holy?

11. How can work be therapeutic in a way often not recognized?

12. Why do you think the devil tempts us Christians to think our work (vocation) is unrelated to God's purpose in it?

CHAPTER 21

Hallmarks of the
Lutheran Reformation

"Unless I am convinced by the testimony of the Scriptures
or by clear reason (for I do not trust either in the pope or in
councils alone, since it is well known that they have often
erred and contradicted themselves) . . . my conscience is
captive to the Word of God. I cannot and I will not retract
anything . . . God help me, Amen."—Martin Luther

This chapter highlights the hallmarks of the Lutheran Reformation,
as opposed to the Reformation more broadly defined that often includes non-Lutheran Protestants. Hence, this chapter confines itself to
the hallmarks that characterized the Reformation only as it pertains to
Lutheran theology.

Ninety-Five Theses

As many Lutherans know, the Lutheran Reformation began in the
small town of Wittenberg, Germany, where on October 31, 1517, Martin Luther posted his Ninety-Five Theses on the door of the All Saints'
Church (also known as the Castle Church). When he hammered to
the door his theses, which, among other things, questioned the selling of indulgences relative to their biblical propriety, he had no idea
what would transpire as a result of his action. He had no intention of
propagating his thoughts on indulgences beyond the halls of the university. Nailing his theses to the door of the university church was not
an out-of-the-ordinary practice. Professors regularly used this method to inform students, professors, and others regarding topics that

would be discussed and debated in the university's classrooms.[1]

As Reformation scholar Roland Bainton says, Luther "was merely inviting scholars to dispute and dignitaries to define"[2] his proposed theses. It was individuals outside of the university, not Luther, who broadcast the theses by translating them into German from Latin. This made the theses available to the populace who had no love for an Italian pope taking money out of Germany's treasury to rebuild St. Peter's Basilica in Rome. The Ninety-Five Theses were the first seeds of the Reformation that spread rapidly across Europe and soon across the world. And soon they had the effect of indirectly spawning a number of significant and wholesome changes, both inside and outside the church. They provided the spirit that "produced wide, immediate, and permanent changes in practically every department of human life."[3] The following are some examples.

> The Ninety-Five Theses were the first seeds of the Reformation that spread rapidly across Europe and soon across the world.

PAPACY DETHRONED

The Lutheran Reformation resulted in the Roman papacy losing its tenacious, controlling grip on the Western world. Emperors, kings, princes, clergy, and congregations were no longer subject to the dictates of the pope. The reduced power of the papacy became evident early in the Reformation when the pope's fierce opposition to reform in the church was not able to squelch it. When Luther first criticized the selling of indulgences, he noted how indulgences had corrupted God's free gift of grace through faith in Jesus Christ. To eliminate indulgences seemed impossible. Tremendous obstacles stood in the way of reforming the church. Hence, soon after Luther had posted his Ninety-Five Theses, Albert Kranz, a Roman Catholic theologian in Hamburg, Germany, informed Luther, "You are speaking the truth, brother, but you will accomplish nothing. Go to your cell and say, 'God have mercy upon me.'"[4]

Kranz understood the entrenched corruption of the church under the power of the papacy. His warning to Luther did not foresee a decline in that power, and there is no evidence that Luther saw it in a different light either, especially when he stood trembling before the Diet of Worms in 1521 as an excommunicated heretic.[5] He may even have recalled Kranz's warning. Yet, by the grace of God, the efforts of Luther and the Reformation to reform the church's doctrines and practices, though not totally achieved, nevertheless dethroned the papacy from much of Western Christendom.

A Restored Gospel

As congregations divorced themselves from the power of the papacy during the Reformation, they were able to restore the pristine Gospel of the apostolic Church because they were now no longer subject to papal dictates that previously contradicted the Gospel in numerous ways. Now *solus Christus, sola gratia, sola fide,* and *sola Scriptura* could be taught and preached freely in many classrooms and pulpits.

Given these teachings of the Reformation, triggered by the Ninety-Five Theses, Philip Schaff, renowned Church historian of the nineteenth century, remarked that the Reformation, "next to the introduction of Christianity, [was] the greatest event in history."[6] Similarly, an unnamed British scholar, one hundred years ago, said, "October 31st should be a festive one in our calendar. . . . There has been no day like it for nineteen-hundred years, but the Day of Pentecost, with its divine consecration and its converting power."[7]

Only Two Sacraments

The Lutheran Reformation redefined the Church's sacraments, teaching there are not seven but two: Baptism and the Lord's Supper. This redefinition was largely derived from St. Augustine's understanding of what constitutes a sacrament. To him, a sacrament (as noted in chapter 8) had to be instituted by God, commanded by God, have visible elements, and convey the forgiveness of sins to repentant Christians. Rome had ignored St. Augustine's definition. Thus, it still teaches there are seven sacraments: Baptism, the Lord's Supper, ordination of priests, marriage, confirmation, penance (absolution), and extreme unction (last rites).

COMMUNION IN BOTH KINDS

The Lutheran Reformation brought back the New Testament's apostolic practice of giving communicants in the Lord's Supper both bread (Christ's body) and wine (Christ's blood). Although the Reformed (non-Lutheran Protestants) also practice Communion in both kinds, many use grape juice instead of wine. None teach that the consecrated bread and wine are the supernatural body and blood of Christ. They deny the words Christ spoke when He instituted the Lord's Supper on Holy Thursday: "This is My body, which is given for you. . . . This cup that is poured out for you is the new covenant in My blood" (Luke 22:19–20). As noted earlier, they also deny that the Lord's Supper is a Means of Grace that absolves repentant Christians of their sins.

CONGREGATIONAL SINGING

The Lutheran Reformation is commonly credited with having reintroduced congregational singing by the laity. For instance, in the early years of the Reformation, the liturgy was first sung in German by the laity in some churches outside of Wittenberg. In 1521, Carmelite monk Kaspar Kantz published a musical setting of the Mass in German. In 1523, Thomas Münzer published a vernacular musical Mass as well as a Matins and Vespers order of service. In 1524, there were also some other versions of the Mass introduced in the German language in some localities.

These different translations of the Mass, however, resulted in liturgical confusion, so Luther's colleagues urged him to produce a translation that would essentially provide liturgical uniformity. Thus, when Luther, in 1526, translated the Latin Mass into the language of the people, he called it *Die Deutsche Messe* (the German Mass). This translation soon spread beyond the confines of Wittenberg, proclaiming God's grace and mercy in German.

Luther's German Mass was designed for lay parishioners to sing, a practice that had been nonexistent for centuries even though laity used to sing hymns in the Early Church. For instance, Bishop Ambrose (339?–97) had the people sing in his cathedral in the latter part of the fourth century in Milan, Italy. His parishioners even sang hymns while they took part in a sit-in to keep the heretical Arians from occupying the cathedral. Ambrose also wrote some hymns for his parishioners. Two of his hymns in particular are still found in many Christian hymnals today; namely, "O Splendor of God's Glory Bright" and "Savior of the Nations, Come."

Ambrose is also credited with having introduced antiphonal singing. However, as noted earlier in chapter 13, long before Luther's time the laity no longer sang in church services. They had become passive observers. Choirs, largely composed of monks and canons, sang or chanted lyrics set to music, commonly sung in plainsong. But now, with the laity singing in church services, as a result of the Reformation, the Lutheran Church became known as "the singing church." Cardinal Thomas Cajetan (1469–1534), who tried to get Luther to recant when he met with him in Augsburg in 1518, later reportedly said of Luther and his songs, "By his hymns, he conquered us."

> The Lutheran Church became known as "the singing church."

Interestingly, almost five centuries after the Reformation began, research shows that members of the Roman Catholic Church still are not greatly interested in congregational singing. This fact is documented in Thomas Day's interesting book *Why Catholics Can't Sing* (1990). Day writes, "A great many people in Catholic churches do not even open their mouths to sing. Whole families, devout people go to church every week, do not even pick up the hymnal."[8] Hence, every time we hear laity singing in churches of various denominations, credit belongs to the Lutheran Reformation and to Luther in particular.

MARRIED CLERGY

In the fourth century, some synods (regional church councils) began mandating clerical celibacy, as did the Synod of Elvira in 305/306. Celibacy was also proposed at the Council of Nicaea in 325, but the council rejected the proposal; thus, many clergy continued to marry. The push of celibacy, however, did not abate. The Synod of Carthage (390) outlawed married men from becoming deacons unless they took a vow of chastity. The Council of Orleans (511) ruled that monks who married were to be expelled from ecclesiastical orders. Later, when the Fourth Lateran Council met in 1215, it outlawed marriage for all clergy. Thus, by Luther's time, clergy celibacy had become normative and firmly entrenched in the Catholic Church.

When the Reformation allowed and encouraged clergy to marry, it restored a practice that once was an accepted part of the Church's life, extending back to the Early Church. Holy Scripture tells us that some of Jesus' apostles were married, and the apostle Paul mentions some apostles taking "a believing wife" with them on their missionary journeys (1 Corinthians 9:5). Additionally, the Gospel of Mark (1:30–31) mentions Peter's mother-in-law, whom Jesus healed.

DAS PFARRHAUS (THE PARSONAGE)

Although some of Christ's apostles were married, we have no evidence that any of them shepherded a congregation or lived in a family parsonage associated with a congregation. But when Luther married Katharina von Bora in 1525, and Elector John in 1532 gave Luther and Katharina the Black Cloister building that once housed Augustinian monks, it became known as *das Lutherhaus.* This was something new and different because for the first time in the history of Christianity, it brought into being *das Pfarrhaus,* the family parsonage. And according to German Reformation scholar Susan C. Karant-Nunn, with this new ecclesiastical concept "the residents of the Lutheran parsonage were expected to epitomize the truly Christian family."[9] Luther and Katharina in their Black Cloister parsonage laudably exemplified this expectation. Their Christian life in the parsonage, and that of succeeding Lutheran pastors, supplanted the common unbiblical cohabitation of the Catholic Church's celibate priests and their concubines, who by definition could not "epitomize the truly Christian family." Following Luther's and Katharina's exemplary parsonage life, other Protestant churches also soon established parsonages in Europe and in the New World. The parish parsonage had become a salutary and highly influential Christian institution.

PRIESTHOOD OF BELIEVERS

First Peter 2:9 states all Christians are members of "a royal priesthood, a holy nation." On the basis of this passage, Luther taught that every Christian was a priest, for in Christ every Christian had direct access to the throne of God without needing an ordained priest to be the intermediary. This was in direct opposition to the official teaching of Roman Catholicism. In opposition to Rome, this doctrine "made for a spiritual democracy, and for religious and civil liberty. Lay people were again given a voice in spiritual matters, and in the government and administration of the church." It also did away with the "unscriptural distinction between a lower morality for the common people and higher morality for priests and monks who formed a spiritual nobility."[10]

It is well for Lutherans to remember that, though the Lutheran Reformation strongly accented the priesthood of all believers, it did not abolish or minimize the pastoral office. Luther did not erase the distinction between the ordained ministry and the priesthood of believers. According to Bernhard Lohse, Luther "used the term *'sacerdotium'* in discussing the universal priesthood, but reserved the term *'ministerium'* for the ordained ministry."[11] As members of the former, every Christian has access to God without an intermediary. This gives every Christian a holy status, but not a holy office with specific functions to perform as a minister or pastor in the church. Pastors were ministers, preachers chosen from the priesthood of the baptized who had special roles to perform as "servants of Christ and stewards of the mysteries of God."[12]

Though the Lutheran Reformation strongly accented the priesthood of all believers, it did not abolish or minimize the pastoral office.

Reformation Day

Luther historian Ernest G. Schwiebert says the Reformation was commemorated "quite early" by the Wittenberg faculty in the *Lutherstube* (Luther's room) with a brief religious service.[13] Later, Lutheran territorial churches in Europe commemorated the Reformation on various days: some on Luther's birthday (November 10), some on the day of his death (February 18), and some on June 25, the date the Augsburg Confession was presented to Emperor Charles V. Then, in 1667, the sesquicentennial year of

1517, the Elector John George II of Saxony set October 31 as the date to celebrate the Reformation.[14] Since then, every year, countless Lutheran churches (and also some Reformed churches) celebrate the Reformation by having special Divine Services on October 31 or the Sunday nearest that date. Currently, in Germany, October 31 is a public holiday in five of its sixteen states.

To celebrate this day in the history of the Christian Church, many Lutheran hymnals contain a special Introit, Collect, Epistle, Gradual, and Gospel lesson. In the Lutheran liturgical calendar, Reformation Day comes near the end of the Pentecost season. The liturgical color for this day is red.

Given that celebrating Reformation Day had become a tradition in Germany, Lutherans brought this custom with them when they migrated to the New World. They celebrated it in a special church service each year on the Sunday nearest October 31, and in some localities, they also held Reformation rallies. The latter brought Lutherans together from numerous congregations, reflecting a bond of Christian fellowship.

In addition to special Reformation Day services, some Lutheran periodicals each year in October still publish articles on the significance of the Reformation. These articles seek to remind Lutherans of the event's importance by underscoring the doctrines of Christ alone, grace alone, faith alone, and Scripture alone. After noting these hallmarks of the Reformation, one article stated, "If the principles are to be more than slogans . . . Lutherans will also make Reformation Day a day of rededication."[15] It is important for us Lutherans to remember that, by celebrating Reformation Day, we are not honoring Luther but commemorating the renewal of the gracious and mighty work of God given to us in the Gospel of Jesus Christ.

In today's secular climate, the celebration of Reformation Day is losing some of its significance. Fewer Reformation rallies are taking place, and attendance at the ones still held is declining. Many Lutherans today are less likely to remember Reformation Day than in the past, unless their pastor reminds them, and when reminded, there is less interest in appreciating this historic day. Some blame the declining interest on Halloween, a secular or neo-pagan day. Halloween has been called "the great cover-up," given that approximately fifty million Americans each year celebrate it on October 31. Others see the decline as a result of our society's growing secularism, which has not left Lutherans unscathed.

VERBUM DOMINI MANET IN AETERNUM
(THE WORD OF THE LORD ENDURES FOREVER)

In 1522, Duke Frederick the Wise, protector of Luther and greatly influenced by Luther, chose these Latin words as his motto. Frederick had them sewn on the sleeves of his court's servants. His successors (dukes) also used this motto. In addition, it was inscribed on banners, flags, uniforms, medals, clocks, and monuments, above church doors, and even on the helmets of war horses. Biblically speaking, this slogan's words are derived from Isaiah 40:8 and 1 Peter 1:25. Both passages contrast the fading and wilting of grass to the Word of the Lord that endures forever.

In 1531, nine Lutheran princes, fearing probable military attacks on their territories by the pro-papal forces of Emperor Charles V, formed a defensive pact. As indicated previously, the princes met in Smalcald, Germany, and named their pact The Smalcaldic League. Following the precedent of Frederick the Wise, the League chose the motto of *Verbum Domini Manet in Aeternum*. It served as a conspicuous hallmark of Lutheran theology and identity.

These words functioned as the League's symbol of unity for clergy and laity alike whose teachings and lives were in constant danger. Thus, the motto became the symbol of the Lutheran Reformation.

Some Lutheran entities still employ this time-honored motto. Quite often, it is abbreviated as VDMA, and sometimes each of these four letters is depicted on a cross with the letter V in the upper-left corner, where the vertical and horizontal arms of the cross intersect, letter D in the upper-right corner, letter M in the lower-left, and letter A in the lower-right corner. The journal *Lutheran Quarterly* depicts this motto in this abbreviated manner too. And The Lutheran Church–Missouri Synod's Concordia Publishing House has adopted this noteworthy Reformation symbol as its official logo, often portrayed in the abbreviated form.

"A MIGHTY FORTRESS IS OUR GOD"

There probably is not a single Lutheran who has never sung Martin Luther's stirring hymn "A Mighty Fortress Is Our God." As noted earlier, this hymn is often called the "Battle Hymn of the Reformation." Although Lutherans greatly cherish this inspiring anthem, it is also sung in many non-Lutheran churches. In recent years, it has even been included in some Roman Catholic hymnals. But because Lutherans have always been identified so closely with this hymn, it is not an exaggeration to call it a highly important hallmark of Lutheran identity.

DATE OF PUBLICATION

Exactly when Luther, the "nightingale of Wittenberg," wrote the lyrics and the music for this hymn is not known for certain. Some historians suggest he composed it when efforts to reform the Church looked bleak and hopeless, given the actions Rome had taken at the Diet of Speyer in 1529. At this diet, Emperor Charles V overturned the decree of *cuius regio eius religio* (the prince determines the religion in his region) that had been issued by the previous Diet of Speyer in 1526. The 1526 decrees resulted in many of Germany's geographic regions implementing specific church reforms. Some even sought to "introduce the whole Reformation."[16]

Other historians think Luther wrote this hymn while he was confined to the castle at Coburg in 1530, before and during the time the Augsburg Confession was presented to Emperor Charles V at the Diet of Augsburg. But Ernest G. Schwiebert is certain that the song appeared even "before 1529 in a hymnal printed around that date." He concludes that Luther composed it "between the summer of 1527 and the spring of 1528."[17]

THEOLOGICAL CONTENT

Some church historians have said "A Mighty Fortress" is a hymn that is as theologically rugged as Luther. As already noted, others have called it "The Battle of Hymn of the Reformation," fighting for the truth and proclamation of the Gospel. Still others, having in mind the French Revolution of the late 1700s, have labeled it as the "Marseilles of the Reformation," giving it the status of a battle hymn.

"A Mighty Fortress" is based on Psalm 46. Its first verse reads, "God is our refuge and strength, a very

> Some church historians have said "A Mighty Fortress" is a hymn that is as theologically rugged as Luther.

present help in trouble." Thus, when Luther wrote the German words *"Ein' feste Burg ist unser Gott"* (A mighty fortress is our God), he made an almost literal translation of the psalm's first line, for the ancient fortress was truly both a refuge and strength, providing people protection from outside enemy attacks. That is how Luther saw God; to him, God was not a pie-in-the-sky concept, divorced from the human scene. Rather, God, through His Word and Sacrament, provided refuge and strength to His people in times of turmoil and trouble. Given that Luther lived constantly with the death decree hanging over his head, along with his struggles against a corrupt papacy, the imagery of God being a mighty fortress in his life described the situation exceptionally well.

Although "A Mighty Fortress" is based on Psalm 46, it also draws from other sections of Scripture. For instance, the words "with might of ours can naught be done" in the second stanza remind us of Christ's words "apart from Me you can do nothing" (John 15:5). The words "Sabaoth Lord," also in the second stanza, are found in Romans 9:29 (NKJV). The words "one little word can fell him" in the third stanza seem like they were drawn from the words Christ spoke to the devil when tempted three times. Jesus rebuffed the devil each time with God's Word, citing three references from Deuteronomy 6. These biblical citations finally prompted the devil to stop tempting Jesus (Matthew 4:11). God's Word did indeed fell him. And not to be overlooked are the words in stanza 2, "And there's none other God." These not only recall the First Commandment, which forbids us to have other gods, but they also recall these words of St. Peter, "There is salvation in no one else, for there is no other name under heaven given among men by which we must be saved" (Acts 4:12). Without noting additional biblical references embedded in this hymn, it is not an exaggeration to say that few other Christian hymns have their phrases and sentences so solidly grounded in Scripture as this one.

Few other Christian hymns have their phrases and sentences so solidly grounded in Scripture as this one.

As noted earlier, during the Reformation era the Lutheran Church was often referred to by many Catholics as "the singing church," and Luther's "A Mighty Fortress Is Our God" reinforced this perception. With respect to this hymn's theological impact, Lutheran hymnist and author W. G. Polack has said,

> The good this hymn has done, the faith it has inspired, the hearts it has comforted, the influence it has exerted cannot be measured and will first be revealed to us in eternity, where the saints of God will praise their Lord and Redeemer for the many blessings, not the least of which will be the privilege of having known and sung this hymn here on earth.[18]

In the 1920s, several coal miners of German extraction were trapped in a mine for three days near Scranton, Pennsylvania. After two days, rescue efforts had brought no results. On the third day, a crowd gathered, saying it was useless to continue; moreover, many in the crowd argued that the miners were probably dead. The owners of the mine were blamed, and the crowd was about to riot. At this juncture, a devout eleven-year-old girl raised her young voice and started singing "A Mighty Fortress Is Our God." Soon others joined her. Singing this hymn changed the crowd's angry mood and digging resumed. Before dawn, the rescue workers found the trapped miners, alive.[19]

One admirer of this hymn expressed its theological value in the following words: "We most likely will not know the same fierce opposition or have our life on the line as did Martin Luther. But we can know the same God as our refuge and strength, who will be for us 'a very present help in trouble.'"[20]

THE HYMN'S WIDE APPEAL

Usages such as the coal-mining incident just cited not only indicate this hymn's wide appeal but also show an appeal that sometimes goes far beyond the pews of churches. It "has been translated into more languages than any other hymn in Christendom."[21] Scholars estimate between two hundred to three hundred translations have been made. One of the better-known translations was made by Thomas Carlyle (1795–1881), known as a Scottish historian, moral teacher, and rector.[22] He rendered the hymn's first line as "A safe stronghold of our God is still."

Odd as it may seem, it is not just Christians who have translated this magnificent hymn. A Unitarian clergyman, Frederic H. Hedge (1805–90), provided an American translation.[23] In 1852, he translated the hymn's first line, *"Ein' feste Burg ist unser Gott,"* to read, "A mighty fortress is our God." And interestingly, this first line became the hymn's present English title, "A Mighty Fortress Is Our God." Not only did a Unitarian clergyman translate and give this hymn its present title, but it even found its way into some Unitarian hymnals.

In the Thirty Years' War (1618–48), Sweden's King Gustavus Adolphus used "A Mighty Fortress" as his army's battle hymn when he fought to preserve the Reformation against the forces of Roman Catholicism. The Swedish king had his troops sing this hymn before at least two battles, at Leipzig and at Lützen, Germany. It was at Lützen where this royal defender of the Reformation was killed in battle on November 6, 1632.

It is not surprising that this inspirational hymn was sung at Luther's funeral in February 1546. And on his tombstone inside the Castle Church in Wittenberg, the church on whose door Luther tacked the Ninety-Five Theses in 1517, are the words *"Ein' feste Burg ist unser Gott"* ("A Mighty Fortress Is Our God"), the hymn's first line, recorded in relief form.

Reportedly, when Luther's wife, Katharina, lay on her death bed with her children present, she asked, "Do you think you children could also sing your father's great hymn of the Reformation?" Without hesitation, they sang, "A mighty fortress is our God, a trusty shield and weapon." Moments later, she took her last breath and went to be with her Lord on December 20, 1552. Her children had her buried in St. Mary's Lutheran Church in Torgau, Saxony. There she rests until the good Lord will come on the Last Day to judge the living and the dead and raise her to everlasting life.

When "A Mighty Fortress" was sung at Luther's funeral, it set a precedent, for since then, it has often been sung at funerals of many prominent individuals, including funerals for some non-Lutherans. In March 1969, it was sung at the National Cathedral in Washington DC, at the funeral of Dwight D. Eisenhower, former World War II general and United States president. And in January 2007, it was sung at the funeral of former United States President Gerald Ford.

Occasionally, "A Mighty Fortress Is Our God" is also sung at other public events. On September 14, 2001, it was sung at the National Cathedral in Washington DC, when hundreds of governmental officials (national and foreign) assembled for an interreligious gathering three days after the Islamic terrorists destroyed New York's Twin Towers and part of the Pentagon Building in Washington, and also crashed a plane in Pennsylvania.

CONCLUSION

As Lutherans, we want to thank God for having given to His Church Martin Luther, who with his biblical and historical knowledge and his dauntless courage, defended the Gospel of Jesus Christ and, as a result, reformed the Church. As Lutherans, we have special reason to celebrate the Reformation on October 31, not because we are members of a church named in honor of Luther, but because, by God's grace, we are spiritually edified by the apostolic teachings that Luther restored in the Church. Hence, we joyfully want to celebrate the Reformation's renewal of the Gospel of Jesus Christ every year on Reformation Day, a distinctive Lutheran hallmark and identity.

Finally, we thank God for having led Luther during the Reformation, in unbelievingly trying times, to compose "A Mighty Fortress Is Our God." His hymn reminds us that God is indeed a spiritual fortress when Christians are maligned or even attacked by anti-Christian forces, or when the devil attacks us by seeking to instill doubts in our minds about the efficacy of God's grace and forgiveness in His Son, Jesus Christ, or to get us to believe that there is also eternal salvation in other gods, contrary to Christ's own words, "I am the way, and the truth, and the life. No one comes to the Father except through Me" (John 14:6). We need to continue to sing this majestic hymn not only on Reformation Day but also on other important occasions, gratefully remembering that by God's grace it is one of the honorable, important hallmarks of our Lutheran theology and identity, all of which we would do well to preserve, teach, and cherish.

CHAPTER 21 DISCUSSION QUESTIONS

1. Why did Luther post his Ninety-Five Theses on the door of the university church?

2. How did Luther in the Reformation restore the Gospel of Jesus Christ?

3. How did the Reformation dethrone the papacy?

4. What significance does Luther's doctrine of the priesthood of believers have for us Lutherans today?

5. Why was the Lutheran Church during the Reformation period called "the singing church"?

6. What biblical precedent did Luther have for encouraging clergy to marry, as well as marrying himself?

7. What effect did Luther's marriage to Katharina and their living in a parsonage have on countless Lutheran and Reformed Protestant parishes?

8. Why did Luther translate the Latin Mass into a German format that he initially called the *Deutsche Messe?*

9. How does Lutheran theology define a sacrament?

10. Why, according to Lutheran theology, are confirmation and ordination not sacraments?

11. Give a couple of reasons why we Lutherans should continue to celebrate Reformation Day each year.

12. Explain how "A Mighty Fortress Is Our God" (*LSB* 656/657) is a spiritual battle song.

13. "A Mighty Fortress" is based on what psalm?

14. What words in that psalm does "A Mighty Fortress" echo?

15. What words in "A Mighty Fortress" are most inspiring to you?

16. Why may Lutherans rightfully see "A Mighty Fortress" as a hallmark of Lutheran identity?

ENDNOTES

INTRODUCTION

1   Merton P. Strommen et al., *A Study of Generations* (Minneapolis: Augsburg Fortress, 1972), 145.

2   Strommen et al., *A Study of Generations*, 148.

3   Lutheran Brotherhood, "Lutheran Brotherhood's Survey of Lutheran Beliefs and Practices" (Photostatic Document: Summer 1998), 11.

4   Mark A. Noll, "The Lutheran Difference," *First Things* (February 1992): 31–40. Noll is a non-Lutheran historian, specializing in the history of Christianity in the United States and Canada.

CHAPTER 1
SOLUS CHRISTUS (CHRIST ALONE)

1   AE 15:339.

2   AE 25:405.

3   AE 15:268.

4   AE 33:26.

5   Martin Luther, "The Earliest Christian Creeds," *Luther's Catechetical Writings*, trans. John Nicholas Lenker (Minneapolis: The Luther Press, 1907), 224.

6   Cited in Hermann Sasse, *This Is My Body: Luther's Contention for the Real Presence in the Sacrament of the Altar* (Adelaide, Australia: Open Book Publishers, 1977), 203.

7   Cited in Michael Reu, *Luther and the Scriptures* (Columbus, OH: The Wartburg Press, 1944), 47. Erasmus of Rotterdam (1469–1536) moved away from Reformation teachings. Luther refuted Erasmus's notion that fallen man had the free will spiritually to choose Christ in God's plan of salvation. See Luther's *On the Bondage of the Will* (1525).

8   Blaise Pascal, *Pensees, The Great Books of the Western World*, ed. Mortimer Adler (Chicago: Encyclopedia Britannica, Inc., 1996), 267. Pascal (1623–62) was a French philosopher and scientist.

9   Wolfhart Pannenberg, *Jesus—God and Man*, trans. Lewis L. Wilkins and Duane A. Priebe (Philadelphia: Westminster, 1968), 19. Pannenberg (d. 2014) was a Lutheran theologian in Germany who defended the historicity of Christ's resurrection.

10 Sasse, *This Is My Body*, 93. Sasse (1895–1976) was an Australian Lutheran theologian.

11 AE 37:364.

12 Strommen et al., *A Study of Generations*, 369.

13 Lutheran Brotherhood, "Lutheran Brotherhood's Survey of Lutheran Beliefs and Practices," (Summer 1998): 10.

14 This heresy refers to Arius (d. ca. 336), a presbyter in Egypt who denied the deity of Jesus Christ.

15 Strommen et al., *A Study of Generations*, 117.

16 *Lumen Gentium* 16, Cited in *Catechism of the Catholic Church* (Liguori, MO: Liguori Publications, 1994), 224.

17 Cited in Francis A. Sullivan, *Salvation Outside of the Church? Tracing the History of the Catholic Response* (New York: Paulist Press, 1992), 115.

CHAPTER 2
SOLA GRATIA (BY GRACE ALONE)

1   *Catechism of the Catholic Church*, 484.

2   Edward W. A. Koehler, *A Summary of Christian Doctrine*, 2nd ed. (Oakland, CA: Alfred W. Koehler, 1952), 79. Koehler (1875–1951) served as a Lutheran professor and theologian.

3   Koehler, *A Summary of Christian Doctrine*, 80.

4   Theodore Hoyer, "The Grace of God," *The Abiding Word*, ed. Theodore Laetsch (St. Louis: Concordia, 1947), 2:203.

5   Followers of John Calvin (1509–64), a French-Swiss theologian.

6   John Calvin, *Institutes of the Christian Religion*, trans. Henry Beveridge (Grand Rapids: Eerdmans, 1957), 2:213.

7   John Calvin, *Calvin's Calvinism: Treatises on the Eternal Predestination of God and the Secret Providence of God*, trans. Henry Cole, 1855 (Grandville, MI: Reformed Free Publishing Association, 1987), 115–16.

8   Francis Pieper, *Christian Dogmatics* (St. Louis: Concordia, 1953), 3:495. Pieper (1852–1931) served as president of The Lutheran Church—Missouri Synod (1899–1911) and as a seminary professor.

9   Arminianism is the theology derived from the Dutch theologian Jacobus Arminius (1560–1609). He, contrary to Calvinism, taught that the predestination of Christians was conditional in that they cooperated in their conversion.

10 Roger E. Olson, *Arminian Theology: Myths and Realities* (Downers Grove: IVP Academic Books, 2006), 14.

11 Philip Melanchthon (1497–1560) wrote the first Lutheran work on dogmatics, which Luther praised. Later, Melanchthon began to espouse some doctrines in conflict with Lutheran theology. Those who followed him were called "Philippists."

12 Chapter 8 provides additional information on the Means of Grace.

CHAPTER 3
SOLA FIDE (BY FAITH ALONE)

1   Ephesus was a pagan city whose citizens worshiped the goddess Artemis (Diana in Latin).

2   J. Gresham Machen, *What Is Faith?* (Grand Rapids: Eerdmans, 1925), 43. Machen formerly served at Princeton Theological Seminary until 1920, when he, an opponent of liberalism, founded Wesminster Seminary in Philadelphia.

3   Paul Tillich, *Dynamics of Faith* (New York: Harper and Row, 1957), 87, 89. Used by permission of HarperCollins. Tillich (1886–1965) was a prominent German liberal theologian, popular in the 1950s and 1960s.

4   Rudolf Bultmann, "The Problem of Miracle," *Religion in Life* (Winter 1957–58): 63–64. Bultmann (1884–1976), a contemporary of Tillich, was an influential liberal German theologian. Bultmann sought to demythologize the New Testament.

5   Dietrich Bonhoeffer, *Wer Ist Und War Jesus Christus?* (Hamburg: Furche-Verlag, 1962), 85. This citation is my translation. Bonhoeffer (1906–45) was a German theologian who was executed by the Nazis in April 1945 for his role in the failed attempt to assassinate Hitler in July 1944, and whom many now mistakenly regard as a conservative Lutheran.

6   Dietrich Bonhoeffer, *Gesammelte Schriften* (Munich: Chr. Kaiser Verlag, 1972), 5:138.

7   Dietrich Bonhoeffer, *Jugend und Studium, 1918–1927* (Munich: Chr. Kaiser Verlag, 1986), 319.

8   Bonhoeffer, *Jugend und Studium, 1918–1927*, 319. Both citations are my translations.

9   Dieter Lührmann, "Faith," *Anchor Bible Dictionary*, ed. David Noel Freedman (New York: Doubleday, 1992), 2:750.

10 Lührmann, "Faith," *Anchor Bible Dictionary*, 2:744.

11 Lührmann, "Faith," *Anchor Bible Dictionary*, 2:752.

12 E. R. Dodds, *Pagan and Christian in an Age of Anxiety: Some Aspects of Religious Experience from Marcus Aurelius to Constantine* (Cambridge, UK: Cambridge University Press, 1965), 121.

13 Wolfhart Pannenberg, *Basic Questions in Theology: Collected Essays*, trans. George H. Kelm (Philadelphia: Fortress Press, 1971), 2:37.

14 John Calvin, *Institutes of the Christian Religion*, ed. John T. McNeill, trans. Ford Lewis Battle (Philadelphia: Westminster, 1960), 1:544.

15 John Warwick Montgomery, *Faith Founded on Fact: Essays in Evidential Apologetics* (New York: Thomas Nelson, 1978), 79. Montgomery is a Lutheran theologian, international attorney, and Christian apologete.

16 J. Gresham Machen, *Christianity and Liberalism* (Grand Rapids: Eerdmans, 1923), 72.

17 Pannenberg, *Jesus—God and Man*, 109.

18 "Lexington: More Than a Hobby," *The Economist* (July 2, 2016): 28.

19 Aristotle, *The Art of Rhetoric*, trans. John Henry Freese (Cambridge, MA: Harvard University Press, 1939), 27.

20 Cited in Robert A. Sungenis, *Not By Faith Alone: The Biblical Evidence for the Catholic Doctrine of Justification* (Santa Barbara: Queenship Publishing Company, 1996), 690.

21 St. Ambrose (340–397), Bishop of Milan and strong opponent of Arianism.

22 Abdel Ross Wentz, "What Is Lutheranism?" in *What Is Lutheranism? A Symposium in Interpretation*, ed. Vergilius Ferm (New York: The Macmillan Company, 1930), 76.

23 Roger L. Sommer, "Sanctification," in *The Abiding Word*, 2:285.

24 Gustaf Wingren, *Luther on Vocation*, trans. Carl C. Rasmussen (Evansville, IN: Ballast Press, 1999), 10.

25 Some of the present discussion on the misuse of the concept of faith is extracted from my chapter "Polytheism: The New Face of American Civil Religion," in *The*

Anonymous God: The Church Confronts Civil Religion and American Society, eds. David L. Adams and Ken Schurb (St. Louis: Concordia, 2004), 193–217.

26 AE 35:370.

CHAPTER 4
SOLA SCRIPTURA (BY SCRIPTURE ALONE)

1 AE 15:339.

2 This epigraph is a paraphrase of these words of Luther: "Here [in the Bible] you will find the swaddling cloths and the manger in which Christ lies." See AE 35:236.

3 AE 32:112–13.

4 Bernhard Lohse, *Martin Luther: An Introduction to His Life and Work*, trans. Robert C. Schultz (Philadelphia: Fortress Press, 1980), 153.

5 Lohse, *Martin Luther*, 154.

6 Erwin L. Lueker, *Lutheran Cyclopedia* (St. Louis: Concordia, 1954), 1116.

7 Boniface VIII, "Titulus II," *Sexti Decretalium Liber Primus* In *Corpus Iuris Canonici* II (Graz: Akademische Druck U. Verlagsanstalt, 1959), 937.

8 Ernest G. Schwiebert, *Luther and His Times: The Reformation from a New Perspective* (St. Louis: Concordia, 1950), 122.

9 Leonard J. Greenspoon, "How the Bible Became the Kynge's Owne English," *Bible Review* (December 2003): 19.

10 John Wycliffe (1320–84), a professor at Oxford University, also encouraged the separation of church and state. In 1415, the Council of Constance excommunicated him, and in 1428 his bones were exhumed and cremated.

11 Schwiebert, *Luther and His Times*, 119.

12 Schwiebert, *Luther and His Times*, 158.

13 Schwiebert, *Luther and His Times*, 158.

14 AE 38:159.

15 Schwiebert, *Luther and His Times*, 149.

16 Roland H. Bainton, *Here I Stand: A Life of Martin Luther* (Nashville: Abingdon Press, 1950), 74.

17 Bainton, *Here I Stand*, 144.

18 Robert A. Sungenis, ed., *Not By Scripture Alone: A Catholic Critique of the Protestant Doctrine of Sola Scriptura* (Santa Barbara: Queenship Publishing Company, 1997).

19 A full list of Feasts, Festivals, and Commemorations can be found in *Lutheran Service Book* (St. Louis: Concordia, 2006), xi–xiii.

20 An ecumenical creed is accepted by most Christian churches. However, some churches—for example, Baptists, who do not believe that Baptism forgives sins—do not accept the Nicene Creed because it asserts, "I acknowledge one Baptism for the remission of sins."

21 During the last two or three decades, some Lutheran congregations have departed from using the historic, traditional liturgy by opting for what is often called "contemporary services."

22 Martin Chemnitz, *The Two Natures of Christ*, trans. J. A. O. Preus (St. Louis: Concordia, 1971), 209. The Romanists called him [Chemnitz, 1522–86] "the second Martin," meaning "if the second Martin had not come, the first one [Luther] would not have prevailed" (J. A. O. Preus, *The Second Martin: The Life and Theology of Martin Chemnitz* (St. Louis: Concordia, 1994), 16.

23 John Eck (1486–1543) opposed Luther and championed papal supremacy.

24 Cited in Bainton, *Here I Stand*, 90.

25 Bainton, *Here I Stand*, 90.

26 Athanasius, "Against the Heathen," *Select Writings and Letters of Athanasius, Nicene and Post-Nicene Fathers* (Peabody, MA: Hendrickson Publishers, Inc., 2004), 4.

27 Henry Alford, *The New Testament for English Readers* (Chicago: Moody Press, n.d.), 511.

CHAPTER 5
NEW TESTAMENT CANONICITY: EARLY CHURCH, LUTHER, AND THE COUNCIL OF TRENT

1 Steven B. Cowan, "Canonicity," *The Encyclopedia of Christian Civilization* (Chichester, UK: Wiley-Blackwell, 2011), 1:370.

2 F. F. Bruce, *The Canon of Scripture* (Downers Grove, IL: InterVarsity, 1988), 41.

3 See *The Qur'an*, A new translation by M. A. S. Abdell Haleem (New York: Oxford University Press, 2004), 416.

4 Joseph Smith, *History of the Church of Jesus Christ of Latter-Day Saints* (Salt Lake City: Deseret Book Company, 1970), 1:18.

5 Marcion was an early Christian heretic who had to be excommunicated by his father, a bishop.

6 Caspar Rene Gregory, *Canon and Text of the New Testament* (Edinburgh: T & T Clark, 1907), 156.

7 Alexander Souter, *The Text and Canon of the New Testament* (London: Gerald Duckworth & Company Limited, 1965), 210.

8 Eusebius (c. 260–c. 339) is often referred to as the father of Church history.

9 Irenaeus, *St. Irenaeus of Lyons: Against Heresies*, trans. Dominic J. Unger, revised Irenaeus M. C. Steenberg (New York: The Newman Press, 2012), 30. Irenaeus (martyred in AD 202) was an Early Church Father who defended Christianity and opposed Gnosticism and other heresies.

10 Irenaeus, *St. Irenaeus of Lyons: Against Heresies*, 30.

11 Lee Martin McDonald, "Identifying Scripture and Canon in the Early Church: The Criterion Question," eds. Lee Martin McDonald and James A. Sanders, *The Canon Debate* (Peabody, MA: Hendrickson Publishers, 2002), 424.

12 AE 35:394–95.

13 AE 35:362.

14 AE 35:396.

15 AE 35:398.

16 AE 35:398

17 AE 35:395.

18 AE 35:396.

19 AE 35:397–98.

20 AE 35:400.

21 Martin Luther, "Die Bücher des neuen Testaments" in *D. Martin Luthers Kritsche Gesamtsausgabe Die Deutsche Bibel* (Weimar: Hermann Böhlaus Nachfolger, 1929), 6:13.

22 Bruce Metzger, *The Canon of the New Testament: Its Origin, Development, and Significance* (Oxford: Clarendon Press, 1987), 239.

23 J. B. Lightfoot, *St. Paul's Epistles to the Colossians and to Philemon* (London: Macmillan and Company, 1993), 299.

24 Henry H. Howorth, "The Origin and Authority of the Biblical Canon in the Anglican Church," *Journal of Theological Studies* (October 1906): 4, 6, 10, 14.

25 F. F. Bruce, *History of the Bible in English* (New York: Oxford University Press, 1978), 31. Used by permission of Oxford University Press, USA.

26 Henry H. Howorth, "The Canon of the Bible among Later Reformers," *Journal of Theological Studies* (January 1909): 202.

27 Metzger, *The Canon of the New Testament*, 246.

28 Martin Chemnitz, *Examination of the Council of Trent*, Part I, trans. Fred Kramer (St. Louis: Concordia, 1971), 190.

29 Chemnitz, *Examination of the Council of Trent*, 180.

30 Chemnitz, *Examination of the Council of Trent*, 189.

31 Chemnitz, *Examination of the Council of Trent*, 176.

32 Chemnitz, *Examination of the Council of Trent*, 177.

33 Chemnitz, *Examination of the Council of Trent*, 177.

34 Nelson Glueck, *Rivers in the Desert: A History of the Negev* (New York: Farrare, Straus, and Cudahy, 1959), 31.

CHAPTER 6
NEW TESTAMENT CANONICITY: LUTHERAN THEOLOGY AFTER THE COUNCIL OF TRENT

1 Edward Reuss, *History of the Canon of the Holy Scriptures in the Christian Church*, trans. David Hunter (Edinburgh: James Gemmel, George IV, Bridge, 1884), 334–35. Reuss (1804–91) was a renowned professor at Strasbourg Theological School in Strasbourg, France.

2 *Württembergisches Glaubensbekenntnis* (*Confessio Württembergica*) (Stuttgart: Evangelische Gesellschaft, 1848), 53. In another edition of this document, Article XXX appears as Article XXVII. See Ernst Bizer, *Confessio Virtembergica: Das württemberrgische Bekenntnis von 1551* (Stuttgart: Im Quell-Verlag, 1952), 178.

3 Chemnitz, *Examination of the Council of Trent*, 181.

4 Chemnitz, *Examination of the Council of Trent*, 176.

5 Bruce M. Metzger, *The New Testament: Its Background, Growth, and Context* (Nashville: Abingdon Press, 2003), 318.

6 Reuss, *History of the Canon of the Holy Scriptures in the Christian Church*, 294.

7   Matthias Hafenreffer, *Theologi-Carum Rerum Summas Suis Ubique Delucidis Scripturae Testimonis* (Tübingen: Typis Philippi Gruppenbach, 1606), 140.

8   Reuss, *History of the Canon of the Holy Scriptures in the Christian Church*, 367–68.

9   Metzger, *The New Testament*, 245.

10 Metzger, *The New Testament*, 245.

11 Metzger, *The New Testament*, 245.

12 The publication was titled *Ausführliche und Gründliche Wiederlegung Des Deutschen Arianischen Catechism, Welcher zu Rakaw in Polen anno 1608 gedruckt ist.* Edward Reuss gives the following title: *Ausführliche Widerlegung des arianische Catechismi welcher zu Rakau 1608 gedruckt . . . durch die Theol. Fakultät zu Wittenberg, 1619.* See Reuss, *History of the Canon of the Holy Scriptures in the Christian Church*, 368.

13 Friedrich Balduin, *Phosphorus veri catholicism: Devia papatus et viam regiam ad ecclesian catholicam et apostolic* (Wittebergae: Caspar Heyden, 1626), 391. C. F. W. Walther, in his article "Ist derjenige für einen Ketzer oder gefährlichen Irrlehrer zu erklären, welcher nicht alle in dem Convolut des Neuen Testamentes befindlichen Bücher für kanonisch hält und erklärt?" *Lehre und Wehre* (1856), 214, cites this work by Balduin, in which he calls the seven disputed books "Apokryphen" (apocrypha).

14 Conradi Dieterici, *Institutiones Catecheticae, B. Lutheri Catechesi* (Norimbergae: Sumptibus Wolfgangi Endteri, 1659), 25.

15 C. F. W. Walther, "Ist derjenige für einen Ketzer oder gefährlichen Irrlehrer zu erklären, welcher nicht alle in dem Convolut des Neuen Testamentes befindlichen Bücher für kannonisch halt und erklärt?" *Lehre und Wehre* (1856): 214.

16 Johannis Gerhardi, *Loci Theologoci* (Bibliopolae Hamburgensis, 1657), 105. This publication is a republished edition of his *Loci Communes*, 1625.

17 Robert D. Preus, *The Theology of Post-Reformation Lutheranism* (St. Louis: Concordia, 1970), 1:305.

18 Preus, *The Theology of Post-Reformation Lutheranism*, 1:305.

19 Preus, *The Theology of Post-Reformation Lutheranism*, 1:386n148.

20 Reuss, *History of the Canon of the Holy Scriptures in the Christian Church*, 370.

21 Werner Elert, *The Structure of Lutheranism*, trans. Walter A. Hansen (St. Louis: Concordia, 1962), 193. Elert (1885–1954) served as a Lutheran professor at Erlangen University.

22 Preus, *The Theology of Post-Reformation Lutheranism*, 1:306.

23 Reuss, *History of the Canon of the Holy Scriptures in the Christian Church*, 394.

24 Elert, *The Structure of Lutheranism*, 193.

25 Howorth, "The Canon of the Bible among Later Reformers," *Journal of Theological Studies* (January 1909): 196.

26 Wilhelm Koepp, *Johann Arndt: Eine Untersuchung Über Die Mystik Im Luthertum* (Darmstadt: Scientia Verlag Aalen, 1973), 67–143.

27 Johann Gerhard, *Theological Commonplaces: On the Nature of Theology and on Scripture*, trans. Richard J. Dinda and ed. Benjamin T. G. Mayes (St. Louis: Concordia, 2009), 52.

28 Reuss, *History of the Canon of the Holy Scriptures in the Christian Church*, 368.

29 Chiliasm is a belief that Christ will return to earth and reign for one thousand years.

30 Walther, "Ist derjenige für einen Ketzer oder gefährlichen Irrlehrer zu erklären, welcher nicht alle in dem Convolut des Neuen Testamentes befindlichen Bücher für kannonisch hält und erklärt?" 204.

31 Walther, "Ist derjenige fur eine Ketzer or gefährlichen Irrlehrer zu erklaren, welcher nicht alle in dem Convolut des Neuen Testamentes befindlichen Bucher fur kanonisch halt und erklart?" 204.

32 See *Neunter Synodal Bericht der Allgemeinen Deutschen Evang. Luth. Synode von Missouri, Ohio u. a. Staaten* (St. Louis: Synodaldruckerei von August Wiebusch u. Sohn, 1858).

33 Francis Pieper, *Christliche Dogmatik* (St. Louis: Concordia, 1924), 1:406–7. My translation.

34 Cited by Francis Pieper, "Dr. Walthers Stellung zur Offenbarung St. Johannis," *Lehre und Wehre* (February 1904): 59. My translation.

35 Pieper, "Dr. Walthers Stellung zur Offenbarung St. Johannis," 59.

36 Luther's Small Catechism by Conrad Dieterich, *Institutiones Catecheticae das ist gründliche Auslegung des Katechismus D. Martin Luthers* (St. Louis and Leipzig Verlag von F. Dette, 1896), 14.

37 Carl E. Braaten, *Principles of Lutheran Theology* (Philadelphia: Fortress Press, 1983), 3.

CHAPTER 7
LAW AND GOSPEL: GOD'S DICHOTOMY

1 AE 26:313.

2 AE 26:313.

3 Walter Geihsler, "Law and Gospel," *The Abiding Word* (St. Louis: Concordia, 1947), 1:111.

4 For a detailed account of this recent controversy, see Scott Murray's excellent defense of Luther's third use of the Law in his book *Law, Life, and the Living God: The Third Use of the Law in Modern American Lutheranism* (St. Louis: Concordia, 2001).

5 AE 13:12.

6 AE 9:136.

7 AE 26:313.

8 AE 26:54.

9 AE 13:86.

10 AE 26:115.

11 C. F. W. Walther, *The Proper Distinction between Law and Gospel*, ed. W. H. T. Dau (St. Louis: Concordia, 1928), 51.

12 Walther, *The Proper Distinction between Law and Gospel*, 6.

13 Siegbert W. Becker, *The Foolishness of God* (Milwaukee: Northwestern, 1982), 230.

14 Cited in Sungenis, *Not by Faith Alone*, 690.

15 Avery Dulles, "Justification in Contemporary Catholic Theology," *Justification by Faith*, eds. H. George Anderson, T. Austin Murphy, and Joseph Burgess (Minneapolis: Augsburg Fortress, 1985), 276.

16 AE 3:225.

17 John Warwick Montgomery, "Law and Justice," *Christians in the Public Square*, eds. C. E. B. Cranfield, David Kilgour, and John Warwick Montgomery (Edmonton: Canadian Institute for Law, Theology, and Public Policy, Inc., 1996), 144.

CHAPTER 8
WORD AND SACRAMENT: TWO MEANS OF GRACE

1 Siegbert W. Becker, *The Scriptures: Inspired Word of God* (Milwaukee: Northwestern, 1971), 24.

2 Becker, *The Scriptures*, 24.

3 Martin Luther, *The Babylonian Captivity of the Church*, trans. A. T. W. Steinhauser and revised by Frederick C. Ahrens and Abdel Ross Wentz (Philadelphia: Muhlenberg Press, 1959), 132. See also AE 36:124.

4 AE 23:92.

5 Augustine, "Reply to Faustus the Manichean," *Nicene and Post-Nicene Fathers of the Christian Church*, ed. Philip Schaff (Grand Rapids: Eerdmans, 1983), 4:244.

6 AE 38:88.

7 AE 40:257.

8 Recorded in J. Gordon Melton, *The Encyclopedia of American Religions: Religious Creeds* (Detroit: Gale Research Company, 1988), 501.

9 Hermann Sasse, "The Lord's Supper in the Life of the Church," *Scripture and the Church: Selected Essays of Herman Sasse*, eds. Jeffrey J. Kloha and Ronald R. Feuerhahn (St. Louis: Concordia Seminary Monograph Series, Number 2, 1995), 4.

CHAPTER 9
THE LORD'S SUPPER: CHRIST'S SUPERNATURAL PRESENCE

1 David Hollaz, cited in Heinrich Schmid, *The Doctrinal Theology of the Evangelical Lutheran Church*, trans. Charles A. Hay and Henry E. Jacobs (Minneapolis: Augsburg Fortress, [1899], 1961), 568.

2 Johann Quenstedt, cited in Schmid, *The Doctrinal Theology of the Evangelical Lutheran Church*, 569.

3 The term *Capernaitic* harks back to the time when the Jews in Capernaum accused Jesus of wanting them literally to eat His flesh and drink His blood in light of what He said in John 6:52–54.

4 John Calvin, *Institutes of the Christian Religion*, ed. John T. McNeill, trans. Ford Lewis Battles (Philadelphia: Westminster, 1960), 2:1293.

5 Calvin, *Institutes of the Christian Religion*, 2:1363.

6 Calvin, *Institutes of the Christian Religion*, 2:1402.

7 Heinrich Schmid, *The Doctrinal Theology of the Evangelical Lutheran Church*, 565.

8 *Catechism of the Catholic Church*, 292.

9   Bainton, *Here I Stand*, 107.

10   Sasse, *This Is My Body*, 35.

11   Sasse, *This Is My Body*, 45.

12   Sasse, *This Is My Body*, 128.

13   Sasse, *This Is My Body*, 137.

14   Sasse, *This Is My Body*, 139.

15   Sasse, *This Is My Body*, 128.

16   Sasse, *This Is My Body*, 81.

17   Johann Gerhard, cited in Charles Porterfield Krauth, *The Conservative Reformation and Its Theology* (Minneapolis: Augsburg Fortress [1871], 1963), 767.

18   Sasse, *This Is My Body*, 132.

19   Sasse, *This Is My Body*, 100.

CHAPTER 10
LUTHER'S SMALL CATECHISM: THE LAITY'S BIBLE

1   Lueker, "Catechetics," *Lutheran Cyclopedia*, 175.

2   Charles Arand, *That I May Be His Own: An Overview of Luther's Catechisms* (St. Louis: Concordia, 2000), 189.

3   Theodore Graebner, *The Story of the Catechism* (St. Louis: Concordia, 1928), 48.

4   F. L. Cross, "Catechisms," *The Oxford Dictionary of the Christian Church* (New York: Oxford University Press, 1997), 299.

5   Colin Buchanan, "Catechisms," in *The New International Dictionary of the Christian Church*, ed. J. D. Douglas (Grand Rapids: Zondervan, 1978), 199.

6   Graebner, *The Story of the Catechism*, 25.

7   Graebner, *The Story of the Catechism*, 27.

8   F. Bente, "Historical Introductions to the Symbolical Books of the Evangelical Lutheran Church," *Concordia Triglotta*, ed. F. Bente, trans. F. Bente and W. H. T. Dau (Minneapolis: Mott Press, 1955), 88.

9   Bente, "Historical Introductions to the Symbolical Books of the Evangelical Lutheran Church," 89.

10   Denis R. Janz, "Catechisms," in *The Oxford Encyclopedia of the Reformation*, ed. Hans J. Hillerbrand, (New York: Oxford University Press, 1996), 1:277. Used by permission of Oxford University Press, USA.

11   Lueker, "Catechetics," *Lutheran Cyclopedia*, 177.

12   Timothy J. Wengert, *Martin Luther's Catechisms: Forming the Faith* (Minneapolis: Fortress Press, 2009), 11.

13   Martin Luther, *A Simple Way to Pray*, trans. Matthew C. Harrison (St. Louis: Concordia, 2012), 15.

14   J. M. Reu, *Explanation of Dr. Martin Luther's Small Catechism*, trans. C. G. Prottengeier (Chicago: Wartburg Publishing House, 1904), 17, 18.

15   David P. Kuske, ed. *Luther's Catechism* (Milwaukee: Northwestern, 1998), 16.

16   Tertullian, "De Capulat or De Corona," *The Ante-Nicene Fathers*, eds. Alexander Roberts and James Donaldson (Grand Rapids: Eerdmans, 1980), 3:94.

17   AE 24:397.

18   Martin Luther, "*Deutsch Catechimus*," in *D. Martin Luthers Werke* (Weimar: Hermann Böhlaus Nachfolger, 1910), 30:126. My translation.

19   Leopold von Ranke, cited in Lueker, "Catechetics," *Lutheran Cyclopedia*, 177.

20   AE 51:135.

21   Hermann Werdermann, *Luthers Wittenberger Gemeinde* (Gutersloh: Verlag von C. Bertelsmann, 1929), 24–25.

22   Bente, "Historical Introductions to the Symbolical Books of the Evangelical Lutheran Church," 76.

23   Luther, "*Vorbemerkungen zu beiden Katechismen*," in *D. Martin Luthers Werke*, 30:441.

24   Henry F. Offermann, "What Is Lutheranism?" in *What Is Lutheranism? A Symposium in Interpretation*, ed. Vergilius Ferm (New York: The Macmillan Company, 1930), 49.

25   Offermann, "What Is Lutheranism?" 49.

26   Leopold von Ranke, *Deutsche Geschichte Im Zeitlater Der Reformation* (Lengerich: Westfahlen, 1839?), 441. My translation.

27   Carol E. Hoffecker et al., *New Sweden in America* (Newark, DE: University of Delaware Press, 1995), 138.

28   Isak Collijn, *The Swedish-Indian Catechism* (Uppsala, Sweden: Almqvist & Wiksells Boktrycheri-A-B, 1937), 12.

29   Hoffecker, et al., *New Sweden in America*, 268.

30   Cited by F. Bente, "Evaluation of the Small Catechism," in *Historical Introductions to the Symbolical Books of the Evangelical Lutheran Church* (Minneapolis: The Mott Press, 1955), 91.

31   Graebner, *The Story of the Catechism*, 78.

32   Luther, *D. Martin Luthers Werke*, 30:126. My translation.

33   Willard Dow Allbeck, *Studies in the Lutheran Confessions* (Philadelphia: Fortress Press, 1967), 224.

34   Cited in Bente, "Historical Introductions to the Symbolical Books of the Evangelical Lutheran Church," 63.

Chapter 11
Luther's Large Catechism: A Teachers' Manual

1   Bente, "Historical Introductions to the Symbolical Books of the Evangelical Lutheran Church," 78.

2   Martin Luther, "Preface to the German Mass and Order of Service, 1526," *Early Protestant Spirituality*, ed. and trans. Scott H. Hendrix (New York: Paulist Press, 2009), 280.

3   Luther, "Preface to the German Mass and Order of Service, 1526," 81.

4   Luther, "Preface to the German Mass and Order of Service, 1526," 81.

5   Luther, "Preface to the German Mass and Order of Service, 1526," 81.

CHAPTER 12
SINNER AND SAINT AT THE SAME TIME

1   Bainton, *Here I Stand*, 23.

2   Luther mentions some of the Old Testament heroes as sinners and saints in various places of his writings. Specifically, the reader may consult AE 3:355, 6:172, and 12:350 to see how Luther saw some of the Old Testament patriarchs as sinners and saints.

3   Sasse, *This Is My Body*, 311.

4   AE 25:258.

5   AE 12:358.

6   AE 16:178–79.

7   AE 26:133.

8   Sungenis, *Not By Faith Alone*, 532.

9   Sungenis, *Not By Faith Alone*, 532.

10   *Catechism of the Catholic Church*, 102.

11   Augustine, cited in Pieper, *Christian Dogmatics*, 1:548n32.

12   AE 26:232–33.

CHAPTER 13
LUTHERAN CHURCH: THE SINGING CHURCH

1   Schwiebert, *Luther and His Times*, 127.

2   Robin A. Leaver, *Luther's Liturgical Music* (Grand Rapids: Eerdmans, 2007), 64.

3   Leaver, *Luther's Liturgical Music*, 47.

4   Leaver, *Luther's Liturgical Music*, 64.

5   Leaver, *Luther's Liturgical Music*, 108.

6   AE 53:193.

7   Carl Schalk, *Music in Early Lutheranism: Shaping the Tradition, 1524–1672* (St. Louis: Concordia, 2001), 31.

8   Homer Ulrich and Paul A. Pisk, *A History of Music and Musical Style* (New York: Harcourt, Brace and World, Inc., 1963), 162.

9   Ulrich and Pisk, *A History of Music and Musical Style*, 36.

10   Markus Jenny, "Luthers Geistliche Lieder und Kirchengesänge," *Archiv Zur Weimarer Ausgabe Der Werke Martin Luthers* (Cologne: Böhlau Verlag, 1985), 4:16.

11   AE 49:428.

12   Editors' comment, AE 49:427.

13   Leaver, *Luther's Liturgical Music*, 209.

14   Richard Taruskin, *The Oxford History of Western Music* (Oxford, UK: Oxford University Press, 2004), 1:755.

15   Taruskin, *The Oxford History of Western Music*, 1:755. Used by permission of Oxford University Press, USA.

16   Charles Sanford Terry, "Chorale," *Grove's Dictionary of Music and Musicians* (Lon-

don: Macmillan and Company, 1954), 2:270. Used by permission of Oxford University Press, USA.

17 Taruskin, *The Oxford History of Western Music*, 1:754. Used by permission of Oxford University Press, USA.

18 Leaver, *Luther's Liturgical Music*, 210.

19 Schalk, *Music in Early Lutheranism*, 22.

20 AE 53:197.

21 Martin Bertheau, *400 Jahre Kirchenlied* (Hamburg: Verlag der Buchhandlung des Nordd. Männer und Jünglingsbundes, 1924), 11.

22 Friedrich Blume, "The Period of the Reformation," revised by Ludwig Finscher, trans. F. Ellsworth Peterson, in Friedrich Blume, *Protestant Church Music: A History* (New York: W. W. Norton and Company, 1974), 43.

23 Theodore Hoelty-Nickel, "The Lutheran Conception of Church Music," *Lutheran School Journal* (January 1942): 220.

24 Hoelty-Nickel, "The Lutheran Conception of Church Music," 221–22.

25 Terry, "Chorale," *Grove's Dictionary of Music and Musicians*, 2:270. Used by permission of Oxford University Press, USA.

26 AE 53:69.

27 Leaver, *Luther's Liturgical Music*, 218.

28 Joseph Herl, *Worship Wars in Early Lutheranism: Choir, Congregation, and Three Centuries of Conflict* (Oxford, UK: Oxford University Press, 2004), 177. Used by permission of Oxford University Press, USA.

29 Ill-ae Rhee, "Liturgical and Musical Reforms from the Middle Ages to Luther" (Rochester, NY: Unpublished Master of Arts thesis, Colgate Rochester Crozier Divinity School, 2009), 19.

30 Leaver, *Luther's Liturgical Music*, 108.

31 Taruskin, *The Oxford History of Western Music*, 1:754. Used by permission of Oxford University Press, USA.

32 Karl Anton, *Luther und die Musik* (Zwickau, Sachsen: Verlag und Druck von Johannes Herrmann, 1928), 11.

33 Luther D. Reed, *Luther and Congregational Song* (New York: The Hymn Society of America, 1947), 10.

34 Christopher Boyd Brown, *Singing the Gospel: Lutheran Hymns and the Success of the Reformation* (Cambridge, MA: Harvard University Press, 2005), 38.

35 Brown, *Singing the Gospel*, 39–40.

36 Brown, *Singing the Gospel*, 80.

37 Brown, *Singing the Gospel*, 42.

38 Brown, *Singing the Gospel*, 148.

39 James Mearns, "Nicolaus Herman," *A Dictionary of Hymnology*, ed. John Julian (New York: Dover Publications, Inc., 1907), 1:513.

40 Justus.anglican.org/resources/bio/12.html (accessed November 29, 2015).

41 Blume, "The Age of Confessionalism," in *Protestant Church Music*, 209.

42 Ulrich and Pisk, *A History of Music and Musical Style*, 272.

43 Johann Friedrich Bachmann, "Über Johann Crüger" in Christian Bunners, *Johann Crüger (1598–1662): Berliner Musiker und Kantor, lutherischer Lied und Gesangbuchschöpfer* (Berlin: Frank & Timme Verlag, 2012), 245.

44 James Mearns, "Martin Rinckart," *A Dictionary of Hymnology*, ed. John Julian (New York: Dover Publications, Inc., 1907), 2:963.

45 David Saul and Inc., Dorling Kindersley, *The Illustrated Encyclopedia of Warfare: From Ancient Egypt to Iraq* (New York: DK, 2012), 174.

46 John L. Flood, *Poets Laureate in the Holy Roman Empire* (New York: Walter de Gruyter, 2006), 817.

47 Gerhard Kappner, "Heermann, Johann," in Wolfgang Herbst, *Wer ist wer im Gesangbuch?* (Gottingen: Vandenhoeck und Ruprecht, 2001), 136.

48 Blume, "The Age of Confessionalism," *Protestant Church Music*, 238.

49 Christian Moller, *Kirchenlied und Gesangbuch: Quellen zu ihrer Geschichte* (Tübingen und Basel: A. Francke Verlag, 2000), 141.

50 In 1610, Arndt published his *Vier Bücher vom wahren Christentum* (*Four Books of True Christianity*), a work that expanded on his first book of 1605.

51 Madeleine Brook, "Paul Gerhardt," sites.google.com/site/germanliterature/early-modern/paul-gerhardt (accessed November 24, 2015).

52 James Mearns, "Gerhardt, Paulus," in *A Dictionary of Hymnology*, ed. John Julian (New York: Dover Publications, Inc., 1907), 1:409.

53 Elke Axmacher, *Johann Arndt und Paul Gerhardt: Studien zur Theologie, Frommigkeit und geistlichen Dichtung des 17. Jahrhunderts*, ed. Hermann Kurzke, Mainzer Hymnologische Studien (Tübingen und Basel: A. Francke Verlag, 2001), xi. My translation.

54 The Center for Church Music: songsandhymns.org/people/detail/paul-gerhardt (accessed November 14, 2016).

55 Brook, "Paul Gerhardt."

56 Brook, "Paul Gerhardt."

57 Frank Senn, *Protestant Spiritual Traditions* (New York: Paulist Press, 1986), 43.

58 Doris Flexner, *The Optimist's Guide to History* (New York: Avon Books, 1995), 100.

59 Charles Sanford Terry, *Bach: A Biography* (London: Oxford University Press, 1928), 275.

60 Henry A. Simon, "Bach at Journey's End," *The Lutheran Witness* (July 2000): 15.

61 Taken from p. 128 of *Spiritual Lives of the Great Composers* by Patrick Kavanaugh, copyright © 1996 by Patrick Kavanaugh. Used by permission of Zondervan. www.zondervan.com.

62 Ulrich and Pisk, *A History of Music and Musical Style*, 272.

63 Herl, *Worship Wars in Early Lutheranism Choir, Congregation, and Three Centuries of Conflict*, 118. Used by permission of Oxford University Press, USA.

64 Timothy J. Deyton, "A Conductor's Analysis of the Lutheran Mass in G Major and Cantata 179, *Siehe zu dass deine Gottesfurcht nicht Heuchelei sei*" (Unpublished Doctor of Musical Arts thesis: Southern Baptist Theological Seminary, Fort Worth, TX, 2001), 25.

65 Deyton, "A Conductor's Analysis of the Lutheran Mass in G Major and Cantata 179, *Siehe zu dass deine Gottesfurcht nicht Heuchelei sei*," 24.

66 Leaver, *Luther's Liturgical Music*, 277.

CHAPTER 14
DIVINE LITURGY TEACHES THE FAITH

1 Brad Thompson, *Liturgies of the Western Church* (Philadelphia: Fortress Press, 1985), 97.

2 Sasse, *Scripture and the Church*, 286.

3 Herman Strathmann, "*Leitourgia*," *Theological Dictionary of the New Testament*, ed. Gerhard Kittel (Grand Rapids: Eerdmans, 1976), 4:216–17.

4 Frank Senn, *Christian Liturgy: Catholic and Evangelical* (Minneapolis: Fortress Press, 1997), 41.

5 Kurt Marquart, "Liturgy and Evangelism," in *Lutheran Worship: History and Practice*, ed. Fred L. Precht (St. Louis: Concordia, 1993), 58.

6 Herman Sasse, "The Lord's Supper and the Life of the Church," *Scripture and the Church*, 10.

7 Marquart, "Liturgy and Evangelism," 61.

8 Theodore Emmanuel Schmauk, *A History of the Lutheran Church in Pennsylvania, 1638–1820* (Philadelphia: General Council Publication House, 1903), 185.

9 Schmauk, *A History of the Lutheran Church in Pennsylvania, 1638–1820*, 181. Beale M. Schmucker states that this liturgy was the product of four continental liturgies. See his "The First Pennsylvania Liturgy," *Lutheran Church Review* (July 1882), 1:162.

10 Abdel Ross Wentz, *A Basic History of Lutheranism in America* (Philadelphia: Muhlenberg Press, 1955), 60.

11 Luther D. Reed, *The Lutheran Liturgy: A Study of the Common Service of the Lutheran Church in America* (Philadelphia: Fortress Press, 1947), 252.

12 James Brauer, *Meaningful Worship: A Guide to the Lutheran Service* (St. Louis: Concordia, 1994), 24.

13 Reed, *Lutheran Liturgy*, 60.

14 Translation from the Didache is mine.

15 *LSB*, Divine Service: Setting Three, 184.

16 *LSB*, Divine Service: Setting Three, 184.

17 Reed, *Lutheran Liturgy*, 247.

18 *LSB*, Divine Service: Setting Three, 185.

19 *LSB*, Divine Service: Setting Three, 185.

20 James Dallen, *The Reconciling Community: The Rite of Penance* (New York: Pueblo Publishing Company, 1986), 125.

21 Dallen, *The Reconciling Community*, 142.

22 Peter Brunner, *Worship in the Name of Jesus*, trans. M.H. Bertram (St. Louis: Concordia, 1968), 133.

23 AE 53:121.

24 Emil Sehling, *Die Evangelische Kirchenordnung Des XVI Jahrhunderts* (Leipzig: O.R. Reisland, 1913), 87. I thank William Weedon for having made me aware of this church order.

25 Richard Charles Wolf, "The Americanization of the German Lutherans: 1683 to 1829" (Unpublished PhD thesis: Yale University, 1947), 439.

26 Wolf, "The Americanization of the German Lutherans: 1683 to 1829," 440.

27 *Kirchen-Agende fur Evangelisch-Lutherische Gemeinden Zusammengestellt aus den Alten Rechtglaeubigen Sachsischen Kirchenagenden, herausgegeben von der Allgemeinen deutschen Evangel. Lutherischen Synod von Missouri, Ohio, und anderen Staaten* (St. Louis: Druckerei der Deutschen Ev. Luth. Synode v. Missouri, O. u.a. St.), 1856.

28 AE 41:154.

29 Charles J. Evanson, "The Divine Service," *Lutheran Worship: History and Practice*, ed. Fred L. Precht (St. Louis: Concordia, 1993), 408.

30 Senn, *Christian Liturgy*, 185.

31 William J. Reynolds and Milburn Price, *A Survey of Christian Hymnody* (Carol Stream, IL: Hope Publishing Co., 1987), 8.

32 Reynolds and Price, *A Survey of Christian Hymnody*, 8.

33 *Egeria's Travels to the Holy Land*, trans. John Wilkinson (Jerusalem: Ariel Publishing House, 1981), 57.

34 Cited in Reed, *Lutheran Liturgy*, 84.

35 Reed, *Lutheran Liturgy*, 277.

36 Hermann Sasse, "Letters Addressed to Lutheran Pastors (Eccelesia Orans)," trans. Ralph Gehrke. *Quartalschrift Theological Quarterly* (April 1951): 89.

37 Henry Ashworth, "Et Cum Spiritu Tuo: An Inquiry into Its Origin and Meaning," *The Clergy Review* (February 1966): 122–23.

38 Gerald L. Bray, "Language and Liturgy," in *Latimer Studies 16: Language and Liturgy*, eds. Gerald L. Bray, Stephen A. Wilcockson, and Robin A. Leaver (Oxford: Latimer House, 1984), 10, emphasis in the original.

39 Evanson, "The Divine Service," 411.

40 Senn, *Christian Liturgy*, 139.

41 Luther D. Reed, *Worship: A Study of Corporate Devotion* (Philadelphia: Muhlenberg Press, 1959), 89.

42 Reed, *Lutheran Liturgy*, 92.

43 AE 53:11.

44 Bainton, *Here I Stand*, 272.

45 Schwiebert, *Luther and His Times*, 453.

46 *LSB*, Divine Service: Setting Three, 194.

47 Reed, *Lutheran Liturgy*, 107.

48 AE 53:29.

49 *Consilia Witebergensia*, III, 50, cited in "Der lutherische Distributionsformel bei Administirung des heiligen Abendmahles," *Lehre und Wehre* (December 1855): 374.

50 *LSB*, Divine Service: Setting Three, 199.

51 Paul Grime, "The Use of the Nunc Dimittis in the Liturgy of the Eucharist" (Unpublished STM thesis, Concordia Theological Seminary, Fort Wayne, IN, 1986), 5.

52 Reed, *Lutheran Liturgy*, 406.

53 Reed, *Lutheran Liturgy*, 406.

54 Scot A. Kinnaman, ed., *Treasury of Daily Prayer* (St. Louis: Concordia, 2012), 18.

55 Peter Brunner, *Worship in the Name of Jesus*, 223.

56 AE 53:19.

57 Charles Porterfield Krauth, "The Relation of Our Confessions to the Reformation and the Importance of Their Study, with an Outline of the Early History of the Augsburg Confession," *Evangelical Review* (October 1849): 240.

58 See David S. Luecke, *Evangelical Style and Lutheran Substance: Facing America's Mission Challenge* (St. Louis: Concordia, 1988).

59 Various authors have in recent years argued that the historic liturgy is irrelevant. For instance, see D. G. Hart, *The Lost Soul of American Protestantism* (Boulder: Rowman and Littlefield Publishers, Inc., 2002), 141–68.

60 John T. Pless, "Divine Service: Delivering Forgiveness of Sins," *Logia* (Reformation 1996): 23.

CHAPTER 15
THEOLOGY OF THE CROSS: LUTHER'S UNIQUE INSIGHT

1 AE 31:53.

2 AE 31:53.

3 Cited in Elert, *The Structure of Lutheranism*, 315.

4 Herbert B. Workman, *Persecution in the Early Church* (New York: Oxford University Press, 1980), 2.

5 AE 30:16.

6 AE 19:183.

7 Martin Luther, *Dr. Martin Luthers Auslegung des ersten Buches Mose*, Joh. Georg Walch edition (St. Louis: Concordia, n.d.), 2:467.

8 AE 30:16.

9 AE 31:243.

10 AE 42:110.

11 AE 22:147.

12 AE 23:360.

13 Albert E. Elsen, *Purposes of Art* (New York: Holt, Rinehart and Winston, 1967), 70.

14 Alister E. McGrath, *Luther's Theology of the Cross: Martin Luther's Theological Breakthrough* (Grand Rapids: Baker Books, 1985), 160.

15 Robin A. Leaver and James H. Litton, *Duty and Delight: Routley Remembered* (Norwich: Canterbury Press, 1985), 54.

16 AE 31:225.

17 AE 31:53.

Chapter 16
The Augsburg Confession: Birth of the Lutheran Church

1   AE 32:112–13.

2   Bente, "Historical Introduction to the Symbolical Books of the Evangelical Lutheran Church," 19.

3   Bainton, *Here I Stand*, 254.

4   Cited by Bente, "Historical Introductions to the Symbolical Books of the Evangelical Lutheran Church," 19.

5   Bente, "Historical Introduction to the Symbolical Books of the Evangelical Lutheran Church," 19.

6   Bente, "Historical Introduction to the Symbolical Books of the Evangelical Lutheran Church," 23.

7   Philip Schaff, *The Creeds of Christendom with a History and Critical Notes* (New York: Harper and Brothers Publishers, 1919), 1:233.

Chapter 17
Two Different Governments: Spiritual and Secular

1   Uwe Siemon-Netto, *The Fabricated Luther: The Rise and Fall of the Shirer Myth* (St. Louis: Concordia, 1993), 99. This book provides excellent insights and understanding of Luther's theology of God's two kingdoms.

2   AE 21:109.

3   Paul Althaus, *The Ethics of Martin Luther*, trans. Robert C. Schultz (Philadelphia: Fortress Press, 1972), 47.

4   AE 30:76.

5   AE 46:69.

6   AE 21:113.

7   AE 21:116.

8   AE 46:186.

9   AE 46:168.

10 AE 21:113.

11 Alvin J. Schmidt, *How Christianity Changed the World* (Grand Rapids: Zondervan, 2004), 151–69.

12 Schmidt, *How Christianity Changed the World*, 160.

13 AE 45:111.

14 "Hosius to Constantius the Emperor," *Athanasius*, in *The Nicene and Post-Nicene Fathers of the Christian Church* (Grand Rapids: Eerdmans, 1980), 4:286.

15 Thomas F. Madden, "Crusade Propaganda: The Abuse of Christianity's Holy War," www.Nationalreview.com (accessed August 18, 2003).

16 Paul Johnson, "Relentlessly and Thoroughly," *National Review* (October 15, 2001): 20.

17 Alvin J. Schmidt, *The Great Divide: The Failure of Islam and the Triumph of the West* (Boston: Regina Orthodox Press, 2004), 153–54.

18 AE 46:168.

19 AE 46:185.

20 AE 46:70.

21 Althaus, *The Ethics of Martin Luther*, 61.

22 AE 13:194.

23 I am grateful to Uwe Siemon-Netto for providing helpful insights he shared with me in personal communication regarding Luther's use of "emergency bishops."

24 Dominique Colas, *Civil Society and Fanaticism* (Stanford: Stanford University Press, 1997), 55.

CHAPTER 18
ADIAPHORA: A LOOK AT CHRISTIAN LIBERTY

1 Lorenz Wunderlich, "Adiaphora," *The Abiding Word* (St. Louis: Concordia, 1947), 2:689.

2 AE 53:80.

3 Arand, "Not All Adiaphora Are Created Equal," *Concordia Journal* (July 2004): 156.

4 Timothy J. Wengert, "Adiaphora," *The Oxford Encyclopedia of the Reformation*, 1:6. Used by permission of Oxford University Press, USA.

5 Theodore Graebner, *The Borderland of Right and Wrong* (St. Louis: Concordia, 1938), 2.

6 Arand, "Not All Adiaphora Are Created Equal," 163.

7 Cited by Bente, "Historical Introductions to the Symbolical Books of the Evangelical Lutheran Church," 103.

8 Theodor Kliefoth, "General View of Divine Worship as Held by the Lutheran Church," trans. B. M. Schmucker, *Evangelical Review* (April 1855): 589.

9 Wengert, "Adiaphora," *The Oxford Encyclopedia of the Reformation*, 1:6.

10 Arand, "Not All Adiaphora Are Created Equal," 161.

11 Arand, "Not All Adiaphora Are Created Equal," 161.

12 Lowell C. Green, "The Distinction of Law and Gospel as the Criterion for Liturgical Forms and Hymnody," *Let Christ Be Christ: Theology, Ethics and World Religions in the Two Kingdoms: Essays in Honor of the Sixty-Fifth Birthday of Charles Manske*, ed. Daniel N. Harmelink (Huntington Beach: Tentatio Press, 1999), 103.

13 Bente, "Historical Introductions to the Symbolical Books of the Evangelical Lutheran Church," 110.

CHAPTER 19
THE BOOK OF CONCORD: LUTHERAN HANDBOOK

1 The exact number of bishops that attended this council is not known. Historians have cited numbers ranging from 280 to 320.

2 Willard Dow Allbeck, *Studies in the Lutheran Confessions* (Philadelphia: Fortress Press, 1968), 143.

3 Allbeck, *Studies in the Lutheran Confessions*, 287.

4 Allbeck, *Studies in the Lutheran Confessions*, 287.

5 Allbeck, *Studies in the Lutheran Confessions*, 196.

6 Allbeck, *Studies in the Lutheran Confessions*, 196.

7 *Concordia*, p. 257.

8 Sasse, *This Is My Body*, 60.

9 Bente, "Historical Introductions to the Symbolical Books of the Evangelical Lutheran Church," 88.

10 Eugene F. Klug and Otto F. Stahlke, *Getting into the Formula of Concord: A History and Digest of the Formula* (St. Louis: Concordia, 1955), 14.

11 Bente, "Historical Introductions to the Symbolical Books of the Evangelical Lutheran Church," 247.

12 Preus, *The Second Martin*, 16.

CHAPTER 20
WORK AND VOCATION: GOD'S MASK

1 Althaus, *The Ethics of Martin Luther*, 38.

2 AE 3:321.

3 AE 12:71.

4 AE 12:71.

5 Emil Brunner, *Christianity and Civilization* (New York: Charles Scribner's Sons, 1949), 61–62.

6 AE 14:114.

7 Schmidt, *How Christianity Changed the World*, 197.

8 Philip Yancey, *Rumors of Another World* (Grand Rapids: Zondervan, 2003), 65.

9 Martin Luther, "*Haus Postille*," *Sämmtliche Schriften*, Joh. Georg Walch Edition, ed. Georg Rörer (St. Louis: Concordia, 1910), 13:2220. My translation.

10 Luther, "*Haus Postille*," 2219. My translation.

11 Plutarch, *Parallel Lives,* trans. Bernadotte Perrin (New York: G. P. Putnam's Sons, 1918), 5:471.

12 Cicero, *De Officii*, trans. Walter Miller (New York: G. P. Putnam's Sons, 1913), 1:153.

13 "Constitution of the Holy Apostles," *The Ante-Nicene Fathers*, eds. Alexander Roberts and James Donaldson (Grand Rapids: Eerdmans, 1982), 7:425.

14 AE 23:323.

15 AE 5:274.

16 AE 5:275.

17 Gustaf Wingren, *Luther on Vocation*, trans. Carl C. Rasmussen (Philadelphia: Muhlenberg Press, 1957), 121.

18 Gene Edward Veith, *The Spirituality of the Cross* (St. Louis: Concordia, 1999), 87.

19 AE 14:114.

20 Althaus, *The Ethics of Martin Luther*, 101.

Chapter 21
Hallmarks of the Lutheran Reformation

1 Erwin Iserloh, *The Theses Were Not Posted*, trans. Jared Wicks (Boston: Beacon Press, 1968) argues that Luther did not post the theses on the church door, but that he had only sent them to some ecclesiastical authorities to read. Iserloh's argument, however, has not been accepted by many Reformation historians.

2 Bainton, *Here I Stand*, 63.

3 Lars P. Qualben, *A History of the Christian Church* (New York: Thomas Nelson and Sons, 1958), 285. Used by permission of Wipf and Stock Publishers. www.wipfandstock.com.

4 Cited in "Reformation Day," *The Lutheran Witness* (October 20, 1914): 169.

5 Luther was formally excommunicated by the pope on January 3, 1521, four months before his appearance at the Diet of Worms.

6 Philip Schaff, *History of the Christian Church* (New York: Charles Scribner's Sons, 1895), 6:1.

7 Cited by Theodore Graebner, "Reformation Day," *The Lutheran Witness* (October 20, 1914): 170.

8 Thomas Day, *Why Catholics Can't Sing* (New York: Crossroad Publishing Company, 1990), 3.

9 Susan C. Karant-Nunn, "The Emergence of the Pastoral Family in the German Reformation: The Parsonage as a Site of Socio-religious Change," *The Protestant Clergy of Early Modern Europe*, eds. C. Scott Dixon and Luise Schorn-Schütte (New York: Palgrave Macmillan, 2003), 93.

10 Qualben, *A History of the Christian Church*, 286.

11 Lohse, *Martin Luther*, 184.

12 AE 36:113.

13 Schwiebert, *Luther and His Times*, 229.

14 "Reformation Day," *Encyclopedia Britannica*, britannica.com/topic/Reformation-Day (accessed May 6, 2016).

15 "In Perspective," *The Lutheran Witness* (November, 1965): 3.

16 Lohse, *Martin Luther*, 82.

17 Schwiebert, *Luther and His Times*, 674.

18 W. G. Polack, *Favorite Christian Hymns: Their Origin and Authorship* (New York: Ernst Kaufmann, 1924), 11.

19 William J. Hart, *Hymns in Human Experience* (New York: Harper and Brothers, 1931), 39–40.

20 Henry Gariepy, *Songs in the Night: Inspiring Stories Behind 100 Hymns Born in Trial and Suffering* (Grand Rapids: Eerdmans, 1996), 191.

21 Fred L. Precht, *Lutheran Worship: Hymnal Companion* (St. Louis: Concordia, 1992), 317.

22 Precht, *Lutheran Worship: Hymnal Companion*, 317.

23 Precht, *Lutheran Worship: Hymnal Companion*, 317.

Subject and Name Index

HALLMARKS OF LUTHERAN IDENTITY

Revelation, Book of, as canonical, 68, 70–73, 79, 84, 89–93

Rinckart, Martin, 103, 168, 174–75, 319

Roebbelen, K. A. W., 89–90

Rogers, John, 73

Roman Catholicism, 7, 12, 21, 22–23, 24, 26, 33, 44–45, 55–56, 59, 63, 83, 87, 88, 91, 102, 111, 118, 123–27, 128, 134, 135, 159–60, 162, 171, 172–73, 183, 216, 218, 221, 224, 252, 257, 265, 266–67, 270–71, 272, 273, 274, 275, 282, 295–97, 303

rosary, 12

Ross, Albert Henry, 77

Salutation (in the Divine Service), 186, 193–94, 199, 206

sanctification, 11

Sasse, Hermann, 18, 117, 124, 125, 126, 127, 157, 185, 193, 205, 307, 315, 316, 318, 321, 322, 326

Schaff, Philip, 223, 235, 293, 324, 327

Schieferdecker, George, 89–90

Schütz, Heinrich, 168, 174

Schwabach Articles, 225

Schwan, Heinrich C., 131

Schwärmerei/Schwärmer. See Enthusiasm/Enthusiasts

Schwenkfelders, 279

Schwiebert, Ernest G., 53, 197, 297, 300, 310, 318, 322, 327

Scrinio pectoris (chamber of the heart), 52

second rank (antilegomena books), 85–90, 93, 95

Selnecker, Nicholas, 82, 103, 275

Senn, Frank, 179, 184, 319, 320, 321

Septuagint, 88

Sergius I (pope), 199

seven sacraments, 111, 252, 293

Shepherd of Hermas, 68

Siemon-Netto, Uwe, 238, 324, 325

sinner-saint, 155–62, 318

Sixtus of Siena, 88

Small Catechism, 10–11, 13, 54, 84, 92, 99, 109, 111, 113, 129–45, 147, 148–49, 151, 153, 189, 215, 240, 263, 272

Smalcald Articles, 31, 54, 263, 267–74, 280

Smalcaldic League, 268, 274, 299

Smith, Joseph, 66, 311

Socinian Catechism, 84

sola fide (faith alone), 7, 13, 15, 24, 35–50, 72, 252, 293

sola gratia (grace alone), 7, 15, 24, 25–33, 293

sola Scriptura (Scripture alone), 7, 13, 15, 24, 51–63, 71, 87, 91, 94, 252, 267, 293

Soldiers' Field, 142

solus Christus (Christ alone), 7, 12, 13, 15–24, 61, 136, 193

Southern Baptists, 114–15

Spener, Philipp, 177

spiritual offense, 252, 257–61, 262, 278

St. Mary's Church, 140, 169, 178

Stump, Joseph, 131, 134

Sungenis, Robert A., 55, 159, 309, 310, 314, 318

synergism, 30

Synod of Elvira, 115, 295

Synod of Tarragona, 52, 53, 59

Synod of the South (Lutheran), 189

Synod of Toulouse, 52, 53, 59

Synodical Conference of North American Lutherans, 189

Syriac Church, 68

Taruskin, Richard, 166, 171, 318, 319

Taverner, Richard, 73

tekmeriois (infallible proofs), 43

Terry, Charles Sanford, 166, 318, 319, 320

theology of glory, 208–10, 221

theology of the cross, 13, 207–15, 219–20, 221, 283, 323

theotokos (God-bearer), 57–58, 63, 277

Thirty Years' War, 175, 176, 178, 303

Thomas (apostle), 37, 40–41, 43

Tillich, Paul, 36–37, 61, 308, 309

Torgau Articles, 225

tradition, Christian, 56–58, 63

transubstantiation, 123–25, 128, 271

TULIP, 29

Turks, 241, 245

two governments/kingdoms, 237–49, 273

Tyndale, William, 73

Una Sancta, 202, 257, 262

University of Wittenberg, 53, 83, 141, 178

Urban II (pope), 244

Vatican II, 193, 194, 195

Veith, Gene E., Jr., 288, 325

Verbum Domini Manet in Aeternum, 299

Vespers, 201–2, 294

Virgin Mary, 57, 60, 63, 137, 193, 226, 227, 277

Voice of the Martyrs, The, 214

Von Ranke, Leopold, 139, 140, 317

Vulgate, 73

Waldensians, 52

Waldo, Peter, 52

Walter, Johann, 164, 172

Walther, C. F. W., 89–92, 100–101

Wengert, Timothy, 133, 315, 324

William (duke of Bavaria), 224

Wingren, Gustaf, 46, 288, 309, 326

Wisconsin Evangelical Lutheran Synod, 9, 135, 190, 217

Wolder, David, 84

Words of Institution, 124, 126, 128, 186, 198, 199, 206

Workman, Herbert B., 210, 323

Wunderlich, Lorenz, 253, 324

Württembergisches Glaubensbekenntnis, 81, 82, 312

Wycliffe Bible, 53

Wycliffe, John, 53, 310

Yancey, Philip, 284, 326

Zwingli, Ulrich, 109, 121–22, 127, 128, 141, 165

SCRIPTURE INDEX

New Testament

Matthew

Mark

Luke

John